FLEXIBLE LIFE SCHEDULING

Fred Best

FLEXIBLE LIFE SCHEDULING

Breaking the Education- Work-Retirement Lockstep

PRAEGER

PRAEGER SPECIAL STUDIES • PRAEGER SCIENTIFIC

Library of Congress Cataloging in Publication Data

Best, Fred.
    Flexible life scheduling.

    Bibliography: p.
    Includes index.
    1. Life cycle, Human. 2. United States--
Social conditions--1960-   3. Life span,
Productive. 4. Time allocation. I. Title.
HQ1064.U5B375   306   80-160
ISBN 0-03-050586-0
ISBN 0-03-050591-7 pbk.

Published in 1980 by Praeger Publishers
CBS Educational and Professional Publishing
A Division of CBS, Inc.
521 Fifth Avenue, New York, New York 10017 U.S.A.

© 1980 by Fred Best

0123456789 038 987654321

Printed in the United States of America

Dedicated with gratitude and love,
to my brother, Sid Brewster

FOREWORD
by Willard Wirtz

Flexible Life Scheduling is basically a brief, taking humanism as its premise, that we are entitled as individuals to treat more of our time as though it belonged to us instead of to somebody else. The argumentation, impressive and persuasive, carries considerably beyond its specific target. Coming at a point when the whole idea of continuing societal and economic growth has been brought into question, Fred Best's study is an invaluable reminder that the only real "limits to growth" are in the conceiving of the kind of growth we are looking for.

The author identifies the book's origins in a college student's "radical humanistic" reactions in the late 1960s against a materialism he found personified particularly in "armies of adults sludging their way through the nine-to-five workday world with almost religious commitment to the golden reward of retirement." Life's division into three time traps—youth for education, maturity for work, older age for denial of either of these vitalizing opportunities—seemed to him a senseless form of vestigial slavery to the tyrannies of archaic employment and education traditions.

Fred Best decided, at the end of his own academic confinement, to take the trouble to check his seemingly deviant opinion against whatever facts and as many other views as he could find; with the consequence that *Flexible Life Scheduling* is a compendium of virtually everything (so far as I know) that has been researched or surveyed or thought, and then reported, of American experience regarding the arranging and scheduling of education and work and leisure.

Voluminous footnotes offer an invaluable index to a currently proliferating literature. This source material is kept in its place, however, by the concise, lean, disciplined synthesizing that is done in the text. The author's scholarship, furthermore, is not permitted either to obscure or diminish his advocacy. He argues strongly and effectively that life would mean a good deal more to millions of people if they could break out of its lockstep; that a majority of working people now place as much premium on getting larger control of more of their own time as they do on making more of somebody else's money; and that the ways and means are now being devised to achieve the desired flexibility. The volume ends, as the college student's thinking started, with the posing of the issue involved here in terms of materialism versus humanism. Its report is that the home team is at least closing the gap.

Complete concurrence with Dr. Best's thesis, including an equal regard for the ultimacy of humanism's values, prompts my emphasizing here the relevancy of this prospect of more flexible life patterns to the broader issue of future "growth" policy. National concern centers today on the implication of increasingly imminent depletions of critical national resources, the metals and fossil fuel supplies lying in the planet's thin crust. Yet that concern includes and reflects a conditioned bias, largely semantic, about the meaning of "growth": that it covers only those elements reflected in the traditional measurement of the gross national product. The term ought to include whatever contributes, on a manageable and self-supporting basis, to the human opportunity to make the highest and best use of the human experience.

Dr. Best is careful to distinguish the idea of flexible life patterns from a simpler notion of spending less time at work. He properly discounts any "work sharing" suggestions that would represent simply a cutting of the present employment opportunity pie into smaller pieces—which would reflect, at least in most senses, a no-growth rather than a growth policy. The attractive prospect is not of people spending less of their lives working but of a better integration of worktime with other types of opportunities.

It is probably important to recognize what is involved here as only superficially a dichotomy between "more money and more time." Despite the survey showings (reported in Chapters 9 and 10) that employees reflect an increasing willingness to make that choice in terms of a preference of more control over more of their own time, a certain skepticism is bound to attach to these findings. What people tell pollsters about their priorities may or may not survive the pressures of actual decision making when the context is double-digit inflation, two children in college, and a mortgage payment due the first of the month. One of the strengths of this volume is its proper emphasis on the particularly strong motivations—in support of time flexibility—of women (who are trying to combine career-motherhood with career-something-else) and older people (who are increasingly disenchanted with life on a shelf called security). But it will be hard to carry the day, or the week, or the year, or a lifetime for any broad proposition cast in naked terms of more time with less money.

It is, of course, the comparative *uses* of the time and the money that present, if they are made clear, the real and operative choice. Although there is repeated reference made to it throughout *Flexible Life Scheduling*, I would emphasize perhaps more basically the vital relationship between this flexibility and the fulfillment of the infinite promise for human and societal and economic growth that lies in what we call—in unfortunately soft phrases—adult education, or lifelong learning. Dr. Best's evidence and argumentation are assembled primarily from a worker and work-place perspective. It is interesting and significant that a closely parallel case can be made on the basis of various developments in the educational system: the almost fantastic increase, for example, in community college enrollments and the rapidly rising median age level of students attending these colleges.

It is the investment rather than the spending potential that gives time its potential attraction advantage over money.

There is appropriate reference in this volume to another relationship between employment—or, more precisely, unemployment—and education. We not only assume that the downtime of unemployment is to be totally wasted; we encourage this by expressly conditioning unemployment insurance benefits on a "work availability" rule that virtually precludes using these periods for education and training. They represent working people's time that is almost ironically free for other uses, and they afford immediately available opportunities for constructive applications of the flexible scheduling concept. It seems reasonable to expect increased recognition in this country of the concept, already accepted throughout much of Western Europe, of countercyclical education and training policy.

So I would only seek to underscore Dr. Best's immensely valuable contribution by suggesting that it has a dimension of importance beyond what he originally intended or now claims for it. He argues in the terms of ultimate significance that more rational life scheduling is vital to "the inner meanings of human existence." I don't believe it debases this argument to point out the equal significance of such a reordering of life's pattern to the attainment of the purpose to find and open up new frontiers of societal and economic growth. Growth in some form or other is probably critical to the meaningfulness, at least to the vitality, of all forms of life, institutional, system, and individual alike. *Flexible Life Scheduling* is a case study in the potential for growth that lies in the improved uses of the sixty or seventy years of time that most of us get as our human endowment.

PREFACE AND ACKNOWLEDGMENTS

How does one choose a few words to preface a book representing several years of effort? Wendell Bell and James Mau, who edited an interesting volume on the future of sociology a few years back, suggested that authors should briefly expose their values as a forewarning of biases that might be interwoven throughout the book. This task seems appropriate enough, but it is not altogether easily accomplished. Stating one's overarching beliefs not only takes more than a few lines but also rears the foreboding possibility that readers may not like the values of an author and therefore disregard the book. Such a thought is enough to cause any author to scurry quickly back into the shadows of personal anonymity.

Nonetheless, some statement on values and why I came to write this book seems merited. The contents and tone of this volume have been affected by my personal experiences, growth, and learning while writing. Originally, the concept of this book was an outgrowth of the radical humanistic values that were in full bloom during the late 1960s at Berkeley and other college campuses. It was easy in those times to look with arrogant detachment at the armies of adults who seemingly sludged their way through the nine-to-five workday world with almost religious commitment to the golden reward of retirement. Subsequent years have not dulled my humanistic concerns, but there have been many sobering insights about life scheduling brought about by the harried pace and economic demands of adulthood; not to mention the dismal "era of limits" spawned by the 1970s and the myriad of scholarly technicalities that accompany prolonged academic training. The reasons for the nine-to-five work-a-day existence have become apparent. Yet there remains the question whether the harried march from school to work to retirement must be as rigid as it has become. Thus, the original impulse that catalyzed my interest in flexible life patterns has grown into an inquiry about why most men and women of today spend the time of their lives as they do, and whether there are desirable and reasonable alternatives. In writing this book I have tried to be scholarly and objective, but I must admit that lingering in the back of my mind has been a personal concern that the value of time must be given more attention relative to the struggle to gain and maintain material well-being. Whether this concern has unduly inflicted this volume is for the reader to decide.

During the time this book has been in preparation, I have been personally amazed at the durability of its major premise. The original proposition that individuals and society would benefit from more freedom to schedule lives has held up as I've explored the issue from the vantage point of education, family life, mid-life pressures, employment, retirement, values, and the ever-present economic constraints on the use of time. To be sure, research and countless discussions have revealed many problems and obstacles that discourage actualization of flexible life scheduling. Nonetheless, research conducted in the preparation of this book has also suggested that there are more problems with retaining the inflexible education-work-retirement lockstep that now prevails.

So many persons have contributed in some way to this volume that I feel frustrated in the attempt to acknowledge all those who have helped. First and foremost, I wish to thank my wife, Fran Corton, who has not only endured the drudgery of writing with me but has also contributed greatly with insights from her own discipline of psychology as well as first-hand perspectives as a member of that emerging majority of women who work and pursue careers of their own. More than anyone else, I owe to Fran the persistent theme advanced within this book that there is no one best way through which we might break loose of today's linear life patterns.

I also owe a great debt to Professor James Wright of the University of Massachusetts and Dr. Barry Stern of the U.S. Department of Health, Education and Welfare. There are few research methodologists I respect more highly than Professor Wright. He taught me that even though the search for knowledge occurs in an imperfect world with limited resources, the results of research ultimately depend on the commitment of the researcher to make the most of tools available with the greatest possible rigor. Barry Stern has been at once a close friend and valued colleague. His enthusiasm for the topic of life scheduling has been at once a source of pleasure and inspiration. I must give him credit for being something akin to the spiritual godfather of this book. I also owe many thanks to Professors Andy Anderson, Harvey Friedman, and Randall Stokes of the University of Massachusetts, who guided my efforts when the seeds of this book were in the form of a dissertation.

A special note of thanks also goes to Gail Rosenberg, Maureen McCarthy, and others at the National Council for Alternative Work Patterns in Washington, D.C. They were a constant source of stimulation and certainly the best source of the most up-to-date information about work-time reforms.

Those who have generously given technical advice, shared ideas and data, and provided encouragement and support have included William Abbott, Paul Barton, Tom Bates, Robert Bednarzik, Bonnie Coe, Walt Davis, Kenneth Fischer, Patsy Fryman, Sam Halperin, Janice Hedges, Emile Heller, Peter Henle, Christopher Hurn, Linda Ittner, Denis Johnston, Carol Jusenius, Ellen Lazer, Gary Lefkowitz, George Pratt, Norman Root, Robert Rosenberg, Isabel Sawhill, Lynda Sharp, Frank Schiff, Jule Sugarman, Alfred Tella, Bernhard Teriet, Dyckman Vermilye, Stephen Wandner,

Anne Young, and Howard Young. While many of these persons do not necessarily subscribe to the total theme or particular parts of this book, the pages that follow have been greatly enriched by their help.

A special note of appreciation is richly deserved by Linda Becker, Barbara Burns, Barbara Katz, and Kathy Redfield, for their splendid work in typing various stages and portions of this book.

Finally, I must pay a special intellectual tribute to Dr. Juanita Kreps, who did most of the ground-breaking research on the topic of life-time distribution of education, work, and leisure. In virtually every aspect of this topic, she has contributed the basic foundations for current and future study.

CONTENTS

LIST OF TABLES

LIST OF FIGURES

PART I

THE ISSUE: THE TIME OF OUR LIVES

Time is weaving the innumerable fine threads of what we now call the future. In the act of searching out the future, man raises to the level of foresight and purposefulness. This represents a transition from man of action, who performs on the basis of the momentary situation, to the man of thought, who takes account of the consequences of his actions and of events to come. This shifting of concern from what is to what may be represents a tremendous spurt of the human spirit. In taking thought for tomorrow, man begins to create tomorrow.

Fred J. Polak
Image of the Future

1

BREAKING THE EDUCATION-WORK-RETIREMENT LOCKSTEP

For most persons in our society, the activities of education, work, and leisure are arranged in what might be called a "linear life plan." Stated concisely, most of us march in linear fashion through school in youth to 40 consecutive years of work or child rearing in mid-life to retirement in old age. While this pattern had healthy features in the past, there are indications that the predominance of this linear life pattern may be stifling the vibrance and productivity of our lives and our society. Indeed, there are increasing indications that we need more flexibility in the ways we schedule the major activities of education, work, and leisure throughout the days, weeks, and years of our lives.

In human terms, there are abundant signs of countless individual problems stemming from the inflexibility of today's linear life patterns. Let me cite a few examples. In Detroit there is a 25-year-old assembly-line worker who left school without completing his high school diploma. Today he would like to finish high school and try college, but his job allows no opportunity to work part time or take a leave of absence to resume his education. In San Francisco, a city planner in her early thirties has just become pregnant. Ideally, she would like to take a year off, then work two-thirds time for a few years before reimmersing herself into a career. Unfortunately, the penalties to her advancement would be tremendous and opportunities for reduced worktime in her current job nonexistent. As a result, she will struggle with 14-hour days between her job and child rearing, contributing less than she would like to both. In the Texas town of Killeen a man in his late forties has worked at the local meat packing plant for over 20 consecutive years. He has the savings and desire to take a year off to travel around the country, but will lose his job if he does so. In New York City a black woman has been unemployed for over a year and wonders why existing jobs cannot be shared. In Salt Lake City a 66-year-old man finds

3

himself bored with retirement, yet unable to find work. The stories are countless: persons trapped unwillingly inside or outside the lockstep flow from school to work to retirement. Each in their own way, they are adding up to a growing demand for more flexible life patterns.

There are also signs that the ways in which we distribute education, work, and leisure over total lifetimes are draining away the productive potential and financial solvency of our society. For a good part of the 1970s, about 7 percent of the U.S. labor force has been unemployed. The cost of this unemployment in human misery, lost productivity, and inflationary tax-raising income maintenance programs has been awesome. If we cannot create enough jobs for those who wish to work, might it not be better to find ways to allow persons in mid-life to reduce or temporarily leave their jobs and thus share their work with others? From another perspective, the competition for work has pushed young persons into ever longer years of schooling and older persons into increasingly earlier retirement. Beyond the social and psychological problems resulting from this pattern, the compression of work into ever fewer years of mid-life has created years of nonincome-earning time at the extremes of life that are leading to poverty, large public expenditures for income maintenance and student aid, and the threatened bankruptcy of the Social Security system. Might it not be better to distribute income-earning worktime more evenly over the total life cycle? Further still, essentially positive forces over the last two decades have led to major increases in educational attainment. Between 1957 and 1978, the portion of the U.S. labor force with one year of college or more almost doubled from 17.5 to 34.0 percent. Today we are finding that our society, as we are currently organized, has a limited need for better trained and educated workers. As a result, there is an awesome waste of productive human potential, growing discontent due to our failure to provide equal opportunity through education, and the possibility of widespread institutional stagnation due to the lack of chances for individual advancement. If we cannot create enough quality jobs to match the skills and aspirations of our population, might it not be better to rotate the more attractive positions among qualified persons by recurrent cycles of education, work, and leisure throughout life?

SURVEYING THE LOCKSTEP

Before diving into the problems of existing life patterns and a discussion of the alternatives, we might do well to ask why the linear life plan has evolved and become so predominant. In the most general sense, the current predominance of the linear life pattern can be attributed to three major causes. First, the natural dynamics of the human life cycle are such that a person gains physical maturity and learns basic skills in youth, works in mid-life when abilities and responsibilities are at their peak, and retires from work as abilities and responsibilities decline in old age.[1] Second, the frequent shortage of jobs in the United States over the last several decades has fostered fierce competition for work that has combined with other kindred forces to hold young people in prolonged years of schooling and push older persons into ever earlier retirement. Third, the explosion of economic productivity brought about by industrialization has allowed tremendous growth in the average person's time away from work.

Some figures on the growth of nonwork time may provide some helpful background. Rough estimates computed by the New York Metropolitan Life Insurance Company of the years of total lifetimes spent on major activities during different stages of history serve to dramatize this growth of nonwork time. These figures estimate that the average lifespans of persons living in primitive (before 4000 B.C.), agricultural (4000 B.C. to 1900 A.D.), and industrial (post-1900 A.D.) eras to be, respectively, 18, 35, and 70 years. In terms of work, these estimates show that about 33 percent of the average primitive person's lifetime was spent on work, 29 percent of an agricultural person's lifetime, and about 14 percent of an industrial person's lifetime.[2] More exact computations based on data from the U.S. Bureau of Labor Statistics indicate that worktime for American males, as a portion of overall waking and sleeping lifetime, has been cut almost in half between 1900 and 1970 from 23.7 to 13.4 percent.[3]

What forms have past increases in nonworktime taken? A good deal of these gains have come in the form of a reduced workweek. Specifically, the average U.S. workweek has declined from approximately 60 to 39 hours over the last century.[4] However, during the last three decades the workweek has remained remarkably stable with significant increases in nonworktime taking the form of longer vacations and more holidays, and more recently considerable increase in the years for education during youth and earlier retirement in old age. In this way, both the options and constraints of advanced industrialization have led to the compression of work into the middle of life and an increasingly pronounced linear life plan.

Just how extensive has this linear life plan become? As one indication, long-range trends show that the proportion of all persons aged 65 and over who were working or looking for work dropped from 35.8 percent in 1900 to 13.1 percent in 1977. Rates for men aged 65 and over show an even more dramatic decline from 63.1 to 20.1 percent over the same period since only one-fifth of the female population worked at the turn of the century. At the other end of the life cycle, the labor force participation rates for all persons aged 14 to 24 declined only slightly from 51.2 to 45.1 percent between 1900 and 1977. For men alone, the labor force participation rate for this age group declined from 73.2 to 49.4 percent. Further still, some 41.8 percent of all voluntary part-time jobs in 1977 were held by persons between the ages of 14 and 24, many of whom were full-time students.[5]

A more graphic indication of the increasing compression of work into mid-life comes from figures calculated to show changes in the proportions of the average male lifespan spent primarily on work and nonwork activities between 1900 and 1970 (similar figures for women were not computed due to technical difficulties).* These figures show that the percentage of the average U.S. male's "lifetime" spent primarily on work or looking for work has decreased from 66.6 percent in 1900 to 59.7 percent in 1970 (see Figure 1.1). Further, computations based on average life longevity, years of school, and average age of retirement indicate that the time spent primarily in work activities has been increasingly compressed into mid-life. Correspondingly, nonworktime has increased substantially in the earlier and later years of life. While this trend was influenced by a dramatic increase in longevity before 1940, the compression of work into an ever smaller proportion of mid-life has increased despite relatively constant life expectancies in recent years. Further still, projections from the Bureau of Labor Statistics suggest an ever more pronounced development of this linear life plan. Specifically, unabated development of current trends will result by 1990 in 44.2 percent of the average U.S. male's lifetime being spent in nonwork activities in youth or old age (see Figure 1.1).

There are, of course, exceptions to this apparent predominance of the linear life plan that are not readily obvious from standard labor statistics. Young persons engaged in prolonged schooling in pursuit of advanced degrees are prone to vacillate between periods of work and school during the later phases of their education.[6] Up to recent times, women have had shorter worklives than men because they have borne the brunt of child rearing responsibilities. However, the current trends show a growing tendency to maintain worklife continuity.[7] For men, there is some incidence of rotation in and out of the labor market during later years, particularly among the less competitive workers. Nonetheless, such tenuous attachment to the labor force has commonly ended in earlier retirement.[8] Although there has been some loosening up of overall life scheduling through limited worktime innovations and atypical individual behavior, it can be said that the linear life plan does represent the prevailing life pattern of persons in late twentieth century American society.

Despite problems associated with this linear life pattern, there can be little doubt that it is more humane and efficient than the life patterns of the nineteenth century and earlier times. In many ways it would appear that this pattern is well attuned to the natural dynamics of the human life cycle. The expansion of school time during youth has increased individual opportuni-

---

*Figures were computed for U.S. males only because of fundamental differences in current lifetime patterns between men and women that made consolidation of figures for both men and women inadvisable. Parenthetically, when "homekeeping" and "child rearing" are considered as "work," the life pattern differences between men and women become more similar. Additionally, while women appear to be pursuing longer and more continuous "worklives," it is unlikely that the average woman will develop a worklife that consumes a longer portion of total lifetime than the average man. In this sense, male lifetime activity estimates present a conservative indication of the linear life plan.

FIGURE 1.1

U.S. Men's Lifetime Distribution of Education, Work, and Leisure by Primary Activity, Actual 1900, 1940, 1960, 1970, and Projected 1980 and 1990

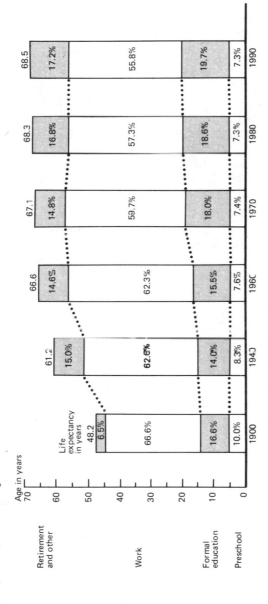

Source: Worklife expectancy figures (number of years in labor force) obtained from Howard N Fullerton and James J. Byrne, "Length of Working Life for Men and Women, 1970," *Monthly Labor Review*, February 1976, pp. 31–35; and Howard N Fullerton, "A Table of Expected Working Life for Men, 1968," *Monthly Labor Review*, June 1971, pp. 49-54. Life expectancy figures (at birth) obtained from *Statistical Abstracts of the United States, 1974* (Washington, D.C.: Bureau of the Census, 1975). p. 55. School years (completed for persons over 25) obtained from *Digest of Educational Statistics for 1975* (Washington, D.C.: U.S. Department of Health, Education and Welfare, Office of Education, 1975), pp. 14–15. Projected figures of worklife and life expectancy from unpublished computations provided by Howard N Fullerton, Bureau of Labor Statistics. Projected years of education are estimates derived from *Current Population Reports,* Series 20, nos. 243 and 293, and Series P-25, no. 476 (Bureau of the Census).

ties as well as broadened personal horizons. For persons in mid-life, it seems only reasonable that work activities should be undertaken while one is at the peak of productive capacities and confronted with the economic dependence of a family. Finally, the release of many aging and often ailing persons from the stresses and ordeals of gainful work through the institution of retirement is truly a humane accomplishment.

While the overall effect of the linear life plan can be viewed as a general improvement of the human condition, it is important to question whether its continuation is desirable or feasible in coming years. Many social conditions have a kind of "life of their own" in which they continue to exist because of institutional inertia and human habits that may be out of step with emerging needs of individuals and society. Thus it is appropriate to question whether the linear life pattern persists in response to real social and human needs or whether more flexible patterns of life might be better suited to late industrial societies such as the United States.

THE GROWING ISSUE OF LIFE-CYCLE PLANNING

Are we approaching, or perhaps well beyond, the point of "diminishing returns" for the compression of work into the middle of life? Is it necessary to have all of one's schooling during youth? Should we remove ourselves from the labor force once and for all in old age? Are there realistic alternatives for the ways we might schedule education, work, and leisure over our total lifespans?

The issue of life scheduling is a vast topic touching upon a multitude of varied and often contradictory social forces. The basic proposition of this book is that the changes in the conditions that determine life patterns are making more flexible timing of education, work, and leisure over total lifetimes both desirable and possible. There is reason to believe that the century-long trend of increasing school in youth and retirement in old age is coming to an end. Indeed, this trend may already have gone too far; the proportion of nonworktime at the extremes of the life cycle may actually be reduced in coming years in favor of more time for leisure and learning during the middle of life. Further still, there is cause to speculate that any increases of nonworktime during mid-life will not come in a monolithic form, such as a standard reduction of the workweek, but rather in a myriad of ways ranging from increased part-time employment to extended sabbaticals.

What basis do I have for forecasting these departures from the past? The answer to this question does not come easily with a few glib phrases. Indeed, we can only assess these possibilities through a widely scoped evaluation of numerous social trends that may attenuate or reverse the forces that originally gave rise to the linear life plan. A few words about these forces may help set the scene for the more detailed discussion of coming chapters.

There are signs that even the seemingly intransigent nature of life and family cycle dynamics may be undergoing transformations supportive of more flexible life patterns. To be sure, the stages of youth, adulthood, and old age will not disappear. However, changing patterns of learning, family life, as well as physiologically based trends in longevity and health are creating lifetime scheduling options that were heretofore nonexistent. In broad overview, people are living longer nowadays, and this is expanding the time frame for distributing education, work, and leisure over total lifespans. In 1900, when the average life expectancy at age 20 was 42 years, the notion of obtaining all of one's schooling in youth in preparation for adulthood was a sound idea. Today life expectancy at 20 is about 55 years, and the idea of recurrent education throughout longer lifespans is both reasonable and increasingly common. Up to recent years, family responsibilities for dependents during mid-life required men to pursue continous employment in order to fulfill a role as "breadwinner" and women to forego or minimize job holding in order to care for children and elderly relatives. Today family units are generally separated from older relatives, couples are having fewer children, and women are seeking career involvements that embellish family incomes. As a result, husbands and wives are beginning to share homekeeping and income earning in ways that may allow more flexible life schedules. Finally, increasing life expectancy and better health among the older population are altering the very definitions of "old age" and "retirement." Life expectancy for persons aged 65 has increased from 12.8 to 16.0 years between 1940 and 1975. This suggests that failure to work in some fashion during the later stage of life may produce severe financial hardships over the increasing length of nonincome-earning retirement years, and that growing numbers of older persons may both prefer and be able to work well beyond current retirement ages. All in all, there are notable indications that the distinctions between the natural stages of life are blurring, and that future years may bring a reversal of the compartmentalization of life into "the three boxes" known as education, work, and leisure.[9]

Competition for jobs, which once fostered the linear life plan, may ironically bring about flexible life patterns in coming decades. In the past, social policies and individual decisions prolonged years of schooling during youth and retirement in part as a kind of work sharing that improved mid-life employment opportunities by reducing the size of the labor force. Today, there is declining benefit to be gained from further expansion of schooling in youth or retirement, and growing desire for more work opportunities among the young and old. If we cannot create an adequate number of jobs in some other way, we may find it desirable to reduce worktime in mid-life in order to spread employment among those ready and willing to work. The idea of reductions of work in mid-life becomes particularly pertinent in view of the increasing labor force activity of women. Current trends show that two out of every three new entrants into the labor force are women. This growing pursuit of paid work on the part of women is causing rapid growth of the working or job-seeking population and intensifying the unemployment problem. This suggests the plausibility of sharing work between the sexes as well as among age groups, particularly if increased family income from married women workers encourages men to forego income-earning work-time for more time off the job. Thus the likelihood that growing numbers of mid-life workers might find it both possible and desirable to reduce work-time may provide a promising opportunity to attenuate persistent unemployment by a variety of worktime reductions during the middle of life.

The last major force that may give rise to new life patterns concerns values toward work and leisure. As a result of social trends already reviewed, there are growing indications that Americans are shifting their preferences toward the amount of paid work they desire, as well as the scheduling of work over short and long periods of time. It is particularly notable that numerous survey studies and work-place experiments indicate that these preferences are not ideal dreams of how the world might be under perfect conditions but responses to hard economic tradeoff choices in which earnings must be sacrificed to reduce or otherwise change worktime arrangements. Additionally, these studies reveal that preferences for alternative worktimes vary tremendously. Although research in this area is still in its exploratory stages, available data strongly suggest the emergence of a new set of values that may catalyze a variety of institutional reforms concerning worktime and life scheduling.

This book will deal at length with substantive discussion of the social forces that may give rise to flexible life scheduling. However, before turning to the task of assessing the impact of these changing conditions, a brief digression will be made to outline possible alternatives and provide a brief history of proposals for more flexible lifetime scheduling.

NOTES

1. Melvin Reder, "Hours of Work and the General Welfare," in *Hours of Work*, ed. Clyde Dankert et al. (New York: Harper and Row, 1965), pp. 179–200.

2. John McHale, "World Facts and Trends," *Futures*, September 1971, p. 260.

3. Fred Best, "The Time of Our Lives: The Parameters of Lifetime Distribution of Education, Work and Leisure," *Society and Leisure* 1, no. 1 (May 1978): 97–98 and 108–09.

4. Fred Best, Phillip Bosserman, and Barry Stern, "Income-Free Time Tradeoff Preferences of U.S. Workers: A Review of Literature and Indicators," *Leisure Sciences* 2, no. 2 (July 1979): 122–25.

5. Figures for 1900 including those in the armed forces were computed from decennial census data cited from *The Statistical History of the United States*, (Stamford, Conn.: Fairfield Publishers, 1965). Figures for 1977 from the *1978 Employment and Training Report of the President*, U.S. Department of Labor, p. 186.

6. *Career Thresholds*, Vol. 6, Research and Development Monograph No. 16, U.S. Department of Labor, 1977.

7. *Dual Careers*, Vol. 4, Research and Development Monograph No. 21, U.S. Department of Labor, 1976.

8. *The Pre-Retirement Years*, Vol. 4, Manpower Research Monograph No. 15, U.S. Department of Labor, 1975.

9. Richard Bolles, *The Three Boxes of Life: And How to Get Out of Them* (San Francisco: Ten Speed Press, 1978).

2

CONSIDERING ALTERNATIVE LIFE PATTERNS

Ultimately, the alternative ways in which we might schedule the days, weeks, and years of our lives are as numerous as the hours in our lifetimes. Before plunging into the reasons for life-cycle reforms, it may be worthwhile to pause a bit to explore the life-scheduling options that might be possible. While the alternatives discussed here have been computed without consideration of the constraints of work organizations, occupational commitments, and personal obligations, they are useful as a means of defining the range of scheduling options that might be evaluated more rigorously.

OUTLINING THE OPTIONS

How might existing amounts of worktime be rescheduled over weeks, months, and years? The average American worker in 1978 had about two weeks vacation, five holidays, and worked about 39 hours a week for 49 weeks every year. This totals about 1,900 hours of work per year. A few examples will illustrate how this amount of worktime might be rescheduled. In terms of the workweek, the average person might work four 10-hour days, three and a half 11-hour days, or three 13-hour days with respective weekends of three to four days' length. In monthly terms, it would be possible to work three 52-hour five- or six-day workweeks and take off one out of every four weeks. Similarly, two concentrated work periods of eight consecutive 10-hour days would allow two extended periods of seven days away from work during the average month. The workyear presents even wider possibilities. Specifically, existing worktime could be rescheduled so that individuals could work forty-four 45-hour workweeks and have eight weeks' paid vacation every year; or work forty 50-hour workweeks with 12 weeks' annual vacation. Along a similar line, persons might work 50-hour workweeks for half the year and 30-hour workweeks for the other half.

Consideration of alternative schedules for overall worklives presents the complications of exploding possibilities and major variations of worklife length between men and women. In 1975 the average American man could expect to work about 40 years out of his 68-year lifespan, and the average woman to work some 24 years out of her 76-year lifespan.[1] Additionally, the average nonstudent man worked 43 hours a week while the average nonstudent woman worked 34 hours a week.[2] These variations require that the worklife alternatives for men and women be considered separately.

Assuming that current life longevity and total workyears remain constant, the average American man might pursue any of a number of worklife alternatives. He could increase his worklife to 45 years by postponing retirement five years in order to work an average workweek of 33 hours. He might also work six more hours a week or postpone retirement five years in order to add 6.5 weeks to his current annual vacation. As yet another alternative, he might leave school two years earlier and retire three years later with the intention of taking six months off work every four years for either education or leisure.

For women, the intertwining of years commonly spent in home keeping, child rearing, and "job employment" complicate the computation of lifetime scheduling options. Among the most viable rescheduling options for women might be to lengthen the worklife to 32 years such that 15 of the total working years would be spent on part-time workweeks of 20 hours. Of course, this is only one of many possibilities.

Problems with the timing of work activities for both men and women go far beyond the need to reschedule existing amounts of worktime. While most men face problems leaving or reducing work, the average woman confronts difficulties obtaining enough "employment" at the right times in her life. Such sex based contrasts beckon us beyond concern with the rescheduling of existing amounts of work to the issue of exchanging income-earning worktime for more free time.

Potential tradeoffs of income for more free time are as varied as the ways of rescheduling work. For the average worker, a forfeiture of 2 percent of annual income would reduce the workweek by 45 minutes, add an additional week of paid vacation, provide for an extended leave with pay (work sabbatical) of seven weeks every seven years, or allow an earlier retirement by about three-fourths of a year. Similarly, a forfeiture of 10 percent of current yearly earnings will reduce the workweek by four hours, add five weeks of annual vacation, provide for a paid sabbatical of 35 weeks every seven years, or allow earlier retirement by four years. It might be anticipated that many full-time workers may prefer such options. At the same time, those with inadequate amounts of work—such as many women, minorities, youth, handicapped, and elderly—might well prefer more work rather than less.

From yet another perspective, potential time-income tradeoffs might be evaluated in terms of future as well as current income. An updating of earlier computations made by Juanita Kreps and Joseph Spengler[3] serves to illustrate the potential increases of free time that might be gained in exchange for portions of expected per-capita economic growth to the year 2000. In a nutshell, these computations show the amount of free time that might be obtained if gross national product (GNP) per capita is held constant at the 1975 level, with all per capita economic growth resulting from increases in output per work hour used to reduce average 1975 worktime.[4] Projections have been computed for healthy and sluggish rates of economic growth. Each will be discussed in turn.

Potential gains in free time that would be possible with a forfeiture of the economic growth expected by the Bureau of Labor Statistics (BLS) would be substantial. Projected and extrapolated BLS growth rates of about 4 percent a year would allow a reduction in the average annual hours of work from 1,911 to 971 hours between 1975 and the year 2000 if real 1975 per capita GNP were held constant and all potential gains in production were exchanged for free-time (see Figure 2.1). Under these conditions any one of the following four options would be possible by the year 2000: a 20-hour workweek, 27 weeks of annual paid vacation, a 39-month paid sabbatical every seven years, or retirement at age 39 (see Table 2.1). A less dramatic exchange of one-third potential per capita economic growth for free time would allow an increase of per capita GNP as well as a decline of worktime to 1,598 hours per year. This tradeoff of one-third of economic growth would give the average worker a 33-hour workweek, 11 weeks' paid vacation, 13 months' paid sabbaticals every seven years, or retirement by age 56 (see Figure 2.1 and Table 2.1). Even a tradeoff of only 10 percent of economic growth would provide by the year 2000 a 37-hour workweek, five weeks' paid vacation, four-month sabbaticals, or an average retirement age of 62. Of course, any range and combination of the above options would be possible.

Less optimistic projections of the GNP based on a 2 percent annual growth rate provide smaller but still significant opportunities for gains in free time by forfeiture of potential increases in per capita production. This sluggish growth rate would allow a reduction in total annual worktime from 1,911 to 1,428 hours between 1976 and the year 2000 if all potential economic growth were exchanged for free time. This would allow a 29-hour workweek, a 15-week annual paid vacation, a 20-month paid sabbatical, or retirement at age 52. An exchange of one-third potential gain in per capita GNP would allow a work year of 1,750 hours and a 36-hour workweek, seven-week vacations, seven-month sabbaticals, or retirement at age 61. A tradeoff of 10 percent of potential growth would allow only minor gains in free-time such as a 38-hour workweek, four-week vacations, two-month sabbaticals, or retirement at age 64. As previously noted, potential time-income tradeoffs might take any number of combinations.

FIGURE 2.1

Alternative Uses of Economic Growth in GNP Per Capita and Hours Worked, 1976-2000 (Based on extrapolations of BLS "slower recovery" economic projections)

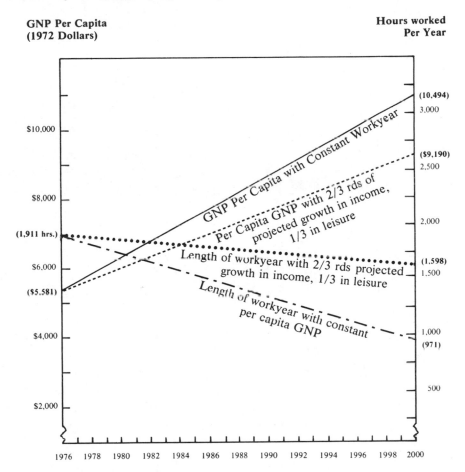

GNP Per Capita
(1972 Dollars)

Hours worked
Per Year

Source: Computed on the basis of economic growth, labor force, and total population projections cited from Charles Bowman and Terry Morlan, "Revised Projections of the U.S. Economy to 1980 and 1985, *Monthly Labor Review*, March 1976; Howard Fullerton, "Revised Projections of the Labor Force to 1990," *Monthly Labor Review*, December 1976; and *Statistical Abstracts of the United States 1976*, Series E Projections, p. 394.

THE SHAPE OF TIME TO COME

It is one thing to outline possible time-income tradeoffs and work rescheduling options but quite another matter to forecast which patterns will

TABLE 2.1

Projected Growth of Productivity and Possible Use of Potential Free Time, 1975–2000 (Bureau of Labor Statistics "slower recovery" projections and extrapolations to 2000, 1972 dollars)

| | Computation of Potential Free Time | | | | Possible Uses of Potential Free Time | | | | | | | |
| | | | | | All GNP Growth to Free Time | | | | One-Third GNP Growth to Free Time | | | |
Year	Actual & Projected Adjusted GNP in 1972 Dollars (billions)	Actual & Projected Total U.S. Population (millions)	Actual & Projected GNP Per Capita in 1972 Dollars	Potential Hrs. Per Yr. Released from Work Per Worker	Work-week (Hrs.)	Vaca-tion (Weeks)	Sabba-tical (Mos.)	Retire-ment (Yrs.)	Work-week (Hrs.)	Vaca-tion (Weeks)	Sabba-tical (Mos.)	Retire-ment (Yrs.)
1975	$1,191.7	213,540	$ 5,581	—	39.0	3.0	—	65.0	39.0	3.0	—	65.0
1980	1,557.8	222,769	6,993	385.0	31.1	13.9	17.6	53.3	36.4	6.4	5.5	61.3
1985	1,865.5	234,068	7,970	572.4	27.3	17.8	23.7	49.2	35.1	7.9	7.9	59.7
1990	2,210.9	245,075	9,021	728.5	24.1	21.7	30.2	44.9	34.0	9.2	10.0	58.3
1995	2,547.1	253,784*	10,036	837.0	21.9	24.5	34.8	41.8	33.3	10.2	11.6	57.3
2000	2,885.8	262,494	10,994	940.5	19.8	27.1	39.0	39.0	32.6	11.0	12.9	56.4

*Interpolation

Notes:

Workweek: The average hours of work per week for the average worker.

Vacation: Total vacation time per year per worker. Potential increased vacation time is added to an estimated 1975 average vacation time of three weeks.

Sabbatical: The amount of extended free time possible every seven years if all potential free time gains are allocated to a sabbatical. 1975 annual vacation time is maintained.

Retirement: Average retirement age for worker aged 21 who allocates all potential free time toward earlier retirement. A 10 percent increase was made over other forms of free time for interest returns on deferred income.

Sources: Actual and Projected Adjusted GNP: GNP for 1975 from *Statisti-cal Abstracts of the United States, 1976,* p. 394; Projections for 1980 and 1985 from "slower recovery" computations by Charles Bowman and Terry Morlan, "Revised Projections of the U.S. Economy to 1980 and 1985, *Monthly Labor Review,* March 1976; and 1990, 1995 and 2000 projections computed by extrapolation of a linear regression based on data and projections from 1965 to 1985. GNP figures adjusted to compensate for .25 percent potential GNP exchanged for free time in BLS projections. Actual and Projected GNP Per Capita: Dollar value of average adjusted GNP per person in U.S. population. Potential Hours Per Year Released from Work Per Worker: The number of hours per year per worker that could be subtracted from 1975 annual work hours if 1975 per capita GNP were held constant and potential per capita economic growth is exchanged for free-time.

actually evolve in future years. Nonetheless, a cautious bit of speculation is called for at this point. It is reasonable to speculate that real economic growth in the United States will average around 3.3 percent per annum over the next two and a half decades, and that the average American worker may be willing and able to forfeit about 25 percent of this growth in exchange for more free time. For the average worker this would mean a decline of total yearly worktime from about 1,911 hours in 1975 to about 1,818 hours in 1985, and something like 1,700 hours by the year 2000. If these speculations are correct, increased free time by 1985 could take the form of a 37-hour workweek, 2 weeks' additional paid vacation, paid sabbaticals of 3.7 months every seven years, or retirement at age 63. By the year 2000, additional free time could take the form of a 35-hour workweek, 5 weeks' additional vacation, 9-month sabbaticals, or retirement at age 61. Once again, such increases in free time would most likely come as a combination of forms.

How might these possible gains in free time be used? First and foremost, a number of social trends suggest that it is unlikely that they would take the form of earlier retirement. Second, it might be expected that more nonwork-time would be used only marginally to increase the amount of time given to schooling during early life. More likely, we might expect a small portion of added free time to come in the form of shorter workweeks and in larger measure to allow extended periods away from work such as longer vacations, holidays, and perhaps some types of work or educational sabbaticals.

The prospect of a shortened workweek is nothing new, but the possibility of substantially extended time away from work raises the possibility of life patterns significantly different from the predominant linear life plan of the present. More specifically, it raises the possibility of widespread "cyclic life plans" in which future gains in free time, and perhaps even existing time given to education in youth and retirement in old age, would be distributed to the middle years of life for extended time away from work for either education or leisure (see Figure 2.2). Of course, a whole range of other flexible life patterns are also possible.

Assuming that there might be some individual flexibility in determining the amount and schedule of worktime, it is likely that life-scheduling patterns would vary significantly according to a person's sex and life-cycle stage. More specifically, persons, particularly women, in early child rearing years might tend to prefer shorter workweeks and perhaps longer vacations. On the other hand, persons in the pre-, late, and postchild rearing stages of life would likely tend toward longer vacations and sabbatical-like leaves from work. In terms of the 3.3 percent growth rate and 25 percent tradeoff rate computations noted above, this would mean that time-income tradeoffs and scheduling of work throughout the lifespan by the year 2000 might resemble the following:

Student Years: Part-time work and extended time for education and leisure.

FIGURE 2.2

Alternative Lifetime Patterns

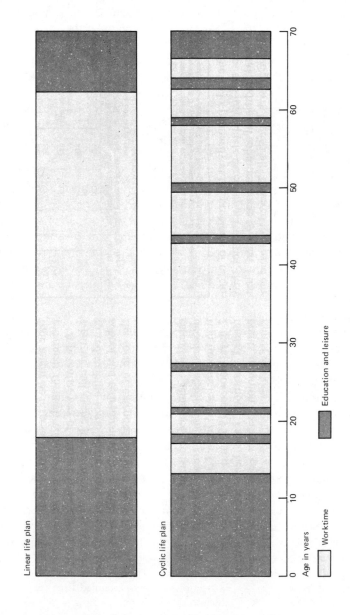

Linear life plan

Cyclic life plan

Age in years

Worktime

Education and leisure

Source: Fred Best and Barry Stern, "Education, Work, and Leisure: Must They Come in that Order?" *Monthly Labor Review*, July 1977, p. 8.

Single and Non-offspring Years:	Longer workweeks of 45 to 50 hours with annual vacations ranging from 8 to 14 weeks and some sabbaticals.
Early Child Rearing Years:	Shorter workweeks of 25 to 40 hours with moderate vacations of two to four weeks.
Late and Post Child Rearing Years:	Moderate to long workweeks of 40 to 45 hours with long annual vacations of five to eight weeks and extended sabbatical leaves.
Old Age:	Short to moderate workweeks of 25 to 40 hours and long vacations and sabbatical leaves.

On the surface this flexible life schedule is appealing to most persons, but the value of such options stems far beyond purely humanistic concerns. Such flexibility may be beneficial to our major institutions and society as a whole. Over the last few decades, countless proposals pertinent to the topic of life scheduling have been made that chronicle the development of a growing chorus of forces that may usher forth life-scheduling options that have heretofore been little more than pipedreams.

NOTES

1. Howard Fullerton and James Byrne, "Length of Working Lives for Men and Women," *Monthly Labor Review*, February 1976, p. 32.
2. John Owens, "Workweeks and Leisure: An Analysis of Trends," *Monthly Labor Review*, August 1976.
3. For a summary of the original computations by Juanita Kreps and Joseph Spengler, see "Future Options for More Free Time," in *The Future of Work*, ed. Fred Best (Englewood Cliffs, N.J.: Prentice-Hall, 1973), pp. 87–92.
4. For an elaboration on the methods of updating these computations, see Fred Best, "The Time of Our Lives: The Parameters of Lifetime Distribution of Education, Work and Leisure," *Society and Leisure* 1, no. 1 (May 1978): pp. 95–124.

3

AN IDEA WHOSE TIME HAS COME ?

In recent years there appears to have been an increasing discussion of the general notion of breaking the education-work-leisure lockstep. To those who favor such notions, the frequency of attention given to this general idea might be taken as a source of encouragement. However, it is sobering to realize that the dream of more individual freedom in scheduling life's activities is far from new. This idea has existed in varying forms among a persistent minority of philosophers, privileged aristocrats, spiritual leaders, and a varied assortment of visionaries since antiquity.

THE HERITAGE OF THE IDEA

Reference to the sanctity of breaks from work—whether in days, seasons, or years—has occurred in the teachings of all major religions. In Hindu writings, withdrawal to retirement is not the last stage of life, but the stage of actively searching for understanding prior to final enlightenment. The Moslem faith requires withdrawal from work and fasting during the month of Ramadan and a pilgrimage to Mecca at least once during the life of a faithful believer.[1] Ancient Hebrew and Arabic writings show that periods of rest from work were advocated and often required. Such breaks from work were advocated for spiritual reasons, but also for the practical economic purpose of establishing a common market day. For the Jewish faith, the Sabbath day dates back to the thirteenth century B.C., and the sabbatical year to the sixth century B.C.[2] The Jewish sabbatical year was to

Portions of this chapter are an abridged updating of a longer paper prepared for the Office of the Assistant Secretary for Education, U.S. Department of Health, Education and Welfare, Fred Best, "A History of the Linear Life Plan and Its Alternatives," Contract No. POO-75-0221, January 15, 1976.

be taken every seven years for purposes of worship, self-renewal, and learning. In some cases, the sabbatical was also intended to foster social justice by relieving the debt burdens of the poor. The notion of the sabbatical year was also incorporated into the Christian faith, and as late as 1940 the U.S. liturgical conference sought to revitalize the tradition.[3]

The idea of breaking from the routine of work existed primarily within religious writings and rare utopian proposals until the late nineteenth century when the academic sabbatical was first established within scholarly communities. Harvard became the first university to instigate a sabbatical with pay for its faculty in 1880.[4] By 1910, some ten major campuses had sabbaticals; in 1922 some 58 out of 590 institutions had such programs.[5] By 1932 the idea had been adopted by 300 of the existing 575 colleges and universities.[6] While the idea of sabbaticals was accepted in principle for public school teachers, it has rarely been put into practice. The City of Boston started a sabbatical program for its elementary and secondary teachers as far back as 1890. By the end of the 1920s, 30 cities had such programs and a National Sabbatical Leave Association had been founded.[7] The push for public school sabbaticals reached its peak in 1925 when New York City enacted a plan providing teachers leave on full pay minus the cost of a substitute. Interestingly, the State of Pennsylvania started a statewide program in 1937 for the purpose of sharing teaching jobs.[8] However, despite the efforts of advocates to spread the sabbatical idea to more schools and noneducational institutions, the idea never really caught hold outside of colleges and universities.[9] One of the reasons for the limited application of sabbaticals is that they were never proposed for humanistic reasons, but rather as an investment in human capital designed to reap returns for sponsoring institutions.[10] This justification has remained dominant up to the present, and it is likely that nonacademic institutions have not viewed sabbatical programs as promising much return in terms of their goals.

In large measure, past concern with life scheduling flexibility was addressed by privileged aristocrats or persons existing outside of main-stream society. Aside from involuntary departures from prevailing patterns of life brought about by social forces beyond the control of the individual, flexible life patterns were rarely pursued. Nonetheless, the notion of flexible life scheduling has reoccurred continually.

A RISING ISSUE

By all accounts, discussion of life scheduling reforms seems to have increased significantly over the last few decades. One of the most interesting things about the growth of attention given to alternative life patterns is that it appears to be coming from highly varied groups. Most notably, discussion and proposals in this area have come from philosophers and humanists, scholars of technology and social change, advocates of lifelong learning, social scientists dealing with labor force problems, persons concerned with the problems of the elderly, and most recently the women's movement.

Popular as well as scholarly literature dealing with human values and philosophies of life have frequently touched upon the theme of flexible life scheduling. During the 1950s, writers such as Erich Fromm and Lewis Mumford praised the virtues of human growth and advocated institutional changes that would encourage pursuit of such goals. Fromm proposed major restructuring of work environments to foster a deeper sense of community and allow more leisure and education throughout all stages of life.[11] Mumford glorified the concept of the Jewish sabbatical as a means of instilling greater reflection and self-understanding.[12] During the 1960s the rise of "humanistic psychology" under the leadership of therapists such as Abraham Maslow and Carl Rogers combined with the youth "counterculture" to foster concern with experiential growth and widespread attention to the notion of periodically or permanently "dropping out" of the work-a-day routine.[13] During this time, one of the clearest manifestos of flexible life scheduling came from Robert Butler, a medical doctor who vividly characterized the dehumanizing rigidity of the education-work-retirement lockstep and proposed more flexible patterns in a nationally syndicated essay.[14]

About the same time, scholars of leisure such as Max Kaplan, Phillip Bosserman, and Stanley Parker were examining the role of leisure within industrial societies and calling for new relations among education, work, and free time.[15] In the 1970s, considerable attention was focused on the stages of human development and changing needs for education, work, and leisure over the lifespan. In 1973, William Irwin Thompson wrote a brilliant expressionistic piece about the stages of the human life cycle and the need for numerous cycles of work and nonwork during life.[16] At the same time, growing scholarly attention was given to the investigation of the changing physical and psychological needs of individuals at different stages of life,[17] and the tremendous popularity of lay writings such as Gail Sheehy's *Passages* indicated a widespread sentiment among the American public concerning the need for change and significant breaks from the institutional routines of life.[18]

Since the late 1950s, a chorus of social critics and scholars concerned with the impact of technology and affluence suggested the necessity for various ways to increase life scheduling flexibility. A good measure of this literature came from overly optimistic visions of how the world might be in coming decades. Futurists such as Robert Theobald suggested that wholesale automation would lead to massive reductions of worktime and the possibility of a leisure society in which cybernated machinery performed most of the work[19] Along similar lines, Herman Kahn and Anthony Weiner forecast gains in affluence that would allow the average worker to accrue unheard of increases of free time as well as life-scheduling flexibility.[20] The effervescent Buckminster Fuller proposed that society simply assume the basic expenses of anyone desiring to leave work under the assumption that one such person in a thousand would discover something that would support all the others.[21] At the same time, discussion of flexible life scheduling also came from less flamboyant thinkers. Most particularly, a presidential commission of prominent scholars and high-level policy makers convened in the mid-1960s to assess the impact of technology. This commission formally recommended policies to increase free time and life-scheduling flexibility as a dividend from expected productivity and a necessity for adjusting to increasing rates of social change.[22]

A somewhat related strain of thought concerning flexible life patterns came from a growing number of individuals and groups advocating "lifelong learning." The idea of lifelong learning first emerged as a humanistic impulse for personal renewal throughout life, then as a response to social change and the need for occupational retraining, and most recently as part of a search for new clientele by educational institutions. Throughout the 1950s and 1960s, Paul Goodman led the attack on the traditional system of linear education by typifying schools as "aging vats" intended to keep young persons out of the labor market and under control.[23] Peter Drucker, Ivan Illich, and others voiced similar views with varying degrees of stridency.[24] At the same time, the foundation of the "lifelong learning" movement was being laid as millions of students paraded through their school years under advice that "learning does not end with your degree." During the 1960s the vague outline of lifelong learning began to take form. Robert Hutchins wrote about the eminent "learning society" in which affluence and automation would leave people with little else to do but return to schools for the intrinsic values of education. About the same time, then Secretary of Labor Willard Wirtz proposed a worker sabbatical allowing people to return to school during mid-life.[25] Similar proposals were forwarded in subsequent years by persons such as Ernest Boyer, Harold Hodgkinson, and Peter Weaver.[26] Little by little, the concept of lifelong learning came to permeate the thought, if not the reality, of society and its educational institutions.

From time to time, writers from various backgrounds have suggested a number of worktime reforms as a means of reducing unemployment and humanizing the work place. In 1929, Walter Teagle, the president of Standard Oil, wrote and spoke nationwide in favor of all manner of ways of reducing worktime as a means of fighting unemployment by spreading work among larger numbers.[27] In 1945, Albert Persoff advocated a worker sabbatical as a means of sharing work.[28] During the mid-1950s, Peter Henle suggested the general idea of providing extended vacation time during mid-life as a possible alternative to shorter workweeks and earlier retirements.[29] The sabbatical idea countinued to receive occasional attention during the 1950s,[30] and appeared again in the late 1960s when Peter Drucker proposed it as a means of encouraging mid-life career changes.[31] About the same time, John Kenneth Galbraith made one of the earliest and widely scoped appeals for overall flexibility.[32]

During the 1970s a deluge of novel worklife scheduling proposals emerged. John Ward Pearson proposed a system of alternating eight-day workweeks to create more work, provide highly desired extended free time, and increase business efficiency through continuous operation.[33] The notion of "flexitime" or "sliding work hours" during the day was proposed by persons too numerous to mention, and a number of proposals came to the fore concerning innovative ways to increase opportunities for part-time work and sharing of jobs by two or more persons.[34] Peter Weaver advocated paying employees with all manner of flexible worktime arrangements.[35] Riva Poor documented and advocated modified workweeks such as the 4-day, 40-hour workweek,[36] and Robert Kahn suggested a unique system of organizing work into task "modules" that would allow workers greater options for arranging their worktime.[37] The idea of "multiple careers" became popular,[38] and with it came renewed advocacy of the worker sabbatical from persons such as James O'Toole, Barry Stern, and Jule Sugarman.[39]

During this time, a number of individuals and groups began to conceptualize a broad notion of worklife flexibility. A number of international studies conducted through the Organisation for Economic Co-operation and Development in Paris chronicled numerous work scheduling reforms and conceptualized the issue within the context of overall life scheduling.[40] Similarly, the National Manpower Institute, under the direction of Willard Wirtz, proposed increased flexibility in schooling, work, and leisure over the total lifespan,[41] and a special report prepared by Albert Glickman and Zenia Brown of the Upjohn Institute concluded that all manner of worktime innovations would become a permanent fixture in the world of tomorrow.[42]

Most recently, persons concerned with the problems of the elderly and working women have expressed considerable interest in more flexible worklives. Growing problems with early retirement have caused a number of social scientists to reflect on whether or not it might be better to increase nonworktime during earlier stages of life and encourage more options for working past the age of 65. Along this line of thinking, Harold Sheppard has advocated flexible and phased retirements, and he has suggested consideration of more broadly scoped life scheduling flexibility.[43] Similarly, Malcolm Morrison has observed that the application of needed flexibility in the retirement system will also require worklife flexibility in earlier years.[44] Juanita Kreps was among a small vanguard of scholars who first pondered the relations between worklife scheduling and the problems of retirement and working women. In a classic study with Joseph Spengler, she charted the economic possibilities for more free time in mid-life, and she has long observed the benefits of flexible retirement and the possible necessity of encouraging some work during retirement years.[45] Kreps also has noted the growth of working women and the resulting family time pressures that are now fostering desires for more free time among many dual-earner families.[46] Isabel Sawhill, Urie Bronfenbrenner, and Ralph Smith are among the many others who have noted this trend and recommended serious considerations of more options for reduced worktime.[47]

A review of literature and proposals concerning flexible life scheduling raises some important questions. By all accounts, the discussion of life-scheduling issues has existed in some form throughout history. Nonetheless, available evidence suggests that concern with this issue has grown tremendously in recent years. Whether or not concern with more flexible life patterns has indeed grown, and whether such concern can be said to reflect real changes in individual and social priorities, are critical questions to be addressed.

While powerful and persistent forces have given rise to the predominance of the linear life plan, a host of important social trends are converging that are likely to encourage individuals to pursue more flexible life patterns in coming years. This shift is not likely to come suddenly through the swift passage of major social legislation or wholesale departure of individuals from existing life schedules. Rather it will occur gradually, as increasing numbers of individuals and institutions grapple with a myriad of novel and interrelated social forces.

NOTES

1. Houston Smith, *The Religions of Man*, (New York: Harper and Row, 1958), pp. 63–65, 240–41.

2. Bruce A. Kimball, "The Origins of the Sabbath and Its Legacy to the Modern Sabbatical," unpublished paper prepared for the Office of the Assistant Secretary for Education, U.S. Department of Health, Education and Welfare, August 1977.

3. Phillip Ritterbush, "Cycles of Education and Experience," unpublished paper prepared for the Quality of Life Research Associates, Washington, D.C., August 20, 1975, p. 11.

4. Ibid.

5. *Association of American Colleges Bulletin*, Vol. 8, 1922, pp. 104–18.

6. Lewis B. Cooper, *Sabbatical Leaves for College Teachers* 1, no. 1 (1932), University of Florida Publications, Educational Series.

7. G. W. A. Luckey, "The Sabbatical Year or Leave of Absence for Teachers in Service for Study and Travel," *School and Society*, 14 (1921) pp. 115–20.

8. Ritterbush, op. cit., p. 13.

9. James B. Dolan, "Extended Leaves of Absence for the Professional Improvement of Public School Educators," dissertation, School of Education, Boston University, 1950.

10. Ibid, pp. 11–13; Cooper, op. cit.; and Walter C. Eells and Ernest V. Hollis, *Sabbatical Leaves in American Higher Education: Origin, Early History and Current Practice*, Office of Education, U.S. Department of Health, Education and Welfare, 1962, p. 3.

11. Erich Fromm, *The Sane Society* (Greenwich, Conn.: Fawcett, 1955), pp. 267–79.

12. Lewis Mumford, *The Conduct of Life* (London: Secker and Warburg, 1952), p. 258.

13. An important element of "humanistic psychology" was the importance of growth and new experience. See Abraham Maslow, *Motivation and Personality*, 2d ed. (New York: Harper and Row, 1970), pp. 35-38. This emphasis on human growth augmented the neoutopian "counterculture" movement of the late 1960s and early 1970s to foster widespread discussion of "alternative lifestyles" which broke the prevailing work "routines." See Ernest Callenbach,

Living Poor with Style (New York: Bantam Books, 1972), pp. 357–77; Charles Reich, *The Greening of America,* (New York: Random House, 1970), pp. 349–96; and Carolyn Symonds, "Technology and Utopia," in *The Modern Utopian,* ed. Richard Fairfield (San Francisco: Alternatives Foundation, 1971), pp. 9–11.

14. Robert Butler, "The Burnt-Out and the Bored," *Washington Monthly*, January 1969, pp. 58–60.

15. Phillip Bosserman, "Implications of Leisure for Youth," in *Technology, Human Values and Leisure,* ed. Max Kaplan and Phillip Bosserman (New York: Abington Press, 1971), pp. 161–63; Max Kaplan, *Leisure: Theory and Policy* (New York: John Wiley, 1975), pp. 187–212; and Stanley Parker, *The Future of Work and Leisure* (New York: Praeger, 1971).

16. William Irwin Thompson, "Walking Out on the University," *Harper's Magazine*, September 1973, pp. 70–76.

17. Daniel Levinson, "The Mid-Life Transition: A Period in Adult Psychosocial Development," *Psychiatry*, May 1977; Roger Gould, "The Phases of Adult Life: A Study of Developmental Psychology," *American Journal of Psychiatry*, November 1972; and Erik Erickson, *Childhood and Society*, 2d ed. (New York: W. W. Norton, 1963), pp. 247–74.

18. Gail Sheehy, *Passages: Predictable Crisis of Adult Life* (New York: Dutton, 1976); and Ellen Goodman, "In Search of the Balanced Life," Washington *Post*, June 14, 1977, p. A19.

19. Robert Theobald, ed., *The Guaranteed Income* (New York: Doubleday, 1966); and "The Triple Revolution," Ad-Hoc Committee on the Triple Revolution, Santa Barbara, Calif., 1964.

20. Herman Kahn and Anthony Weiner, *The Year 2000* (New York: Collier-Macmillan, 1965), pp. 193–202 and 213–17.

21. Hugh Kenner, *Bucky: A Guided Tour of Buckminster Fuller* (New York: William Morrow, 1973), pp. 188–97.

22. *Technology and the American Economy*, Vol. 1, Report of the National Commission on Technology, Automation and Economic Progress (Washington, D.C.: U.S. Government Printing Office, February 1966), pp. 64–65 and 90–91.

23. Paul Goodman, *Compulsory Mis-Education* and *The Community of Scholars*, (New York: Random House, 1962), pp. 18 and 54.

24. Peter Drucker, *The Age of Discontinuity* (New York: Harper and Row, 1968), pp. 221–23; Ivan Illich, *Deschooling Society* (New York: Harper and Row, 1970); and Lord Bowden, "Learning All Our Lives" in *The World in 1984*, Vol. 2, ed. Nigel Calder (Middlesex: Penguin Books, 1964), pp. 73–76.

25. Robert M. Hutchins, *The Learning Society* (New York: Praeger, 1968), pp. 122–36, 134.

26. Charles Benson and Harold Hodgkinson, *Implementing the Learning Society* (Washington, D.C.: Jossey-Bass, 1974), p. 113; Philip Semas, "Workers' Sabbaticals Eyed as Key to Lifelong Education," *Chronicle of Higher Education*, March 18, 1974.

27. Arthur Weinberg and Lila Weinberg, *Passport to Utopia: Great Panaceas in American History* (Chicago: Quadrangle Books, 1968), pp. 241–47.

28. Albert M. Persoff, *Sabbatical Years with Pay: A Plan to Create and Maintain Full Employment* (Los Angeles: Charter Publishing Company, 1945).

29. Peter Henle, "Proposals for Reducing the Workweek," *Monthly Labor Review*, November 1956, p. 1267.

30. M. Glen Miller, "Sabbatical Leaves for Workers?" *The Rotarian*, August 1952, pp. 26–28.

31. Drucker, op. cit., pp. 221–23.

32. John Kenneth Galbraith, *The New Industrial State* (New York: Signet Books, 1967), pp. 369–72.

33. John Ward Pearson, *The 8 Day Week* (New York: Harper and Row, 1973).

34. *Job Sharing: A Guide to Developing a Job Sharing Project* (Palo Alto, Calif., New Ways to Work, February 1976); and *Changing Patterns of Work in America*, Hearings of the

Subcommittee on Employment, Poverty and Migratory Labor, Committee on Labor and Public Welfare, U.S. Senate, April 7–8, 1976.

35. Peter Weaver, *You, Inc: A Detailed Escape Route to Being Your Own Boss* (New York: Doubleday, 1973).

36. Riva Poor, *4-Days, 40-Hours* (Cambridge, Mass.: Bursk and Poor Publications, 1970).

37. Robert L. Kahn, "The Work Module: A Proposal for the Humanization of Work" in *Work and the Quality of Life* ed. James O'Toole (Cambridge, Mass.: MIT Press, 1974), pp. 199–226.

38. Drucker, op. cit., pp. 221–23; Dale L. Hiestand, *Changing Careers After Thirty-Five: New Horizons Through Professional and Graduate Study* (New York: Columbia University Press, 1970); Damon Stetson, *Starting Over* (New York: Macmillan, 1971); and *An Evaluation of Policy Related Research on Programs for Mid-Life Career Redirection*, Vol. II (Santa Monica, Calif. Rand Corporation, 1975).

39. *Work in America* (Cambridge, Mass.: MIT Press, 1974), pp. 122–34; Barry Stern, *Toward a Federal Policy on Education and Work*, U.S. Department of Health, Education and Welfare (Washington, D.C.: U.S. Government Printing Office, 1977), pp. 98–103; and Jule Sugarman, "The Decennial-Program," *Journal of the College and University Personnel Association*, Summer 1977, pp. 47–52.

40. Archibald A. Evans, *Flexibility in Working Life* (Paris: Organisation for Economic Co-operation and Development [OECD], 1973), International Conference, *New Patterns for Working Time* (Paris: OECD, 1973); J. deChalendar, *Lifelong Allocation of Time* (Paris: OECD, 1977); and Gosta Rehn, *Prospective View on Patterns of Working Time* (Paris: OECD, 1972).

41. National Manpower Institute, *The Boundless Resource* (Washington, D.C.: New Republic Book Company, 1975); and Willard Wirtz, "Education for What?" in *Relating Education and Work*, ed. Dykman Vermyle (Washington, D.C.: Jossey-Bass, 1977), pp. 268–75.

42. Albert S. Glickman and Zenia H. Brown, *Changing Schedules of Work*, (Kalamazoo, Mich.: Upjohn Institute, 1974).

43. Harold Sheppard, *Research and Development Strategy on Employment-Related Problems of Older Workers* (Washington, D.C.: Center for Work and Aging, American Institutes for Research, October 1977), pp. 105–19, 83–85; and Harold Sheppard, "The Allocation of Work Time Over Longer Life-Span," paper delivered to the Institut de la Vie, Vichy, France, April 1977.

44. Malcolm H. Morrison, "Flexible Distribution of Work and Leisure: Potentials for Aging," unpublished paper, Antioch College, 1974.

45. Juanita Kreps and Joseph Spengler, "The Leisure Component of Economic Growth," in *Automation and Economic Progress*, ed. Howard Bowen and Garth Mangum (Englewood Cliffs, N.J.: Prentice-Hall, 1966), pp. 128–34; and Juanita Kreps, *The Lifetime Allocation of Work and Income* (Durham, N.C.: Duke University Press, 1970).

46. Juanita Kreps and R. John Leaper, "Home Work, Market Work, and the Allocation of Time," in *Women and the American Economy: A Look to the 1980's*, ed. Juanita Kreps (Englewood Cliffs, N.J.: Prentice-Hall, 1976), pp. 61–81.

47. *Changing Patterns of Work in America*, op. cit., pp. 467–74; "Statement by Urie Bronfenbrenner," in *Part-Time Employment and Flexible Work Hours*, Subcommittee on Employee Ethics and Utilization, U.S. House of Representatives, May 24, June 29, July 8, and October 4, 1977, pp. 277–92.

PART II

WHY FLEXIBLE LIFE SCHEDULING IS POSSIBLE

It is but natural, we reason, for youth to be fashionably impoverished and for old age to be only meagerly financed. A lengthening of both these nonearning periods, which during the twentieth century has resulted in an additional decade of time free of work, now poses a new set of questions regarding the appropriate allocation of work and income through the lifespan.

Juanita Kreps
Lifetime Allocation of Work and Income

4

NEW RELATIONS BETWEEN
EDUCATION AND WORK

Few institutions have been exposed to as much turmoil and change in recent decades as those concerned with education. Schools of all types and levels have been profoundly affected by a torrent of varied social forces; and they have in turn exerted considerable impact upon society in general. One of the most important outcomes of this ongoing interaction has been the generation of a number of trends that are likely to alter the distribution of education and work, as well as leisure, over total lifetimes.

In terms of life scheduling, trends in the relationship between education and work that deserve special attention are as follows:

Increasing flexibility and diversity in the methods of education may undermine the traditional assumption that most formal education should be acquired in consecutive years of full-time schooling during youth.

Increasing incidence of occupational change within longer life spans and the desire for "second chances" at school are likely to foster pressures for more time and opportunity to pursue educational activities during mid-life.

The growing mismatch between educational attainment and occupational opportunity is likely to foster a greater value for leisure and pressure for sharing of quality jobs through cycles of education, work, and leisure.

Growth in the years of prolonged schooling during youth causes extended financial hardships for students that might be attenuated by intermittent periods of education and work in the earlier part of life.

These four trends will do much to increase the incidence of work during what have come to be viewed as the "school years" of youth, and education and leisure during the "work years" of mid-life.

THE CHANGING NATURE OF EDUCATION

Changes in the lifetime distribution of education and work will stem in part from major realignments in the nature of schooling. In addition to teaching skills and knowledge, schools have also provided a mechanism for distributing social opportunity by "sorting and selecting" students according to demonstrated traits and abilities, socializing students with the values and perspectives required by society, and performing custodial roles that keep students from undesirable activities. These functions have evolved and changed over past years, and a brief look at the history of education will provide a useful background for assessing current realignments and their implications for life scheduling.

From the first primitive tribes to the beginning of the industrial era in the mid-eighteenth century, the vast portion of educational activities took place without formal schooling. With the exception of a small number of elites, who had the privilege of private tutors or attendance at church-run universities, education of the young was accomplished informally through personal relations with kinship groups and one's immediate community. Most education took the form of apprenticeship-like relations in which young persons sought to emulate the skills demonstrated by their elders. Basic literacy and mathematical skills were rarely taught, and even members of the aristocracy were frequently unable to read and write.[1]

The emergence of industrialization and accompanying social changes brought the rise of schooling as the principal means of educating youth. Foremost, the increase of affluence accompanying industrialization made it possible for growing proportions of young persons to spend increasing amounts of time and resources for educational endeavors. Additionally, the ongoing disappearance of old occupations and emergence of new ones made it less feasible for parents to pass on their skills to their children, thus giving rise to schools to train and select young persons for a shifting variety of jobs.[2] Further, the need for basic skills such as reading to cope with an increasingly complex society coupled with greater job skill requirements brought about by technological advances fostered the emergence of schools to train children in ways that parents and elders were not prepared to teach. As industrial societies matured, these and other forces not only gave rise to schooling, but also increased the number of social functions provided by schools.

Little was accomplished in the way of providing publicly funded schooling during the first 100 years of the industrial era.[3] Prior to the 1870s, children were commonly put to work at home or in factories with little schooling at early ages. In these times, it was not unheard of for children to be working full time at age seven or eight. During the first half of the nineteenth century in the United States, it was estimated that one child in six attended elementary school, and only one man in 10,000 attended a college or university.[4]

As the affluence grew and the nature of industrial society matured, school systems assumed a focal role along with increasing functions. Tax-supported compulsory education did not emerge until the 1850s, but spread rapidly after that time. Up to 1900, the major advance in public education was the spread of elementary schooling. During this period, public school systems appeared to have the dual objectives of teaching the basic "three R's" of reading, writing, and arithmetic, as well as keeping custody of children who were increasingly prevented from employment through "child labor laws."[5] As a result, illiteracy declined from approximately 50 percent in 1800 to about 11 percent in 1900.

During the first 40 years of the twentieth century, educational attainment and the roles of school systems within the United States increased dramatically. The main thrust during this period was the expansion of free secondary education. Between 1900 and 1940, the proportion of persons 17 years of age graduating from high school skyrocketed from about 7 percent to 53 percent. This general increase in schooling not only reduced illiteracy to about 3 percent by 1940 but also altered the social purposes of educational systems. Most particularly, high schools shifted emphasis from preparation for college to providing vocational training. Thus the role of public schools grew increasingly into the area of vocational education that had formerly been accomplished through some form of on-the-job experience.

Between 1940 and 1975 American educational institutions continued to perform their heretofore acquired roles, as well as assuming growing responsibilities for increasing labor skills to meet the demands of an ever more technical society, providing a productive custodial environment for young persons unable to find employment, and insuring equal opportunity to all social classes and groups. The increasing job skills required for advanced industrial employment, coupled with a surge of political support for accelerated technological advancement wrought by the post-Sputnik "arms race," led to an intense national commitment to produce a highly skilled labor force through higher educational attainment. These new priorities intermeshed with the problems of providing entry-level jobs for the maturing post-World War II "baby boom" generation and led many social policy makers to encourage prolonged schooling in order to remove young persons from the labor force.[6] Finally, the educational system became the primary mechanism for insuring equal social opportunity: first by expanding educational options to GI's returning from World War II, then working class children, minorities, women, and the handicapped.

This thrust toward increasing social opportunity, combined with other previously mentioned forces to further expand the roles of educational institutions, fostered growth of school enrollments and educational attainment. The goal of universal secondary education was progressively achieved, with some 94.1 percent of persons aged 14 to 17 attending school in 1970 as compared to 79.6 percent in 1947. The most dramatic advances came in higher education, with the proportion of persons between the ages of 25 and 29 with four years or more of college increasing from 5.8 percent in 1940 to 22.0 percent in 1975.[7]

In the future, the American educational system can be expected to consolidate the multifaceted purposes acquired over the past century, as well as assume new functions. Increased attention will likely be directed to providing skill renewal and retraining opportunities for adults, as well as teaching basic knowledge and vocational skills to youth. Further, it is likely that schools will redouble emphasis placed upon screening students to insure that persons of similar capacities are given equal opportunities to achieve. Finally, increased educational attainment is likely to create an appetite for learning programs designed for self-enrichment and recreational purposes. This ongoing realignment of the social functions performed by schools can be expected to foster a reexamination of the timing of education over lifetimes.

SCHOOL, WORK, AND NONTRADITIONAL EDUCATION

The traditional system of school instruction is changing in ways supportive of more flexible life patterns. As most of us know all too well, most schools, from elementary through graduate levels, have been modeled after a traditional system typified by a straight succession of courses with teachers providing lectures, reading assignments, and grading tests within a classroom setting. Starting in the 1960s, educational research and the political pressures fostered by a larger and more diverse student constituency forced a widespread recognition that different individuals learn best under varying methods and time frames. A wave of educational innovations followed, including nongraded studies, academic credit for work and other experiences, vouchers and "learning contracts," residential colleges, decentralized campuses, ethnic curricula, and equivalency examinations. Such reforms are likely to alter life patterns by combining work and school during youth and reducing the tendency to restrict formal education to youth.

It is becoming apparent that many important skills and traits are best learned through direct personal experience outside of the classroom. Indeed, it is increasingly recognized that work in itself has important educational value. Further, there is a growing awareness that prolonged schooling without work experience may have many negative consequences. For example, students can train for occupations with unrealistic assumptions about job opportunities, or prepare for careers in which they later find themselves to be unsuited by temperament or ability. Prolonged education, when confined to the classroom, can foster false assessment of one's preparation for work.[8] In some cases, the absence of work experiences during school can create student suspicions that employment opportunities will not result from educational attainment and can therefore undermine motivation to stay in school.[9] Finally, it is becoming apparent that career-related work experience, as well as educational attainment, is an increasingly important prerequisite for finding a job. As a result, schools are seeking to better integrate work experiences into their curriculums through a variety of cooperative programs, work-study arrangements, internships, job simulations, and career exploration programs.

A number of studies indicate that efforts to integrate education and work would be well received by students. One particularly interesting 1973 survey by Daniel Yankelovich posed a number of novel posthigh-school options to a national sample of youth between the ages of 16 and 25:

A start-your-own-business program featuring training and interest-free loans.

New types of technical schools offering certified training for skills needed in expanding industries.

A career-planning year exposing the person to many different fields and job opportunities and featuring career counseling.

New types of apprenticeship programs in industry, the arts, unions, or service organizations, where the person is paid minimum wages while he or she learns high-paying skills.

A six-year job-and-college program where the person works steadily at the job and gets a college degree for both work and formal courses taken at a nearby college.

A majority of both college and noncollege youth stated that they would "seriously consider" all but the "start your own business program." More specifically, over 70 percent expressed "serious" interest in the "career-planning year" and "six-year college-and-work plan." [10] These and other survey responses indicate that student-age youth have a strong interest in spreading the work years generally restricted to mid-life into the school years of youth and early adulthood.

In addition to spreading work into the domain of school years, the premium placed upon individualized methods of learning can be expected to foster values and expectations for more personal discretion in scheduling education, work, and leisure. This will greatly reduce traditional social stigmas and institutional rigidities that have restricted formal education primarily to youth and early adulthood. While such liberalization in the scheduling of school programs does not insure commensurate adjustments in the world of work, it is likely to pave the way toward more learning opportunities for persons who are middle aged and older.

SOCIAL CHANGE, ADULT DEVELOPMENT, AND LIFELONG LEARNING

Today people are confronting constant social and personal change throughout ever longer lifespans, and resulting occupational transitions and

FIGURE 4.1

Employment by Major Occupational Group, Actual 1960, 1972, and Projected 1980, 1985

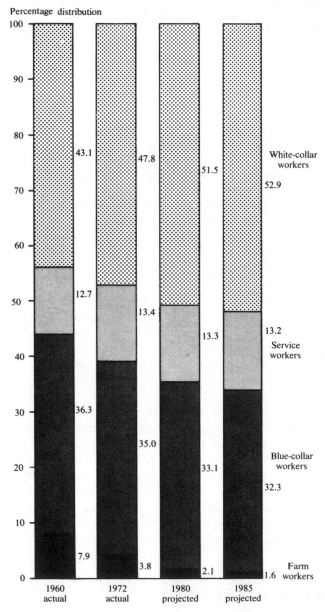

Source: *The Condition of Education*, U.S. Department of Health, Education and Welfare, 1976, p. 121.

postyouth schooling are likely to foster still more pressure for life-scheduling flexibility. Occupational displacements and opportunities resulting from social change may require mid-life retraining; continuing aspirations for upward social mobility may encourage many middle-aged persons to return to school in order to enhance their status; and human needs for growth and change may cause a demand for a variety of educational experiences during mid-life and later. Additionally, educational institutions searching for a new clientele in the wake of the maturing "baby boom" generation will be likely to adjust their curriculums to attract older students.

Rapid rates of social change are likely to cause frequent occupational adjustments and some need for retraining throughout life. Recent projections estimate that between 1974 and 1985 the average growth of all occupations will be 20 percent, but the growth and decline of specific occupations will range from plus 158 percent for dental hygienists to minus 39 percent for farmers and farm workers.[11] These projections suggest that occupational change, which has always been a common phenomenon,[12] will certainly persist and perhaps increase for many workers (see Figure 4.1).

As one indication of current occupational change, a study by James Byrne found that 8.7 percent of all U.S. workers changed major occupational categories during 1972.[13] Another study based on different data by Dixie Sommers and Alan Eck found that almost a third of all workers in 1966 who were still working in 1970 had changed to a different detailed occupation, and about 18 percent had changed major occupational categories.[14] Both these studies underscore the general reality of occupational change. Of course, much of this change occurs among younger age groups,* and within firms as promotions or horizontal transfers facilitated by various forms of on-the-job training. However, it is also true that a good deal results from involuntary dislocations and self-motivated pursuit of better jobs, both of which may necessitate a return to school for retraining.

Aspirations for upward social mobility combined with job dissatisfaction and new occupational opportunities are also likely to cause growing numbers of persons to return to school during mid-life. A number of survey studies conducted over the last 20 years have shown that 8 to 19 percent of the working population are consciously dissatisfied with their jobs,[15] one-fourth to one-third feel that their abilities are underutilized by their employers,[16] and about 40 percent would like to change their occupations.[17] Thus we can expect that intense labor market competition in coming years is likely to encourage return to school by many dissatisfied workers as one of the most accessible routes to upward social mobility. Further, there is also likely to be notable return to school among persons seeking "second chances" at education foregone in younger years due to economic, emotional, and cultural reasons independent of their abilities. Even those who

---

*The rate of occupational change declined with age and was lower for women. However, women were more prone to withdraw from the labor force.

were relatively successful in school during youth may undertake retraining in order to maintain and enhance their standing in the labor force.

Life-cycle dynamics may also foster more mid-life education. Several scholars have hypothesized that adults, like children and adolescents, have developmental stages. There appears to be a growing consensus that most adults progress through successive phases of stabilization and consolidation followed by change and growth as they come to pursue new goals and confront changing problems that come with different ages.* If this is true, it can be expected that the personal discretions of modern affluence coupled with longer lifespans may cause many adults to pursue more flexible life patterns in order to facilitate new experiences, self-evaluation, and mid-life career changes.

Finally, the declining proportion of the U.S. population under 25 is likely to cause many educational institutions to encourage adult enrollment. Between 1980 and 1990 there will be a 20 percent decline in the traditional school-aged population between 18 and 25 years old.[18] As one college official put it, schools are simply "running out of kids," and they are seeking an older student clientele in order to avoid serious financial problems. Anecdotal reports of this interest in adult students is plentiful, and college enrollment figures confirm its existence. In 1970, some 22 percent of the college student population was over 25 years of age; in 1975 the proportion was 34 percent, and the 1980 proportion is in the neighborhood of 40 percent.[19] Increasingly, colleges and other educational institutions are likely to develop programs to meet the needs and encourage participation of postchild rearing women, retired persons, and the underemployed seeking new occupational opportunities and various forms of personal development.

While there is little in the way of trend data, a number of opinion surveys indicate considerable interest on the part of adults for educational activities. A 1974 Harris survey found that 49 percent of those over 18 years old were interested in the specific educational goal of "learning new skills and participating in job training programs in order to take a different job."[20] More recently, a 1977 Gallup Poll of the U.S. population over age 18 investigated why adults might go back to school and what types of schooling they might pursue. When asked to choose four major reasons why they might "go back to school," some 49 percent reported that they would pursue

---

*A review of the literature in this area suggests about six stages and junctures during the human lifespan are commonly cited: First, there is the generalized stage of childhood in which the individual seeks to learn rudimentary skills. Second, the stage of adolescence in which the major concerns shift toward the development of identity and psychological severance from parents. Third, early middle years in which the individual seeks a place in the adult world in terms of mature relationships and economic autonomy. Fourth, mid-life where the individual confronts aging and reevaluates his or her general course in life. Fifth, late middle years in which the individual confronts what he or she has become and is likely to become. Sixth, old age, with the realization of death and the necessity for finding and maintaining ongoing interests and engaging purposes.

"personal improvement and enrichment," 4 percent said they would "take classes leading to a bachelor's degree," 11 percent claimed they would "take classes that would help get a better job," and 17 percent stated they would take classes that would help them gain promotions in their existing jobs.[21] These studies indicate that the desire for education declines but does not disappear as age increases and that there is substantial latent interest in mid-life education.[22]

Actual participation in mid-life schooling lags far behind stated interest. However, available data indicate that involvement in adult educational programs is both rising and changing. One series of studies found that the proportion of the U.S. population over age 35 who are enrolled in formal degree-earning programs has increased from 1.7 to 2.1 percent between 1972 and 1977. Further, participation in these programs has shifted somewhat dramatically away from elementary, secondary, and vocational school to colleges, with full-time college attendance growing faster than part-time attendance (see Table 4.1). Four other studies found that the proportion of those between the ages of 35 and 54 who were enrolled in one or more activities of organized instruction outside of the workplace other than full-time high school or college steadily climbed from about 8.7 percent in 1957 to 11.1 percent in 1969 and 13.3 percent in 1975.[23] About one-half of these participants were pursuing occupational training, about one-fourth general education, and another one-fourth programs related to personal development.[24]

The growth of educational activities during mid-life is likely to foster more flexible life patterns in three ways. First, the increasing incidence of school enrollment during mid-life, particularly full-time college attendance, will break down the traditional assumption that formal schooling should occur in youth and encourage the redistribution of formal educational undertakings into mid-life. Second, the pursuit of educational activities during mid-life, be they formal or informal, will require time. As a result, any growth in the need or desire for education during the work and child rearing years of mid-life is likely to foster a growing demand for more individual opportunities to take time away from work. Third, it has been suggested that educational attainment increases both independent thinking and the capacity for leisure.[25] If this is true, it can be expected that increased education during both youth and mid-life may engender a greater appreciation and demand for nonwork time.

"OVEREDUCATION" AND ROTATING SOCIAL OPPORTUNITY

In previous decades, the rising needs for a highly skilled and educated labor force have merged with widespread desire for personal achievement within the context of equal opportunity to make extended years of schooling

TABLE 4.1

Adults over Age 35 Enrolled in Degree-Granting or Certified Educational Programs by Type of School, 1972, 1974, 1976, and 1977

Year	Total Number (000s)	Percent of U.S. Population over 35	Percent of U.S. Labor Force over 35	Total Percent Enrolled	Type of School Attended		
					Elementary & Secondary School	Technical & Vocational School	College
October 1972	1,458	1.7	2.3	100.0	6.9	39.1	54.1
October 1974	1,502	1.7	2.4	100.0	5.3	26.8	67.9
October 1976	1,604	1.8	2.4	100.0	4.1	21.9	74.0
October 1977	1,860	2.1	2.4	100.0	4.6	24.0	71.4

Source: Anne M. Young, "Going Back to School at 35," *Monthly Labor Review,* October 1973, pp. 39–42; Anne M. Young, "Going Back to School at 35 and Older," *Monthly Labor Review,* December 1975, pp. 47–50; Anne M. Young, "Going Back to School at 35 and Over," *Monthly Labor Review,* July 1977, pp. 43–45; and data for October 1977 provided courtesy of Anne M. Young of the U.S. Bureau of Labor Statistics.

the central avenue of social mobility. For many years, schooling represented the "meritocratic" ideal: The rewards and valued positions in society would be distributed on the basis of proven effort and skill as evidenced primarily by educational certification. Today we are beginning to realize that the developed skills, not to mention the undeveloped potentials, within our population are considerably greater than the demands of our labor market. Nonetheless, young people are continuing to stay in school longer in order to first avoid and then overcome competition with older workers and each other (see Figure 4.2). As a result, more and more education is required for jobs with relatively stable skill requirements.[26] In the absence of other channels of opportunity, the true meaning of education to both occupational achievement and human fulfillment is being lost as those seeking advancement compete by rushing to ever higher levels of "overeducation."

The increasing problem of overeducation can be illustrated by comparing the actual and projected growth in the proportion of college graduates in the labor force with the growth in the number of professional and technical jobs (the kind most college graduates seek). While the proportion of workers with college degrees is expected to rise rapidly in coming years, the number of professional and technical jobs is projected to grow only slightly. As a result, the proportion of workers who are in professional and technical occupations by the year 1990 is expected to be about 15.7 to 15.9 percent, while the proportion of college graduates in the labor force will increase to about 21.7 percent (see Table 4.2). These projections indicate an expected surplus of about 6 million college graduates in 1990.[27] Other data suggest that these figures may underestimate future underutilization of educational attainment. Indeed, the percentage of the labor force with four years of college was 17.0 in 1978, a figure that already surpasses the projected percentage for 1980.[28] In terms of occupations, Joseph Froomkin has predicted that the demand for professional and technical workers may actually decline because of technological advances and stabilized growth of public–sector employment.[29]

Projected levels of overeducation will likely foster serious problems in coming years. Not only will it result in widespread suboptimization of human resources, but also political discontent, job dissatisfaction, and the counterproductive effects of dampened occupational aspirations. The signs of these problems are rapidly becoming apparent. Even in 1972, about half of recent college graduates who were employed reported that they held jobs that were unrelated or only partially related to their studies.[30] In 1958 the proportion of recent graduates reporting such lack of relationship between their studies and jobs was only about 17 percent.[31] Furthermore, this may be only a partial indicator of future dissatisfaction.[32] When one considers that 50 percent of high school graduates in 1974 expected to be professional or technical workers by age 30,[33] it becomes apparent that the high educational and occupational expectations of today's youth can only lead to serious social tensions in coming years.

FIGURE 4.2

Educational Attainment of the Labor Force, Actual 1957–59, 1970–72, and Projected 1980, 1990

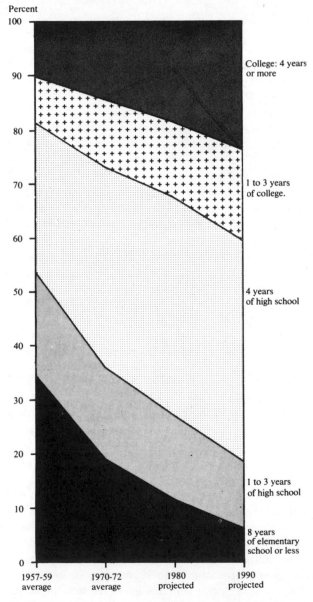

Source: *The Condition of Education*, U.S. Department of Health, Education and Welfare, 1976, p. 120.

TABLE 4.2

Actual and Projected Shares of Professional-Technical Employment for College Graduates, 1960–90

Year	Percent of Labor Force over Age 16 with Four Years or More of College	Professional-Technical Workers as a Percent of Total Civilian Employment
1960	10.0	11.4
1965	11.6	12.5
1970	12.9	14.2
1975	15.7	15.0
1980	16.4	15.3
1985	19.2	15.5
1990	21.7	15.7–15.9

Sources: Actual percent of labor force over age 16 with four years of college or more cited from *1977 Employment and Training Report of the President*, U.S. Department of Labor, Table B-9, p. 203. Projected percent of labor force over 16 with four years of college or more cited from Denis F. Johnston, "Education of Workers: Projections to 1990," *Monthly Labor Review*, November 1973, p. 24. Actual proportion of professional and technical jobs as a percent of total occupations cited from *1977 Employment and Training Report of the President*, Table A-15, p. 162. Projected percents of professional and technical jobs for 1985 cited from Max L. Carey, "Revised Occupational Projections to 1985," *Monthly Labor Review*, November 1976, p. 12. The percent of professional and technical jobs for 1980 was estimated on the basis of actual growth rates from 1970 to 1977, and the percents for 1990 were estimated by using the actual and projected growth rates for the 1977–85 and the 1970–85 periods to calculate a minimum to maximum range.

In a society in which human capacities for achievement blatantly surpass the opportunities for achievement, it becomes necessary to either expand the opportunities, redistribute opportunities, or confront declining aspirations and likely stagnation. Although the schools can be partially faulted for the failure of education to provide social opportunity, the problem lies primarily with the world of work and the dismal fact that there simply are not enough quality jobs. As a result, it may be necessary to develop new channels, and perhaps new definitions, for social opportunity and personal achievement.

There are four general responses to the overeducation problem, three of which are likely to encourage movement toward more flexible life scheduling. First, opportunities for educational attainment might be reduced. Of course, this response would gravely impair the long-standing American commitment to equal opportunity. Second, programs might be instigated to improve the "quality of work" through job redesign and participative decision making so that more jobs become acceptable to better educated workers. While a great deal can be done in this area, including a number of worktime reforms to increase individual freedom and provide breaks from boring or disagreeable work, it is crucial to recognize that the fundamental nature of most occupations is such that efforts to improve the "quality of work" would reduce but not resolve tensions resulting from the underutilization of education. Third, individuals and possibly American society as a whole may realign aspirations and values to place greater emphasis on the nonwork parts of life.[34] The likely result is that there may be a growth in the desire for free time during mid-life that would certainly contribute to the evolution of more flexible life patterns. Fourth, ways may be found to expand occupational opportunities by moving toward rotational systems for sharing not only the number of jobs but the quality of work.[35] A variety of rotational systems in which most workers open jobs and advancement opportunities to others by periodically leaving or sharing their work could become at once a major thrust toward more flexible life patterns as well as the next step in America's traditional pursuit of achievement·and equal opportunity.

PROLONGED SCHOOLING AND LIFETIME DISTRIBUTION OF INCOME

Past growth of years spent in schooling has prolonged the nonincome-earning years of youth and increased financial hardships during the early stages of life. In 1975 about 62 percent of the total U.S. population over age 25 did not enter the labor force in other than incidental ways until at least age 18, and approximately 14 percent did not enter the labor force for more than short periods until age 22 because of college enrollment.[36] Those who continued school in pursuit of advanced degrees were not likely to enter the labor force until age 26 or later. Continued extension of such consecutive nonearning or low-earning school years cannot help but foster high incidence of economic dependence, debt accumulation, and near poverty status among many young persons.

The problem of inadequate income accompanying prolonged school attendance is worsening due to the declining lifelong economic return of education and the cumulative costs of extended training. While education is an investment, and highly educated persons are still likely to earn substantially more over their lifetimes than those with less education, this relative advantage has been eroding. Incomes of college graduates continue to surpass those of high school graduates, but the advantage dropped from 53 percent to 40 percent more between 1969 and 1974; and among younger persons aged 25 to 30, the advantage fell from 39 percent to 23 percent.[37] In addition, fees and living expenses for college or other extended schooling have risen. Thus substantial debts are frequently incurred that must be repaid with declining future earnings.

The idealistic notion of a straight progression through school in order to maximize earnings in mid-life becomes less viable as the years of schooling increase. For many, if not most, the interspacing of work through the school years would relieve student financial problems, reduce the need for government and family support, and provide work experience to guide and enrich educational pursuits. As a result of these considerations, work is likely to be increasingly combined with education, and education is likely to be extended further into the life cycle.

In a nutshell, a variety of forces that are changing the nature of American education may also foster more flexible life scheduling. For educational and economic reasons, work is likely to be increasingly interspaced with education during youth, with the result that youth may no longer be primarily reserved for schooling, and formal education will be extended into the center of the life cycle. Correspondingly, the need and desire for retraining and self-enrichment may foster interest in "lifelong learning," a trend that will be encouraged by school systems searching for a new supply of students to bolster declining enrollments. Finally, increasing levels of educational attainment may further encourage flexible life patterns by fostering work scheduling reforms in response to the needs of better educated workers, new values toward leisure, and pressures for the rotation and sharing of limited quality jobs. While alteration of prevailing life patterns will ultimately require fundamental changes in the world of work, changes currently occurring within educational institutions are likely to play an important role in paving the way to flexible life schedules.

NOTES

1. Crane Brinton, John Christopher, and Robert Wolff, *A History of Civilization*, Vol. 1, 2d ed. (Englewood Cliffs, N.J.: Prentice-Hall, 1960), pp. 130, 175, 213, 326, and 330.

2. One recent U.S. study suggests that only one child in four currently assumes the same occupation as his or her parents. See Peter Blau and Otis Duncan, *The American Occupational Structure* (New York: John Wiley, 1967), pp. 23–47.

3. Massachusetts came close to a public education system as early as 1647 by requiring by law that townships of over 50 persons should pay the salary of a schoolmaster. See T. Harry Williams, Robert Current, and Fred Freidel, *A History of the United States to 1876* (New York: Knopf, 1961), pp. 78–79.

4. Williams et al., op. cit., pp. 202 and 403.

5. Brinton et. al., op. cit., p. 403; Michael Katz, *School Reform: Past and Present* (Boston: Little, Brown, 1971), pp. 65–71; and Robert Havighurst and Bernice Neugarten, *Society and Education*, 4th ed. (Boston: Allyn and Bacon, 1975), pp. 1–182 and 197–98.

6. While there is little direct empirical evidence to attest to the assertion that educational opportunity was expanded to keep young persons out of the labor market, most policy makers from these times agree that unemployment was a consideration in prolonging school years. See Phyllis Lehmann, "Willard Wirtz: Candid Answers About Joblessness," *Worklife*, February 1979, pp. 2–5.

7. *Digest of Educational Statistics 1977–78*, National Center for Educational Statistics, U.S. Department of Health, Education and Welfare, 1978, pp. 18; 14.

8. Not only does a lack of real work and job-searching experience allow the perpetuation of faulty assumptions, but inadequate educational evaluation can foster gross ignorance of

students' real educational advancement. "Grade inflation" and passage of courses without satisfying minimum requirements have contributed to this problem recently. As one example, a 1975 survey of 50,000 college students found that 60 percent described their grade average as B or better as compared to 36 percent in 1969. Those reporting a C average or lower shrank from 45 percent in 1969 to 25 percent in 1975. See William Delaney, "Traditional Values Return to Campus," Washington *Star*, January 14, 1977, pp. Al and Al8; and Barry Stern, *Toward a Federal Policy on Education and Work*, U.S. Department of Health, Education and Welfare (Washington, D.C.: U.S. Government Printing Office, 1977), pp. 34–41.

9. Anecdotal evidence recently presented to the National Commission for Employment Policy indicates that many minority high school students are refusing to continue school because the perceived absence of job opportunities provides no incentive for further educational effort. See *1978 Annual Report* of the National Commission for Employment Policy, Washington, D.C.

10. When asked to select the one plan in which they were most interested, the "six-year college and work plan" was chosen most frequently by 48 percent of the college respondents and 31 percent of the noncollege respondents. The "career-planning" year was the next most frequent choice of about one-fourth of both college and noncollege youth. See Daniel Yankelovich, *The New Morality* (New York: McGraw-Hill, 1974), pp. 111–14.

11. Max L. Carey, "Revised Occupational Projections to 1985," *Monthly Labor Review*, November 1976, pp. 13–14.

12. Sociologists Harold Wilensky and Harold Sheppard have independently estimated that the average worker of the 1950s and 1960s held about 12 jobs during the worklife. Between 1900 and 1970, the proportion of the labor force working in the agricultural sector has declined from about 60 percent to about 4 percent. More recently, the labor force has been shifting about 1 percent a year.

13. James J. Byrne, "Occupational Mobility of Workers," *Monthly Labor Review*, February 1975, pp. 53–59.

14. Dixie Sommers and Alan Eck, "Occupational Mobility in the American Labor Force," *Monthly Labor Review*, January 1977, pp. 3–17. This study revealed labor force entry and withdrawal, unemployment, and transfer between about 300 detailed occupational categories.

15. *Job Satisfaction: Is There a Trend?* Manpower Research Monograph No. 30, U.S. Department of Labor, 1974, pp. 4–5. It should be noted that direct questions about job satisfaction underestimate discontent because respondents tend to justify their current status and work. See Robert Blauner, "Work Satisfaction and Industrial Trends in Modern Society," in *Class, Status and Power*, ed. R. Bendix and S. M. Lipset (New York: The Free Press, 1965), pp. 473–87; and Harold Wilensky, "Varieties of Work Experience," in *Man in a World of Work*, ed. H. Borow (Boston: Houghton Mifflin, 1964).

16. Robert P. Quinn and Thomas W. Mangione, *The 1969–1970 Survey of Working Conditions* (Ann Arbor: Survey Research Center, University of Michigan, 1973), p. 121.

17. Unpublished study cited in John Robinson, Robert Athanasious, and Kendra Head, *Measures of Occupational Attitudes and Occupational Characteristics* (Ann Arbor: Survey Research Center, University of Michigan, February 1969), pp. 47–58 and 78.

18. David J. Graulich, "Graying of Campus: Adult Students Alter Face of U.S. College as Enrollments Falter," *Wall Street Journal*, January 24, 1977, pp. 1 and 20.

19. Graulich, op. cit., p. 1. Figures for the proportion of college students over age 35 estimated from data available from *The Conditions of Education*, U.S. Department of Health, Education and Welfare, 1976, p. 226. It is noteworthy that the proportion of college students aged between 25 and 34 years rose from 16.4 percent in 1965 to 25.0 percent in 1974. In citing these figures it should be noted that these proportions are strongly influenced by demographic trends and historic influences such as postwar GI benefits.

20. Elizabeth Meier, *Aging in America: Implications for Employment*, Report No. 7, National Council on the Aging, Washington, D.C., 1976, p. 15.

21. *A Gallup Study on the Image of and Attitudes Toward America's Community and Junior Colleges* (Princeton, N.J.: The Gallup Organization, August 1977), pp. 5–10.

22. To illustrate the extent of potential adult interest in education, a somewhat dated but instructive 1965 national survey found that 78.8 percent of persons aged 30 to 49 and 54.1 percent of persons aged over 50 stated that they "have something they would like to learn more about." Figures are calculated from data cited in Mitilda Riley and Anne Foner, eds., *Aging and Society* (New York: Russell Sage Foundation, 1968), p. 527.

23. Data from 1957 roughly comparable to 1969 and 1975 data. The 1957 data computed from *Current Population Reports*, P-20, No. 80, (1958), p. 4; 1969 and 1975 data computed from *Social Indicators 1976*, Office of Federal Statistical Policy and Standards, U.S. Department of Commerce, December 1977, p. 309. For breakdowns of data for persons over 17 years of age by occupation for years 1969, 1972, see Fred Best and Barry Stern, "Education, Work and Leisure—Must They Come in that Order?" *Monthly Labor Review*, July 1977, p. 6.

24. Barry Stern, "Desire of Workers for Education and Training," unpublished paper prepared for the Office of the Assistant Secretary for Education, Department of Health, Education and Welfare, May 1975, pp. 14–15; and *Social Indicators 1976*, p. 286. Since a great deal of adult learning occurs on the job and through informal channels such as lectures and individual studies, it is likely that adult enrollment figures underestimate the extent of mid-life educational activities. For example, a dated but still relevant 1962 national survey found that about 20 percent of the U.S. population reported "studying any subject by any method." See Riley and Foner, op. cit., p. 116.

25. It has been hypothesized that those with high levels of education are more likely to have the knowledge and skills to structure their lives to undertake rewarding occupational as well as leisure activities. See Harold Wilensky, "The Uneven Distribution of Leisure," *Social Problems*, Summer 1960, pp. 32–56. While the choice between valuable and rewarding work and leisure may swing toward work as well as leisure, there are indications that both the value given to leisure and willingness to exchange income for more leisure increases with education. For example, one 1974 national survey found college graduates to be more likely than high school graduates to prefer shorter working hours to other job characteristics including increased pay. See Garth Taylor, "Job Characteristics: Short Working Hours," National Opinion Research Center, April 1975. At the same time it must also be noted that more highly educated persons tend to receive higher incomes, and therefore may have increased incentives to work greater amounts of time. This may be particularly true if persons with higher education feel they must recover their investment of time and money spent on education. See John Owen, *The Price of Leisure* (Montreal: McGill-Queens University Press, 1970), pp. 12–17.

26. For example, James Bright has noted that the job of department store sales clerk generally required completion of eight years of schooling in 1900 and now commonly requires two years of college. Today the same job is, if anything, less demanding. See James Bright, "Does Automation Raise Skill Requirements?" in *Exploring the Dimensions of the Manpower Resolution*, Subcommittee on Employment and Manpower, U.S. Senate, 88th Cong. 2d sess. (Washington, D.C.: U.S. Government Printing Office, 1964), pp. 558–80.

27. It has been suggested by some that college-educated persons would not be "underemployed" in managerial jobs, and that such jobs will abound in future years. See Neugarten and Havighurst, op. cit., pp. 302–5. In many cases this is true. However, it should be noted that just as many professional and technical jobs do not require college degrees, and that many managerial positions such as foreperson positions and small proprietorships would "underemploy" persons with college educations. All in all, the growth of professional and technical positions is a good index of the number of jobs that can utilize college graduates. This point is generally confirmed and elaborated by a recent study of educational attainment within all occupational categories between 1950 and 1970. See Orlando Rodriguez, "Occupational Shifts and Educational Upgrading in the American Labor Force Between 1950 and 1970," *Sociology of Education*, January 1978, pp. 55–67.

28. Kopp Michelotti, "Educational Attainment of Workers—Some Trends from 1975 to 1978," *Monthly Labor Review*, February 1979, p. 56.

29. Joseph Froomkin, *Supply and Demand for Persons with Post-Secondary Education*, Policy Research Center paper prepared for the Office of the Assistant Secretary for Education,

Department of Health, Education and Welfare (Washington, D.C., 1976). Current data support Froomkin's projections. The proportion of professional and technical jobs in 1976 was 15.2 percent. The estimated seasonally adjusted proportion for 1977 was 15.18 percent, and 15.13 for January 1978. See J. Bregger and K. Hoyle, "The Employment Situation: January 1978," Bureau of Labor Statistics News Release, February 3, 1978, Table A-3.

30. Anne McDougall Young, "Labor Experience of Recent College Graduates," *Monthly Labor Review*, October 1974, p. 36.

31. Figures for 1958 as well as comparison to Young's above-noted study and reasons for reported job situation have been consolidated in Richard B. Freeman, *The Over-Educated American* (New York: Academic Press) p. 19.

32. In the 1960s it was argued by the "human capitalists" that increased educational attainment would stimulate faster economic growth on the assumption that an upgrading of the labor force through more schooling would lead to greater worker productivity. Ivar Berg, *Education and Jobs: The Great Training Robbery* (New York: Praeger, 1970), pp. 86–104, has argued that the reality of the process is quite different from the economists' model. What actually happens is a process of unproductive job dislocation by more highly qualified workers who may be forced to stay in or accept jobs not utilizing their education and bump slightly less qualified workers from their jobs. No increase in productivity occurs because the nature of the jobs is usually such that they do not require higher skills. Productivity may actually drop because the more highly qualified worker is likely to be dissatisfied with the job.

33. *The Condition of Education*, op. cit., p. 123.

34. Research tends to indicate that a lack of interest in work activities will cause workers to focus their major life concerns upon nonjob activities. See Curt Tausky and Robert Dubin, "Career Anchorage: Managerial Mobility Motivations," *American Sociological Review* 30 (1965): 725–35.

35. A number of ways are being developed to share available quality jobs among qualified persons. A number of "job rotation" mechanisms have been developed within progressive work organizations. See *Work in America* (Cambridge, Mass.: MIT Press, 1973), p. 111. Also, the concept of "job sharing" in which two persons hold one job has frequently been used to allow qualified workers to pursue demanding careers. See Barney Olsted, "Job Sharing—A New Way to Work," *Personnel Journal*, February 1977, pp. 78–81; William Arkin and Lynne R. Dobrofsky, "Job Sharing in Academia," paper delivered at the 72nd Annual Meeting of the American Sociological Association, Chicago, September 9, 1977; and "At Fillmore, Principal is Actually Two Women," Washington *Post*, December 26, 1977, p. All. Another example of such "job rotation" comes from a number of county public defender offices across the country that allow their lawyers to take a voluntary three-month leave every year with a commensurate loss of pay. As a result, new lawyers can be hired on a permanent basis. See "Statement of James Hooley, Public Defender of Alameda County," *Leisure Sharing*, California State Senate, Sacramento, November 1, 1977.

36. *Statistical Abstracts of the United States, 1976*, Bureau of the Census, p. 124.

37. Andrew Spekke, "Is Going to College Worth the Investment?" *The Futurist*, December 1976, p. 297.

5

CHANGING FAMILY LIFE AND SEX ROLES

One prominent labor economist has called the changes currently occurring in family life and sex roles "the single most outstanding phenomenon of our century."[1] His comment may not be far from the truth. Changes in the nature of families and relations between the sexes will affect all of us in countless ways at every stage of our lives. Of particular concern to the issue of life scheduling, these changes are ushering in new views concerning the uses of time and choices of life's basic activities.

Why will the growth of women workers and accompanying changes in sex roles alter life patterns? The answer lies in the tremendous impact that family life has on the stages of the life cycle. Very generally, variations of human activities over lifespans are attributed to two major factors. First, the human development and aging process is such that individuals naturally tend to learn basic skills during youth, work in mid-life while at the peak of their productive capacities, and retire in old age when abilities decline. Second, the stages of parenthood and family development have great impact on the scheduling of work and nonwork over the life cycle. Indeed, it is safe to suggest that few factors are more powerful in prompting continuous work activities during mid-life than the unrelenting financial and temporal demands of parenthood.[2] As a result, family-cycle dynamics have combined with the natural aging processes to encourage the prevalence of the current education-work-retirement lockstep. In speculating about the future, no one in their right mind would claim that these natural dynamics of the life cycle will disappear. However, a number of fundamental changes occurring within modern families are likely to reduce many of the constraints that have made flexible life patterns implausible in the past.

Of the host of forces that have been reshaping family life and sex roles, three deserve particular attention because of their emerging impact on the scheduling of work and nonwork activities:

Responsibilities for dependents are declining due to the combined trends of fewer children and increasing independence of aging relatives, thus allowing more economic and personal discretion to pursue new combinations of work and leisure.

The proportion of women who are working on paying jobs in increasing, particularly among wives and mothers, thus fostering pressures for worklife flexibilities allowing both men and women to pursue the "dual careers" of parenting and holding a job.

Family roles between husbands and wives are becoming more flexible and egalitarian, thus creating new values that are conducive to life scheduling variations and a redistribution of time given to employment within family units.

The combined impact of these trends upon the way time is allocated to work and nonwork must be judged against the backdrop of major transitions occurring within contemporary family life.

THE FAMILY IN TRANSITION

The changes currently evolving in family life and sex roles are not occurring overnight. Rather, they are the ongoing result of social forces that have been at work for centuries.[3] Through all stages of human development, the family has been a multidimensional institution serving a variety of biological, psychological, and social purposes. And, like many other institutions, the family and related sex roles have changed dramatically with the emergence of new social conditions.

In primitive, preagrarian times the family was focused heavily upon child rearing and provision of protection from enemies and a hostile environment. Under these conditions, men pursued the role of warrior-hunter and women become mate-mother-campkeepers. The value of human labor coupled with what must have been high infant mortality rates fostered a premium for large families, which further solidified the nurturient roles of women.

The advent of agrarian civilization and the development of a protective larger society shifted family purposes to economic production and consumption. Farming and the performance of rudimentary tasks became the focus of family life. The role of men shifted to the performance of heavy labor and accompanying skills, and women continued to perform home tasks and rear large numbers of children. Under these conditions the family became a highly integrated unit of economic production.

Industrialization, with its specialization and separation of work and nonwork activities, reduced and altered the economic purposes of the family but increased its importance as a source of intimacy and personal support. With industrialization came increasing economic interdependence with society at large, greater reliance on money as a unit of exchange, and separation of income-earning work activities from the family. As a result, what we now call "traditional sex roles" emerged in which men were expected to work on paying jobs while women kept house and raised children.

Today there is compelling evidence that a host of interrelated social forces have emerged over the last several decades that are causing an ongoing and profound realignment of family and sex roles.[4] Within the overall scope of human history, these changes are occurring rapidly; but within the context of the more human timeframe of years and decades, this realignment is gradual, originating over the last century with the sparse employment of women and the early feminist drives for legal equality, and likely to continue a good century or more into the future.

What are these changes, and how might they influence life patterns in the future? As a broad speculation, the "traditional" sex role dichotomy in which men are employed as "breadwinners" and women are "housewives" is likely to become progressively less distinct. This general trend will present the need for numerous reforms in the timing of paid work. For individuals, particularly married couples, the increase of total family time given to the employment of both husband and wife will create a tremendous pressure for more flexibility over the course of the life cycle to allow time away from the job to pursue family responsibilities and leisure activities. From the stand-point of society, the prospect of continuing growth in the size of the labor force due to women workers raises the question of whether worktime should be reduced in a number of ways so as to more equitably distribute available job opportunities among the increasing number of persons desiring work and between spouses within family units.* The likelihood of such long-run changes and their potential impact on life patterns can best be assessed by looking more closely at the key social trends of smaller families, more women workers, and changing sex roles.

DECLINING FAMILY RESPONSIBILITIES FOR DEPENDENTS

The declining size of most families is likely to have noteworthy effect on future life patterns. Specifically, a shrinking number of dependents within family units will reduce the financial and personal responsibilities of most mid-life men and women. In turn, families are likely to have more financial discretion to exchange income for free time and more personal discretion to utilize potential gains of free time.

Couples are having fewer children and, when this is combined with

---

*Among other things, the rise of employment among both men and women from upper socioeconomic family units may take available jobs away from both men and women in lower socioeconomic family units, thus fostering increasing inequality of opportunity and attainment.

increasing independence of elderly relatives,[5] the net result is a significant reduction in the number of dependents within the average family unit.[6] In terms of actual fertility, the number of births per 1,000 women has declined from 122.9 in 1957 to 68.4 in 1974.[7] Use of contraceptives, later marriages and resulting postponement of birth of first child, and new values concerning the ideal size of families have been major forces driving down birth rates. For example, national surveys show that 59.3 percent of wives of childbearing age wanted two or less children in 1975 as compared to 38.6 percent in 1967.[8]

The emergence of smaller families has important economic and social implications for the evolution of flexible life patterns. While families with fewer children are likely to spend more per child, they are still likely to spend less on children out of their family budgets and thus have greater financial discretion to exchange income for more time away from work. A consideration somewhat divorced from economics is that children take time and that fewer children are likely to demand less time from their parents.[9] This is particularly important when one considers the time spent on children over the span of the family cycle. Most persons do not have children in consecutive years, but space the birth of offspring two or three years apart. Thus, every child added to a family unit not only adds to the time burden at any given point in time but also means that parents will have the economic and social responsibility for a dependent child for two or three more years of their lives. Over both the short and long run, smaller families will increase the financial and temporal options for more flexibility in the scheduling of their lives. For women, this means increasing opportunity to pursue other than a "homemaker role," most notably to take paying jobs.

THE RISE OF WORKING WOMEN

The prospect of continued growth of women workers has a number of important implications for life scheduling. First, many working women pursue "dual careers" as home keepers and job holders, and the requirements of these two responsibilities are fostering a growing demand on the part of many women for work scheduling flexibility and opportunities to work less than full time. Thus, as the proportion of women in the labor force rises, it can be expected that pressures will grow for a number of worktime reforms. Second, the increase of dual-earner families that is accompanying the rise of working women will increase the financial discretion of family units to forego earnings for more free time. Finally, the time pressures occurring within dual-earner families, particularly families with young children, are likely to foster realignments of family roles and an increasing premium for more free time among both men and women.

A quick look at key social trends dramatizes past growth of women workers. Over the last few decades the increasing proportion of women who work has been staggering. The labor force participation of women has been increasing and is expected to continue to increase at a rate of about 1 percent a year.[10] Of the 2.2 million new workers who entered the U.S. labor force in 1976, 1.4 million were women. In 1960, some 32 percent of the labor force were women. By 1978 the figure passed 41 percent. Further, the increase of working women has not been restricted to pre- and postchild rearing years. About 61.3 percent of the working women in 1977 were working wives (see Table 5.1), half of whom had children under the age of 18.[11] For economic and noneconomic reasons, the incidence of women workers has risen dramatically over the last few decades, and there is every indication that this rise will continue for a good many more years.

The rising educational attainment has been one of many forces contributing to the increase of women workers. Growth in school opportunities and increased discretion brought about by fewer and later children have contributed to higher educational attainment for both men and women, in turn fostering growing labor force participation among women (see Figure 5.1). Among other things, the number of preferred children generally declines with educational attainment, which over the long run increases the discretion of women to work during mid-life. Further, the degree of sex role flexibility (that is, women working, men assuming childcare tasks, and so on) increases with educational attainment and thus engenders a family climate conducive to working wives. Further still, the educational attainment of women is equaling and perhaps overtaking that of men;[12] as educational attainment rises, we can also expect that occupational aspirations and competitive standing in the job market will likewise increase.[13] The result is likely to be a continuing rise in the work aspirations, labor force participation, and occupational standing of women relative to men.

In addition to a growing aspiration to work, many women also find it necessary to hold a job for economic reasons. Later marriage requires most women to earn their own livelihood; and high rates of divorce force large numbers of women, particularly those who are single heads of dependent households, to pursue income-earning work activity. The longer lifespans of women coupled with current social security and pension inequities also require a growing proportion of older women to support themselves after the death of their husbands. Further still, the continuing existence of financially troubled households requiring the added income of women members makes it apparent that increasing numbers of women will find it necessary to work.

Finally, equal opportunity initiatives and the changing occupational structure are providing more job opportunities for women. Although the changes are not overwhelming, women are currently making inroads as workers in what were previously considered "male occupations."[14] Beyond the slight but continuing growth of women in traditionally "men's jobs," the most rapid job growth has taken place in economic sectors with traditional "women's jobs." The white-collar occupations, including sales, clerical, and

TABLE 5.1

Women in the Population and Labor Force by Marital Status, March 1940, 1970, and 1977

Characteristics of Women Workers	1940	1970	1977
Population			
Single	27.6	22.1	15.6
Married	59.6	61.9	65.3
Widowed or divorced	12.9	16.0	19.1
Total percent	100.0	100.0	100.0
Total (000s)	50,549	69,994	77,947
Labor Force			
Single	48.5	22.3	24.1
Married			
Husband present	30.3	59.8	56.8
Husband absent	6.1	4.6	4.4
Total married	36.5	63.4	61.3
Widowed or divorced	15.1	14.3	14.8
Total percent	100.0	100.0	100.0
Total (000s)	13,840	31,233	39,374
Labor Force Participation Rate			
Single	48.1	53.0	48.0
Married			
Husband present	14.7	41.4	47.1
Husband present, child under 18	8.6	40.1	48.3
All married women	16.7	41.4	47.1
Widowed or divorced	32.0	36.2	39.0
All women	27.4	42.6	48.0
Total (000s)	13,840	31,233	39,374

Note: Figures for 1940 based on women over 14 years of age; figures for 1970 and 1977 based on women over 16 years of age.

Source: 1975 Handbook on Women Workers, Bulletin 297, Women's Bureau, U.S. Department of Labor, pp. 17 and 28; *1978 Employment and Training Report of the President*, U.S. Department of Labor, pp. 232, 235, 236; and 1978 *Statistical Abstracts of the United States*, Bureau of the Census, pp. 40–41, 401.

professional work, have expanded faster than the more toilsome manufacturing and construction occupations, and this is a major force fostering the growth of women workers.[15]

In terms of life scheduling, it is likely that the rise of women workers

FIGURE 5.1

Labor Force Participation of Persons 25–34 Years Old by Sex and Education, 1964, 1968, 1972, and 1975

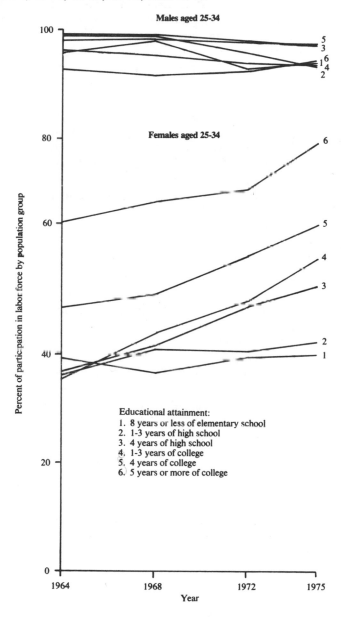

Source: The Condition of Education, U.S. Department of Health, Education and Welfare, 1976, p. 116.

and dual-earner families is likely to foster a growing need for more free time within family units. The simultaneous rise of both the proportion of women who work and the occupational status of working women may foster increasing equality and sharing of roles between men and women. Correspondingly, the time given to work by employed wives is likely to reduce the time available within family units for homekeeping, childcare, and leisure activities. This will force working husbands and wives to more equally share homekeeping as well as income-earning responsibilities, thus creating a pressing premium for more free time on behalf of both men and women within dual-earner families.

Correspondingly, the decline in the number of family dependents coupled with the added income earned by working wives is increasing the financial discretion of more and more family units to allow one or both spouses to forego what we now call "full-time work" in favor of more free time. To illustrate, the median income of families with both spouses in the labor force was $14,885 in 1976, as compared to $12,360 for families where only the husband was employed.[16] Such increased financial discretion brought about by the growth of dual-earner families is likely to encourage a kind of "work sharing" within family units in which the average man works less while women work more. While this realignment is not likely to reduce family income, it is likely to foster major changes in the quantity and scheduling of worktime.

It is probable that the pressures and discretions of the changing American family will foster a high premium for flexibility in adjusting the quantity and scheduling of worktime to match the changing needs of different stages of the family cycle. Although the time taken away from work by women during pregnancy and early child rearing is declining,[17] we can expect that such leaves and worklife departures will persist, and that the growing number of working women will cause more acceptance for worklife junctures for both men and women. For parents, particularly women, who wish to continue working during the early child rearing years, there is likely to be a growing interest in "permanent part-time work" with standard benefits and career advancement potentials. As the family cycle progresses and children enter the school years, there is likely to be a desire for shorter workweeks among both working mothers and fathers. Finally, as children pass from adolescence to adulthood, the added financial discretion resulting from a return to full-time work by both husband and wife and the declining dependence of children may lead to increasing desires for longer vacations and possibly sabbatical leaves.

FLEXIBLE AND EGALITARIAN SEX ROLES

The growth of women workers is a comparatively new trend that is likely to continue, fostering major economic and cultural changes. The underlying premise of this trend is that the "traditional" sex roles of "breadwinner" and "homekeeper" will be shared more equally within the family of the future.[18] While the growth of women workers has been clearly documented (see Table 5.1), the secondary realignments of family life are somewhat less apparent. Nonetheless, there are signs of fundamental sex-role changes within family units that are likely to foster values highly conducive to flexible life patterns.

One indication of changing family and sex roles, and their implications for worktime reforms, comes from studies of the amounts of time given each day and week by men and women to family and nonfamily activities. While there are a number of such "time budget" studies dating back to 1934, the only comparable trend data of this kind are two national surveys conducted in 1965 and 1975. These two studies confirm the long-range trend toward sharing of work and home responsibilities and underscore the gradual pace of these changes (see Table 5.2). Specifically, married men increased time spent on family care by a slight 7.8 percent (from 9.0 to 9.7 hours a week), and a growing number of working wives reduced family care time some 13.5 percent (from 28.8 to 24.9 hours a week).[19] While interpretation of these surveys is complicated by a number of considerations,* the results do indicate a changing but inequitable distribution of domestic chores within families where both spouses work.[20] Although available data from these studies do not indicate a loss of free time, they do substantiate the existence of overloading with multiple responsibilities and growing time pressures within dual-earner families that are likely to catalyze increasing interest in less work and more flexibly scheduled jobs.

Another sign of changing sex roles and life patterns comes from labor force statistics citing the rise of "househusbands" who perform housekeeping tasks while their wives work on paying jobs. Men are increasingly withdrawing, either temporarily or permanently, from the labor force while growing numbers of their spouses are performing the "breadwinner" role by holding a job. While the labor force participation of married women between the ages of 20 and 54 has climbed from 41.6 percent to 52.4 percent between 1967 and 1976,[21] the rate for men of the same age has declined from 94.6 to 91.5 percent.[22] The number of men who are neither working nor seeking work and have working wives increased from 1.6 percent of the working-age male population in March 1965 to 2.2 percent in March 1975.[23] The reasons

---

*According to these two studies, the average married woman appears to be reducing time spent on family care regardless of worktime commitments. There are a number of plausible but untested explanations for this observation. Most notably, the analysis of data reviewed for this chapter do not reflect family time pressures among parents with young children specifically. Additionally, women as well as men may be increasing family care efficiency. Married women may be neglecting family care responsibilities. Smaller families may not require as much family care time as in the past. Husbands and wives may be bargaining within family units concerning the balance of family care responsibilities, with husband assuming only a portion of what wives refuse to do.

TABLE 5.2

Hours Allocated to Major Activities over Week by Sex and Marital Status, 1965 and 1975

Activity	Total		All Men		All Women		Married Men		Married Women	
	1965	1975	1965	1975	1965	1975	1965	1975	1965	1975
Sleep	53.3	54.7	52.8	53.6	53.7	55.7	53.1	53.4	53.9	56.0
Work for pay	33.0	32.5	51.3	45.5	19.4	20.0	51.3	47.4	14.1	14.3
Family care	25.4	20.5	8.8	9.5	37.7	30.8	9.0	9.7	42.4	35.5
Personal care	21.5	21.8	21.1	21.0	21.8	22.8	20.9	21.4	21.8	23.6
Free time	34.8	38.5	34.0	38.4	35.4	38.7	33.7	36.1	35.9	38.6
Total hours	168	168	168	168	168	168	168	168	168	168
Number	1218	726	521	332	697	394	448	245	531	258

Source: Table computed from data cited in John P. Robinson, *Changes in Americans' Use of Time:*
1965–1975, Progress Report, Communication Research Center, Cleveland State University, August 1977, Table 4.

for this nonparticipation in work activities among mid-life men include illness, return to school, inability to find work, and personal preferences.[24] While most of this nonparticipation is most likely temporary, data suggest that there is not only a growing number of husbands and wives who share income earning and home tasks but that many may be reversing or rotating these responsibilities.

Further indication of changing family and sex roles comes from survey studies. The best overall indicator of changing attitudes deals with preferences between a "traditional marriage" and a "sharing marriage." The specific options presented to survey respondents were:

"A traditional marriage with the husband assuming the responsibility for providing for the family and the wife running the house and taking care of the children."

"A marriage where husband and wife share responsibilities more— both work, both share homemaking and child responsibilities."

A spring 1974 survey of a nationally representative sample of 4,008 persons over age 18 found that about 49 percent favored the "traditional marriage" and 45 percent favored the "sharing marriage."[25] The same question posed to 1,063 adults during late October 1977 found that a reduced 43 percent chose the "traditional marriage" and an increased 48 percent selected the "sharing marriage."[26] Preferences for the "sharing marriage" were greatest among young persons, suggesting that desire for more flexible and equal sex roles may increase with the attrition of older generations.

Other survey findings also indicate significant shifts in sex-role attitudes. One series of studies requested respondents from four consecutive national samples of persons aged 14 to 24 to state their agreement or disagreement with the statement: "While there are some exceptions, the statement that 'women's place is in the home' still makes sense." The proportion of respondents from this age group expressing disagreement with this statement rose from 40 percent to 51 percent between 1970 and 1976.[27] Similarly, two national surveys of first-year college students conducted in 1967 and 1974 found that the proportion of respondents agreeing that "a women's place is in the home" declined from about 54 percent to 30 percent.[28] As yet another indicator of changing sex role attitudes, the proportion of respondents from five consecutive national surveys of the American public who expressed general agreement with the women's liberation movement increased from 49 percent in 1972 to 60 percent in 1976.[29]

As an overview, a study by Karen Mason, John Czaika, and Sara Arber used special statistical techniques to evaluate five national surveys taken between 1964 and 1974 dealing with women's sex-role attitudes. The results of their review found that "there has been considerable movement toward more egalitarian role definitions in the past decade, with such change occurring equally among higher and lower status women." Their analysis also found that educational attainment and labor force participation were closely associated with new sex-role attitudes.[30] Of course, the importance of these responses must be qualified with the observation that what people say they prefer and how they actually behave are often two different things. Nonetheless, the results of these survey studies indicate that the views of today's men and women are moving away from traditional sex roles toward more flexible and equal relations between the sexes and within family units.

Shifting behaviors and attitudes supportive of nontraditional sex roles not only present an image of changing family life but also point to major realignments in the ways we use the time of our lives. One scholar of changing family patterns put the matter well:

> Rather than be confined to sex-stereotyped activities or try to meet rigid timetables of accomplishment, men and women may do best to adopt a flexible time perspective that permits them to negotiate twists and turns as they appear. . . . Timing regulates the interplay of one individual's needs with those of others. It is too soon to describe all the principles of this new "family clockwork." But some evidence is available to suggest that a new set of norms is emerging to govern the interaction of paid employment, parenthood, and household work. The new normative ideal appears to be one that encourages flexibility over the life span in the tasks that one takes up at each age and in the sex-typing of these tasks.[31]

Contrary to the rigid division of paid and nonpaid work that evolved during the early and middle stages of industrialization, there are indications that both men and women are changing their values and behaviors to better integrate employment with other dimensions of their lives. Increasingly, there appears to be a growing realization that income-earning work and family work cannot be arbitrarily compartmentalized according to sex or age.

There are strong indications that important structural relationships exist between nontraditional sex roles and the desire for alternative work patterns. Both attitudinal and behavioral data suggest that we are now at some mid-point in a long-term redistribution of work between men and women. In coming years men are likely to work less on paying jobs and more on family chores while women work less as homekeepers and give more time to income-earning employment. Labor force participation rates for men have declined from 86.8 to 78.3 percent between 1947 and 1977, while the rates for women have climbed from 31.8 to 48.5 percent over the same period.[32] Projections from the U.S. Bureau of Labor Statistics indicate that participation rates for men will decline further to 76.4 percent by 1990 while rates for women will rise to 57.1 percent.[33] More significantly, a larger portion of the total population is likely to participate in the labor force, but the amount of time given to the job by the average worker may be notably less than what we currently call full-time. In addition to redistribution of the amount of paid work between the sexes, changing family patterns are also likely to stimulate growing pressures for more flexibility in the scheduling of work. As spouses come to share breadwinning efforts, they must likewise share and integrate homekeeping tasks. This will require more options to adjust the scheduling as well as the amount of job time, not only over the short spaces of days and weeks but the long-run time span of the family and life cycles.

NOTES

1. Quote from Eli Ginzberg cited from Kathy Sawyer, "Keeping up with the Jones Beginning to Lose Appeal," Washington *Post*, December 25, 1977, p. A14.

2. Richard Estes and Harold Wilensky, "Life Cycle Squeeze and Morale Curve," *Social Problems* 25, no. 3 (February 1978): 277–92; and Gilbert Ghez and Gary Becker, *The Allocation of Time and Goods Over the Life Cycle* (New York: Columbia University Press, 1975).

3. William J. Goode, *World Revolution and Family Patterns* (New York: The Free Press, 1970).

4. Some of these forces include widespread use of contraceptives, declining birth rates, independence of elderly parents, breakdown of extended kinship networks due to geographic and social mobility, changes in the structure of occupations, longer years of schooling, rise of single-parent households, later marriage and child bearing ages, equal opportunity statutes, and the increase of women workers. For some discussion, see Janet Zollinger Giele, "Changing Sex Roles and Family Structure," *Social Policy*, January–February 1979, pp. 32–43.

5. The proportion of persons aged 65 and over who are living as household heads or primary individuals has risen from 60.2 percent to 77.8 percent for men between 1955 and 1975, and from 35.4 percent to 48.3 percent for women for the same period. See *Social Indicators 1976*, Office of Federal Statistical Policy and Standards, U.S. Department of Commerce, December 1977, pp. 42, 50, and 64. Opinion surveys also indicate that grown children resist caring for older parents. One 1975 national survey found that 53 percent of respondents felt that it was a "bad idea" to have "older people share a home with their grown children." Some 31 percent thought it was a "good idea" and 16 percent were undecided. See *Codebook for the Spring 1975 General Social Survey*, National Opinion Research Center, University of Chicago, July 1975, p. 58.

6. The average size of U.S. families has declined from a peak of 3.70 members in 1965 to 3.59 in 1970 and is projected to decline to 3.04 by 1990. See *Social Indicators 1976*, op. cit., pp. 45 and 62.

7. In the past there has been fluctuation of fertility rates. For example, the fertility rate in 1940 was 54.1. For rates from 1940 to 1974, see ibid., p. 26.

8. Ibid., p. 16. Preferences for larger families was even greater in the 1950s. See *The Virginia Slims American Woman Opinion Poll*, Vol. III, The Roper Organization, 1975, p. 65.

9. The temporal and economic demands of child rearing are, of course, not totally divorced. In many cases time and money can be substituted for each other. For example, money can buy child care assistance, and parental time can sometimes be used to provide home tutoring to make up for private education that a family cannot afford. See Gary Becker, "A Theory on the Allocation of Time," *Economic Journal*, September 1965, pp. 493–517.

10. Ralph Smith, *The Subtle Revolution* (Washington, D.C.: The Urban Institute, 1979); and 1976 *Statistical Abstracts of the United States*, Bureau of the Census, p. 355.

11. *1977 Employment and Training Report of the President*, U.S. Department of Labor, pp. 135–36, 189, and 194.

12. While the average male has recently attained parity of educational attainment with the average female (*Statistical Abstracts of the United States 1976*, op. cit., pp. 123–25), there are signs that women are equaling and surpassing men in higher education. While stated plans to attend college among high school seniors were essentially equal in 1972, more women seniors planned to attend college in 1974 by a margin of 46.2 to 40.9 percent (*Social Indicators 1976*, op. cit., pp. 269–97). These stated plans are manifesting themselves in college enrollments. Specifically, the percentage of women aged 18 to 19 enrolled in college climbed from 30.3 to 36.7 percent between 1965 and 1975, while the rates of enrollment for men of the same age declined from 40.1 to 36.7 percent over the same period (ibid., pp. 273 and 301).

13. Using labor force participation rates as an indicator of occupational aspirations, the 1974 participation rate for women with less than high school education was 32.2 percent as compared to a rate of 58.8 percent for women with four years or more of college (*1975 Handbook on Women Workers*, Women's Bureau, U.S. Department of Labor, p. 23).

14. There are numerous indicators of the participation of women in "men's occupations." See *Women and Work*, Research and Development Monograph 46, Employment and Training Administration, U.S. Department of Labor, 1977, pp. 38–40; and *1975 Handbook on Women Workers*, op. cit., pp. 83–101. In terms of managerial jobs, resistance to women is gradually declining (while the increase is not overwhelming, the proportion of all managerial jobs held by women has grown from 15.5 to 18.6 percent between 1959 and 1974 [ibid., p. 87]); and many jobs commonly associated with heavy labor have become less physically demanding in recent years. For example, workplace technology and job safety regulations on most construction jobs have made these occupations more suitable for women workers. As a partial result the proportion of all craft and kindred jobs held by women rose from 2.5 to 4.2 percent between 1959 and 1974 (ibid., p. 87).

15. Valerie Oppenheimer, "Demographic Influence on Female Employment and the Status of Women," in *Changing Women in a Changing Society*, ed. Joan Hamber (Chicago: University of Chicago Press, 1973).

16. Howard Hayghe, "Families and the Rise of Working Wives—An Overview," *Monthly Labor Review*, May 1976, pp. 12–19.

17. Juanita Kreps and Robert Clark, *Sex, Age and Work* (Baltimore: Johns Hopkins University Press, 1975), pp. 8–9.

18. Michael Young and Peter Willmott, *The Symmetrical Family* (New York: Pantheon, 1973).

19. John P. Robinson, *Changes in Americans' Use of Time: 1965–1975, A Progress Report* (Cleveland: Communication Research Center, Cleveland State University, August 1977); and John P. Robinson, *How Americans Use Time* (New York: Praeger, 1977).

20. This observation is supported by a number of additional studies. See Janice Neipert Hedges and Jeanne K. Barnett, "Working Women and the Division of Household Tasks," *Monthly Labor Review*, April 1972, pp. 9–14; and Kathryn E. Walker, "Time-Use Patterns for Housework Related to Homemaker's Employment," paper presented to New York State College of Human Ecology, February 18, 1970. Although more time series data are necessary, analysis of the National Longitudinal Surveys of mature women sponsored by the U.S. Department of Labor indicate that working wives with husbands present continue to assume "responsibility" for most household tasks, although to a lesser extent than non-working wives. See Frank L. Mott, "The NLS Mature Women's Cohort: A Socioeconomic Overview," paper prepared for the Secretary of Labor's Invitational Conference on the National Longitudinal Surveys of Mature Women, National Commission on Manpower Policy, Washington, D.C., January 26, 1978.

21. Figures cited from "The Great Male Cop-Out from the Work Ethic," *Business Week*, November 14, 1977, p. 156.

22. Figures computed from data cited from *1977 Employment and Training Report of the President*, op. cit., pp. 139 and 144.

23. Elizabeth Waldman and Vera Perrella, *Marital and Family Characteristics of Workers*, Special Labor Force Report 64, U.S. Department of Labor, Appendix p. A-20, Table Q, March 1965; Howard Hayghe, *Marital and Family Characteristics of the Labor Force*, Special Labor Report 183, U.S. Department of Labor, Appendix p. A-19, Table D, March 1975; also see *1975 Handbook of Women Workers*, op. cit., p. 22. Further, it is reported that among the male labor force "drop-outs" between the prime ages of 25 and 34 in 1976, some 63 percent had working wives ("The Great Male Cop-Out," op. cit.).

24. About half prime-age male nonparticipants are disabled, but there is cause to suspect that disability compensation programs are being used by many to finance withdrawal ("The Great Male Cop-Out," op. cit.). About 200,000 prime-age male nonparticipants are minority men between the ages of 20 and 54 who have withdrawn from the labor force as discouraged job seekers (estimates based on computations based on data from *1977 Employment and Training Report of the President*, op. cit., pp. 141 and 144).

25. *The Virginia Slims American Women's Opinion Poll*, op. cit., p. 51.

26. Data cited from a New York Times-CBS Poll, Richard J. Meislin, "Poll Finds More Liberal Beliefs on Marriage and Sex Roles, Especially Among the Young," New York *Times*, November 27, 1977, p 75.

27. Data provided courtesy of the American Council of Life Insurance from report entitled *Youth 1976*, p. 52.

28. *National Norms for Entering Freshmen, Fall 1967* 2, no. 7 (American Council for Education): 19 and 27; and *The American Freshman: National Norms for Fall 1974*, University of California, Los Angeles, pp. 24 and 26.

29. Data provided courtesy of American Council for Life Insurance from report entitled, *Current Social Issues: The Public's View*, Spring 1977, p. 13.

30. Karen Oppenheim Mason, John L. Czaika, and Sara Arber, "Change in U.S. Women's Sex-Role Attitudes, 1964–1974," *American Sociological Review* 41, no. 4 (August 1976): 573–96. An analysis of the National Longitudinal Surveys of Mature Women indicates that nontraditional sex role attitudes contribute to the propensity of women to work, which in turn fosters even more nontraditional sex role attitudes. See Anne Statham Macke, Paula M. Hudis, and Don Larrick, "Sex Role Attitudes and Employment Among Women: A Dynamic Model of Change and Continuity," in *Women's Changing Roles at Home and on the Job*, Special Report No. 26, National Commission for Employment Policy, Washington, D.C., 1979.

31. Giele, op. cit., p. 33.

32. *1978 Employment and Training Report of the President*, U.S. Department of Labor, pp. 179 80.

33. Bureau of Labor Statistics, "New Labor Force Projections to 1990: Three Possible Paths," News Release, U.S. Department of Labor, August 1978.

6

OLDER WORKERS AND
RETIREMENT REFORM

Among the forces that may foster a realignment of the ways we distribute work over the life cycle, few are likely to have greater impact than the growing host of changes affecting older workers and the institution of retirement. For decades, American workers have come to expect and look forward to pension incomes to finance ever earlier retirements. More recently, this dream has been subject to skepticism and reassessment. For many, the social and economic benefits of retirement do not outweigh the costs, and there is resistance to laws and social norms that dictate a set age for retirement. For all, there is increasing concern that the fiscal solvency of both private and public pension programs is in grave danger.[1] These problems can be expected to grow in coming decades, and the result is likely to be increasing pressure for more flexibility concerning the interrelations of work and retirement during the later years of life.

The doubts now being expressed about retirement are the result of a number of intertwined social trends. Four of these trends merit special attention:

Committed pension payments are becoming greater than future funding sources due to sluggish economic growth and a growing number of dependent older persons who are living longer.

Pension incomes are inadequate for large portions of the retired population, and this problem may worsen due to scarcity of revenues and increasing longevity of the older population.

There is growing resistance to retirement due to the increasing health of older workers and declining physical demands of most jobs.

Intense labor market competition for jobs is forcing many older workers into premature retirement and making it extremely difficult for postretirement persons to resume necessary income-earning work activities.

The combined impact of these four trends is reversing many of the conditions that originally gave rise to the practice of retirement as we know it today.

THE EMERGENCE AND MATURATION OF RETIREMENT

Over the last several decades the proportion of lifetimes given to retirement during later life has increased dramatically. Compared to preindustrial societies in which the elderly continued to work up to the point of physical incapacitation, industrial societies have devised mechanisms to both force and allow ever larger proportions of the older population to pursue increasingly longer periods of nonwork at the ends of their worklives. By 1963, Lenore Epstein and Janet Murray estimated that nine out of ten men over age 65 were retired.[2] Subsequently, the proportion of older persons working in later life has continued to decline. As one illustration, the percent of all U.S. men and women over age 65 not in the labor force rose from 62.6 percent in 1947 to 86.8 percent in 1976.[3]

The growth of retirement can be largely attributed to increasing longevity, economic surplus capable of supporting a work-free existence for the elderly, and pressures to replace older workers with younger employees. Increasing longevity is, of course, no surprise. Data from the Bureau of the Census indicate that the average lifespan has increased from 48 to 70 years between 1900 and 1970,[4] and that years of remaining life for the average 50-year-old person grew from 23 to 26 years between 1940 and 1970.[5]

While it is true that economic affluence has allowed the spread of retirement, it is also true that many elderly persons cannot accumulate adequate personal wealth to sustain prolonged retirement without some form of social assistance. These financial constraints, combined with the decline of extended families capable of supporting aging relatives and pressures forcing older workers to withdraw from the labor force, made development of pension plans an essential prerequisite to the extensive retirement evidenced today.

Proposals for pensions plans gradually emerged as a humanistic reform to ameliorate the displacement of older workers brought about by industrialization. The first practical application of the idea within the United States was initiated in 1875 by the American Express Company. However, there were comparatively few pension plans put into effect during the nineteenth and early twentieth centuries, and most of these were restricted to the white-collar employees of the largest corporations. Indeed, 50 years after the American Express Company first instigated its pension system there were only 400 plans in operation covering 4 million workers—one-third of the grand total coming from four companies.[6] Unions typically opposed such plans as paternalistic.

As late as 1940, less than one-fifth of all U.S. commercial and industrial employees were covered by private retirement plans. However, growth of such programs increased rapidly in subsequent years. This growth has commonly been attributed to belief among employers that retirement provided a humane way of dealing with less-productive older workers. Following World War II, unions began to push for blue-collar pensions and businesses came to emphasize pensions as a significant labor recruitment and maintenance incentive. Union interest increased as a result of government tax exemptions for pension plans and the enhanced appeal of fringe benefits due to recurrent wage and price controls.[7] Innovations such as "industry-wide" and "portable" pensions evolved to meet the needs of fluid labor groups such as construction workers and seamen. As a result, about 50 percent of all U.S. employees were covered by private pension plans by 1970.

The idea of extending the pension plan concept from isolated private firms to a general public program was "in the air" by the late-nineteenth century. American social reform leaders such as Richard Ely, Edward Bellamy, and John Gregory advocated various versions of "social insurance" for the elderly during the 1880s.[8] However, the earliest public pensions plans were initiated by European nations. Germany became the first under Bismarck in 1889.[9] In turn, most modern European countries implemented some form of old age and illness insurance by the turn of the twentieth century.[10]

The United States, which confronted the full impact of industrialization later than Europe, was slower to move toward public retirement programs. It was not until 1914 that the State of Arizona enacted the nation's first public old age pension.[11] The plan was declared unconstitutional by the state's supreme court but movement toward a national old age pension system continued. The economic depression of the 1930s catalyzed widespread agreement that the efficiency-oriented labor market of mature industrialization, coupled with forces separating older persons from family assistance, were making it increasingly impossible for many elderly persons to support themselves. It was also frequently suggested that increased options to retire would reduce labor force size and ease the critical unemployment problem. Despite opposition from business and organized labor, a national Social Security system was passed by Congress in 1935. President Franklin D. Roosevelt considered this bill to be the hallmark of his New Deal and expected that its provisions would expand as the idea gained greater favor with the public.[12]

Roosevelt's expectations have proven to be more than true. Today, retirement is a permanent fixture in the fabric of American life. The combination of national Social Security, private pensions, and old age savings plans has come to cover the vast majority of American workers with increasing benefits and options for earlier retirement. In 1976, over 90 percent of the population over age 65 was covered by some form of pension.

For the average person in this age group, benefits provided some 50 percent of their preretirement earnings. Finally, the retirement age has been declining steadily. Alterations of the Social Security system in the 1960s have allowed and encouraged considerable retirement at age 62,[13] and early vesting of private pensions allows retirement as early as the mid-50s.[14]

ECONOMIC GROWTH, POPULATION TRENDS, AND FUTURE OF RETIREMENT

Contemporary economic and population trends are disrupting the basic assumptions upon which many retirement programs were founded. Social Security, as well as many private pension plans, was initiated as an intergenerational transfer program that uses the economic productivity of mid-life workers to finance the retirement incomes of older generations.[15] In the past, this system functioned quite well for two reasons. First, population growth insured that the size of younger working generations had always been considerably larger than the retired population they supported. Second, reasonably constant economic growth since the 1940s had allowed expansion of retirement programs. As a result, it had been possible to provide growing pension incomes and other benefits to an increasing number of older persons tending to retire at earlier ages.

It appears increasingly unlikely that economic and population trends will allow a continuation, let alone an increase, of current retirement programs. In addition to a long-run likelihood of sputtering economic growth, declining birth rates and existing age distributions within the U.S. population will create a long-range situation in which fewer rather than larger numbers of mid-life workers must provide the retirement incomes of the older population. Specifically, as the large, post-World War II "baby boom" generation approaches retirement age after the year 2000, the ranks of the retired will bulge and the smaller younger generation will be called upon to finance their retirement.

The problem of financing retirement programs will be further complicated by the fact that life expectancy at age 65 is increasing. While average life expectancy for both sexes at age 65 was 12.2 years in 1930, it was 16.0 in 1976.[16] Further, it is projected to increase to 16.8 years by 2000 and rise still further in the more distant future.[17] This will lead not only to longer years of dependency for those who are retired but also to a larger group of "very old" over age 75 who will likely require greater medical services (see Figure 6.1).

Current and projected ratios of dependent retirees to workers provides an overview of the problem that lies ahead. There were 11.7 persons over 65 for every 100 working-age persons between 20 and 64 in 1940, 18.4 persons over 65 for every hundred working-age persons in 1970, and the number is projected to rise to 32.8 per hundred workers by year 2030 (see Table 6.1).[18]

FIGURE 6.1

Percent of the Total Population in the Older Ages, 1900–2040

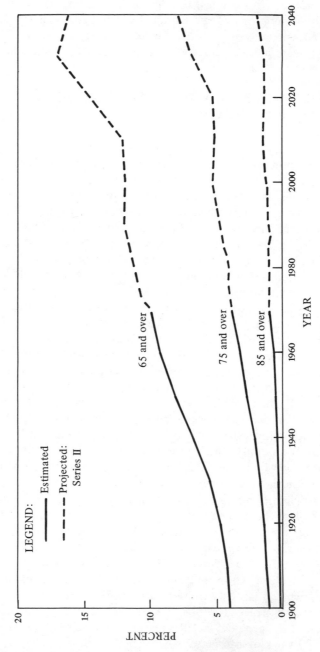

Note: Estimates and projections as of July 1, except for 85 and over, 1900-1930, which relate to April 1. Points are plotted for years ending in zero except for 1975.

Source: Demographic Aspects of Aging and the Older Population in the United States, Current Population Reports, U.S. Bureau of the Census, Special Studies Series P-23, No. 59, May 1976, p. 4.

TABLE 6.1

Actual Past and Projected Future Dependency Ratios, Selected Years, 1930–2050

Year	Under 20	65 and over	Total
1930	69.6	9.7	79.3
1940	58.5	11.7	70.2
1950	59.2	14.1	73.3
1960	74.1	17.4	91.5
1970	71.7	18.4	90.0
1975	64.1	19.2	83.3
1990	48.1	19.6	67.7
2000	45.9	19.3	65.2
2010	42.0	19.8	61.7
2020	42.4	25.8	68.2
2030	43.9	32.8	76.7
2040	43.2	32.6	75.8
2050	43.5	31.9	75.4

Note: The dependency ratio is the total number of people under 20 and over 64 per 100 people aged 20 to 64.

Source: Alicia Munnell, *The Future of Social Security* (Washington, D.C.: Brookings Institution, 1977), p. 110.

In sum, the proportion of the U.S. population that is retired will grow dramatically in future years, and the costs of supporting this population will likewise increase.

As a result of economic and population trends, the long-run fiscal outlook for social security and many other pension programs is somewhat glum. In some cases, many of these problems can be painlessly overcome by a series of informed technical adjustments.[19] In terms of the burden to be endured by future mid-life workers, there will be some relief brought about by declining birth rates and fewer dependent children (see Table 6.1).[20] However, a likely increase of family expenditures on individual children, coupled with the fact that the cost of supporting a retired person is now approximately three times the cost of supporting a person under age 18, makes this source of relief limited. Further, if the current trend toward early retirement continues, the public cost of supporting tomorrow's retired population will be even higher (see Table 6.2). Assuming that needed technical adjustments are made in the Social Security system, and that retirement age does not decline further, population trends alone will require that Social Security taxes increase some 23 percent between 1975 and 2010, then almost double by 2030.[21]

TABLE 6.2

Public Costs of Supporting Elderly Dependents as a Percentage of Disposable Personal Income under Different Retirement Ages

Retirement Age	1975	1990	2000	2010	2015	2020	2025
55		14.88	15.06	17.40	18.85	19.95	20.24
62		10.53	10.24	11.07	12.13	13.39	14.46
65	7.74	8.71	8.60	8.80	9.67	10.74	11.85
70		5.74	6.07	6.08	6.46	7.09	7.85

Source: Cited from Harold Sheppard and Sara Rix, *The Graying of Working America* (New York: The Free Press, 1977), p. 29 (based on data from Robert Clark, "The Interaction of Retirement Age and Future Dependency Costs by Continuing Low Fertility Rates," Department of Economics, North Carolina State University, 1977, p. 17).

The increasing cost of retirement costs to working generations will give rise to considerable social tensions in coming decades. Social Security deductions are well on the way to becoming the largest tax bite withheld from the average worker's paycheck.[22] Presumably, there will be a reluctance on the part of future working populations to provide tax revenues for public pensions.[23] At the same time, the growing proportion of older persons with direct interests in retirement benefits will foster a formidable political force for the maintenance and possible increase of these benefits. Congressional debates on the extent of taxation for Social Security are already heated. As public sentiment responds to still higher levies in the future, it can be expected that pressures will give rise to a search for alternative retirement policies.

There are three major responses to the growing problems of financing existing retirement programs. First, taxes might be raised. Second, retirement pensions and benefits might be reduced or restricted to select groups. Third, the age of retirement might be increased in order to readjust the ratio of workers to retired nonworkers. Realistically, we can expect that attempts will be made to enact all these responses. One major result will be reexamination of the role and timing of retirement in our society, thus stimulating realignments in the relationship between work and nonwork activities among the older population.

LIFETIME DISTRIBUTION OF INCOME AND POVERTY IN OLD AGE

Although 90 percent of the aged population have retirement pensions of some sort,[24] the level of income provided from these sources is frequently inadequate. Due to the absence of work-related expenses and lower taxes, retirees require between 65 and 80 percent of their preretirement earnings to maintain a standard of living equivalent to that in their later work years.[25] Yet the 1974 median income for families headed by persons aged 65 and older was only 51.8 percent of the median for families headed by persons aged 14 to 64.[26]

While many older persons are reasonably well off due to high Social Security benefits supplemented by other sources of income,[27] a disproportionately large portion of persons over age 65 are officially classified as "poor" or "near poor." Amendments to the Social Security Act in 1962 to neutralize the impact of inflation have greatly reduced poverty among the elderly.[28] Nonetheless, in 1975 some 15.3 percent of those over 65 fell under the "poverty line" as compared to 12.0 percent for those under age 65.[29] More important, about 25 percent more of the total population over 65 had annual incomes that were no more than $1,000 (1975 dollars) above poverty status. Many more are living on very modest incomes. For example, in 1975 only 15.8 percent of the aged population had incomes over $10,000[30] as opposed to 64.7 percent of the total population.[31]

Current trends toward earlier retirement and increasing life expectancy at age 65 present an even more dismal picture of the economic status of the elderly. Even if the average retirement age does not decline, a large portion of the future older population will have to live an increasing number of years with inadequate incomes, and the likelihood that a growing proportion of persons will find it necessary or desirable to retire before age 65 will further worsen this problem. For those who are "poor" or "near poor" at the start of retirement, this problem will be critical, particularly as medical costs increase toward the end of life. However, even those who are relatively well-to-do will experience problems due to more years of nonincome-earning retirement.

The problem of an inadequate livelihood during retirement is further complicated by Social Security restrictions limiting the amount of income that beneficiaries can earn by work activity without losing benefits.[32] The issue of whether or not to continue these earnings restrictions is not easily resolved. There has, nonetheless, been a gradual liberalization of these provisions to allow more income-earning work activities among Social Security recipients.[33] Such liberalization will likely continue, and with it a progressive blurring of the distinction between the retirement and work stages of life.

The problem of inadequate incomes during retirement is largely determined by how income-earning worktime is distributed over the total lifespan. As Juanita Kreps so aptly noted:

> The timing of work largely dictates the pattern of income and our views on
> the adequacy of income at different ages; it is but natural, we reason, for
> youth to be fashionably impoverished and for old age to be only meagerly

financed. A lengthening of both these non-earning periods . . . now poses a new set of questions regarding the appropriate allocation of work and income through the lifespan. . . . Although low levels of income may be acceptable for short periods of time, they cannot be lightly dismissed when they prevail during as much as two decades at the end of life.[34]

While the problems of inadequate retirement income might be reduced by increasing voluntary and forced saving during midlife, this would be an unlikely solution for persons with low incomes and an unpopular social policy for the better off. There is, however, much to be said for spreading work over a larger portion of the life cycle. Policies directed to this end would even out income over the stages of life, allow individuals more direct control over their personal finances, reduce the cost and inconvenience of massive government transfer mechanisms, and attenuate some of the negative social effects of sudden departures from work to retirement.

The worklife could be spread into the later years of life in a number of ways. First, part-week and part-year work for the elderly might be promoted. Second, older persons might be encouraged to pursue retraining and "second careers" in occupations more appropriate to their age.[35] Third, the average age of retirement might be gradually increased to 68 over the next two or three decades. Consideration of these options not only opens the possibility of increasing the flexibility of an overly rigid retirement system but also of spreading the worklife more flexibly over the mid-life period.

IMPROVING HEALTH AND WORK CAPACITIES OF THE ELDERLY

A major assumption of existing retirement policies is that older persons must be removed from work because they are no longer mentally or physically capable of performing job responsibilities. Recently, the idea of removing older workers by an across-the-board mandatory retirement age has been attacked as grossly inappropriate. Proponents of this point of view observe that there is no compelling reason for setting retirement at age 65. Indeed, it is commonly noted that the norm of retirement at age 65 was set in 1889 by Bismarck, not because this age marked a point at which most persons could no longer work, but because average life expectancy in Germany at that time was such that the fiscal requirements for a public old age pension starting at that age would be negligible.[36]

While available data provide no clear-cut answers concerning the work capacities of older persons, evidence does suggest that any assumption about declining abilities must be rigorously qualified in terms of individual differences and the type of capacities required for specific types of jobs. Indeed, growing knowledge about the process of aging, increasing health among the elderly, and the changing nature of work suggests that growing proportions of the post-65 population may be well suited to continue at least some form of work activity.

Data concerning the human aging process indicate that many older persons are capable of continuing work activity. While individual differences are extremely varied, some individuals at age 65 are every bit as functional as a person 20 years their junior.[37] Beyond individual differences, research on aging is demonstrating that the average decline of specific mental and physical abilities with age is uneven. For example, sight, hearing, endurance, strength, and physical dexterity all decline with age. However, these and other capacities decline at widely varying rates and generally do not fall below the requirements of most jobs as individuals enter the later stages of life.[38] Further, there is no age at which a person can be generally proclaimed nonfunctional.[39] It is also important to note that most persons learn to adapt to declining capacities. Knowledge and experience can be expected to increase with age, and these traits have important implications for job performance. As an illustration, job-related accidents and absences in manufacturing industries decline with age.[40] Many older people are capable of continuing some form of work, and a blanket age criteria for retirement does not adequately recognize the diversity of individual abilities.

There are also important indications that the degenerative effects of aging are declining for the average person. As already noted, average life expectancy at age 65 has increased some 3.5 years between 1930 and 1976. Additionally, the health of older persons appears to be increasing. HEW data show that "healthy life expectancy" has grown faster than overall life expectancy since 1958,[41] with the average number of days of reported sickness a year for persons over age 65 declining from 47.3 in 1958 to 38.0 in 1974.[42] While it is unlikely that health and longevity among older persons will increase dramatically in the foreseeable future, it is plausible that improved medical care and environmental conditions will further forestall the degenerative effects of age. One impact is that a growing proportion of older persons may be physically capable of continuing some form of work activity well after the age of 65.

Finally, changes in the nature of work itself are likely to alter both the ability and desire of older persons to continue working. There can be little question that the nature of work influences both the necessity and desirability of retirement. Workers employed in the more toilsome manual occupations generally exhibit a much greater desire for retirement than those in the white-collar occupations.[43] In addition to physical demands, the chance of injury and resulting incapacitation are also greater among manual lines of work. However, even these manual occupations are becoming less exhausting and dangerous. More important, they are accounting for an ever smaller portion of available jobs, as less strenuous service and white-collar jobs become more prevalent. Work is becoming less physically demanding, and it can be expected that a greater number of older persons will therefore be able and willing to continue working in future years.

Of course, the physical demands of a job are not the only reason why older workers may be judged incapable of continued work. Obsolete skills and declining motivation have frequently been cited as reasons for retiring. While this problem unquestionably exists, it must also be acknowledged that a lack of training opportunities and declining possibilities for promotion or job change during preretirement years tend to have a stultifying effect upon older workers. Many white-collar jobs may entail undue bureaucratic routines that foster an accumulative decline of morale and skill obsolescence.[44] Thus, while many workers may evidence declining performance as they grow older, such "incapacity" is often the result of the social environment as well as the aging process.

What we are discovering about the aging process and the impact of work conditions upon job performance suggests a need to depart from a monolithic retirement age norm and move toward more flexibility. This would entail new relations between work and retirement. For many, longer worklives and postponed retirement might be both necessary and desirable. For others, partial retirement with part-time or part-year work might be preferred. For others, the prospect of a longer worklife coupled with a career change might prove both personally and socially beneficial. And for many, the existing retirement norm may be fully appropriate. In sum, current data concerning the physical and mental capacities of the elderly suggest that flexible approaches to work and nonwork during old age would be far more sensible than an across-the-board retirement age of 65.

PREFERENCES FOR VOLUNTARY AND FLEXIBLE RETIREMENT

Up to very recent times retirement has been viewed as a welcome reward for a life of hard work. Today, there are growing signs that increasing numbers of older workers are not retiring out of personal preference or physical necessity, but because institutional and economic forces are pushing them unwillingly out of the labor force. For many, retirement is becoming a forced decision, and growing numbers of persons of all ages are rebelling against it.

There are important institutional forces at the firm level that tend to make retirement an involuntary inevitability. Particularly important is the high cost of older workers to firms. As seniority increases with age, wages and salaries also tend to rise, due in many cases as much to length of service as merit of performance.[45] In many cases, a profit-optimizing firm will come to realize that even though senior workers are performing well, the productivity of such older employees may not justify their pay levels. However, unless there is gross negligence on the part of such workers, the firm is likely to continue to employ them and even raise their pay in order to honor union agreements and avoid morale problems among younger workers who are concerned about how they may be treated later in their careers.

In addition to the high cost of senior employees, a number of additional considerations cause firms to push for the eventual termination of older employees through retirement. First, an important management tool for the motivation of employees is the ability to offer advancement, and the departure of older employees opens opportunities for the promotion of younger workers. Second, in some cases the skills of older workers may become obsolete, and it may be less expensive and provide more long-run returns to hire and train a qualified younger person rather than retrain an older worker.[46] Third, it can be assumed that some portions of a firm's senior employees—possibly in response to firm neglect—develop a counterproductive attitude of doing only enough to get by while waiting for the inevitability of retirement. Whether or not these observations are valid, they represent common assumptions that encourage many firms to seize upon retirement as a convenient, humane, and relatively inexpensive way of replacing older employees[47] with less costly and often better trained younger adults.[48]

Firms encourage the retirement of older employees in a number of ways. One study of 23.3 million workers enrolled in defined private pension plans during 1974 found that about 45 percent were subject to some form of "mandatory retirement" provision.[49] The incidence of such forced retirement appears to have grown over the last two decades,[50] but federal and state legislation is now restricting such provisions.

For the most part, firms encourage retirement through establishing norms and incentives that are also supported by public retirement programs. Most private pension plans have followed the Social Security norm by establishing age 65 as the standard retirement age.[51] In most cases, these plans, like Social Security, allow more flexibility for early retirement rather than later retirement.[52] Some union and firm agreements have actually developed policies encouraging early retirements for all workers. A notable case in point is the "30 years and out" negotiated by the United Auto Workers to allow retirement with a fully vested pension by age 55.[53] Many workers are also pushed into unwanted retirement by a number of informal pressures. While most evidence of such sanctions is anecdotal, survey studies of both supervisors and employees tend to support the often-stated belief that there is widespread bias against older workers that is likely to foster retirement by or before age 65.[54]

Beyond firm pressures to retire, there are also powerful labor market forces causing undesired labor force withdrawal among older workers. When the number of available jobs falls substantially below the number of persons seeking to work, labor market competition tends to push the more vulnerable workers out of the labor force.[55] Because senior-level pay is high and limited returns on job training tend to dissuade employers from hiring workers in their mid-fifties and older, the impact of more-than-temporary unemployment can ultimately lead to withdrawal from the labor force. This is particularly true of individuals, especially minority workers, who have always had marginal positions in the work force. For such persons, early retirement with a meager but regular pension income can serve as an honorable but undesired escape from prolonged unemployment or demeaning work.[56] Similarly, already retired persons seeking to return to work also confront difficulties finding acceptable reemployment, and the likely result is continued retirement.[57] Labor market competition, coupled with employers' biases against older workers, tends to force many older persons into unwanted and premature retirements and to keep them retired.

Survey studies concerning retirement can provide some insight into the changing nature of retirement decisions and the extent to which workers are resisting retirement. A series of national studies conducted primarily with male samples since the early 1940s indicates a declining necessity to retire due to health problems, a rise in voluntary preference for retirement, and most recently a growing confusion about the value and nature of retirement. A survey undertaken by the Social Security Administration in 1941–42 found that only 5 percent of the sample voluntarily retired out of a desire for leisure, while the bulk of the sample retired involuntarily due to health problems.[58] Another 1951 survey confirmed these basic responses by finding that only 3.8 percent retired voluntarily and most retired because of poor health.[59]

Surveys conducted in the 1960s revealed a growth in voluntary retirement. A 1963 study found that 19 percent of men who retired at age 65 and 11 percent of those retiring earlier stated that the desire for leisure was their reason for retirement.[60] Other surveys conducted in the late 1960s found that about half of the respondents retired willingly without health problems or institutional requirements.[61] Notably, one of these studies also found that about half the men who had recently retired wanted to return to work.[62] While interpretation of these studies is subject to some specifications, these results indicate that the view among workers of retirement as a positive goal grew over the last three decades, but that the actuality left many with much to be desired.

Two recent national surveys conducted in 1974 and 1977 by Louis Harris and Associates found a surprising contradiction of opinions about retirement.[63] In 1974, more than one-third of those over age 65 and retired reported that they did not retire by choice but were forced to retire.[64] Attitudes about forced retirement were ambivalent. In both 1974 and 1977, some 86 percent of respondents aged 18 and over felt that "nobody should be forced to retire because of age if he wants to continue working and is still able to do a good job." However, about half of the 1974 sample also agreed that "since many people are ready to retire at 65 years of age, and it's hard to make exceptions for those who are not ready, it makes sense to have a fixed age for everyone."[65] With the exception of those aged 40 to 55, large majorities of all other age groups in the 1974 study did not look forward to stopping work at retirement age.[66] Correspondingly, 31 percent of those aged 65 and not working in 1974 stated that they would like jobs. Nonetheless, retirement at age 65 or between ages 60 and 64 were selected as the most preferred ages for retirement by all respondents. However, it is notable that while 47 percent of workers aged 55 to 64 chose 60 through 65 as preferred retirement ages, some 43 percent of this same group chose over 65 or "late as possible" as the most desirable ages for retirement. Paradoxically, there were also signs of growing resistance to earlier retirement. In 1974, a narrow 45 to 40 percent plurality (15 percent were "not sure") thought it was "a good thing" that "the age at which people are required to retire has become younger in recent years." In 1977, a 51 to 39 percent majority (10 were "not sure") thought that lowering the retirement age was "not a good thing."

In sum, the contradictions of opinion uncovered by the Harris surveys and other studies reflect a genuine multiplicity of views concerning retirement. Available survey studies indicate support for the basic institution of retirement, growing reservation about reducing the average age of retirement, varied views concerning the proper retirement age, a general opposition to the idea of forced retirement at a given age, and a desire for more personal flexibility concerning retirement arrangements.

The likelihood that many older workers will resist current retirement age norms in favor of retirement sometime after age 65 reveals an important contradiction in retirement trends. While an increasing proportion of older persons will find it necessary and desirable to resist retirement in favor of longer worklives, labor force competition and the economics of individual firms are manifesting powerful forces pushing workers toward retirement by age 65 or earlier. These conflicting forces have important labor market implications. If the average retirement age had been increased to 68 in 1975, about 4 million additional jobs would have been necessary to accommodate the increased size of the labor force.[67] Considering that the total number of unemployed for that same year was 7.8 million, there can be little doubt that such later retirement would have gravely aggravated an already pressing unemployment problem. The unavoidable implication is that new relations between work and retirement must be found.

EMERGENCE OF FLEXIBLE RETIREMENT AND LIFE SCHEDULING

Movement toward more flexible worklives is likely to be encouraged by trends that contradict traditional assumptions about retirement:

Public pension programs were established as an equitable and reliable intergenerational transfer of funds from younger workers to retired older persons; but current economic and population trends are greatly expanding the tax burden of workers and causing political tensions that will place the reliability of future retirement pensions in doubt.

Retirement programs were designed to provide persons with a decent standard of living during retirement; but likely constraints on retirement revenues and increasing longevity are likely to foster long-run financial problems for many older persons.

Retirement was conceived to provide for older persons when they were no longer capable of working; but longer life expectancy, better health, and easier work make it possible and often desirable for larger portions of the older population to continue working.

Retirement was originally developed as a reward to elderly persons for a life of work; but retirement is frequently the alternative to older workers who are being forced unwillingly out of the labor force by a lack of jobs and competition from younger workers.

In short, many of the original assumptions upon which current retirement policies were founded are no longer true. The result will be a growing necessity to realign the balance of work and nonwork among both the older and younger population. What is the likely nature of this realignment of work and retirement? Two general speculations might be made.

First, the scope of individual differences and likely magnitude of future social changes make it unlikely that today's overly rigid and monolithic retirement policies will persist. Even more important, powerful demographic and economic forces will require more flexibility. The large post-World War II baby boom generation will start withdrawing from the labor force around the year 2005. Just as this generation will be crowding the labor force for the remainder of the twentieth century, it will leave a wake of empty jobs when it reaches retirement age. The result will be a retired population too large to support and a tremendous demand for labor.[68] Additionally, international competition and depletion of raw materials is likely to cause a volatile economy in coming decades in which the demand for labor may fluctuate dramatically.[69] Considering these conditions, and the possibility that last-minute adjustments may not be feasible, private and public retirement policies are likely to incorporate a number of incentives and options allowing a wide range of retirement alternatives for both employers and employees. Such options might entail postretirement recall provisions and rights, phased retirement options such as reduced or part-time work opportunities after age 60, provisions for reverse-seniority pay scales to allow older workers to continue working at a lower pay scale, and opportunities to change jobs and occupations.[70]

Second, the shortage of jobs in the foreseeable future will require that any large-scale postponement of retirement age will in turn require at least a commensurate reduction in worktime among younger workers. It is particularly noteworthy that a recent proposal made by Juanita Kreps to gradually increase the average retirement age to 68 was also accompanied by a less–publicized observation that such an increased retirement age might require downward adjustments in worktime earlier in life in order to better spread available worktime over the life cycle and to provide political accommodation for those losing expected retirement years.[71] Along this line, Kreps and others have also suggested sabbaticals, longer vacations, and increased part-time work opportunities for all ages. In this context, it can be expected that evolving changes in the nature of retirement may not only influence the relations between work and leisure during the later decades of life but also provide a powerful force toward reducing worktime and increasing worklife flexibility for the younger population.

NOTES

1. One national survey found that the proportion of the American public expressing confidence in the Social Security system declined from 63 percent in 1975 to 50 percent in 1977. Additionally, the proportion of persons stating that they were "very confident" declined substantially, and the proportion declaring that they were "not at all confident" rose from 10 to 20 percent in the same time period. Data courtesy of the American Council for Life Insurance from report entitled *MAP '77*, p. 71.

A more recent nationally representative survey conducted in August 1978 found that more than two-fifths of American workers have "hardly any confidence at all" that the Social Security system will ever pay them benefits and another two-fifths had "less than full confidence." See Spencer Rich, "Many Doubt They'll Get Social Security Benefits," Washington *Post*, March 1, 1979, A6.

2. Retirement was defined as working less than 35 hours a week for less than 50 weeks a year. Lenore Epstein and Janet Murray, "Employment and Retirement," in Bernice Neugarten, ed., *Middle Age and Aging* (Chicago: University of Chicago Press, 1975), p. 354.

3. *1977 Employment and Training Report of the President*, U.S. Department of Labor, 1978, p. 154.

4. Fred Best, "Recycling People: Work Sharing Through Flexible Life Scheduling," *The Futurist*, February 1978, p. 8.

5. *Social Indicators 1973*, Office of Federal Statistical Policy and Standards, U.S. Department of Commerce, p. 3.

6. These companies were U.S. Steel, Pennsylvania Railroad, New York Railroad, and American Telephone and Telegraph. See *Collier's Encyclopedia*, Vol. 18 (New York: Cromwell-Collier Educational Corp., 1971) p. 564.

7. *Encyclopedia Americana*, Vol. 21 (New York, 1969), p. 544.

8. Sidney Fine, *Laissez Faire and the General-Welfare State* (Ann Arbor: University of Michigan Press, 1956), pp. 236, 298, 300, and 324.

9. John McDowell, "Social Security," *Encyclopedia Americana*, op. cit., Vol. 25, p. 186j.

10. Great Britain enacted national social security in 1897 and compulsory health insurance in 1911. France instigated a comprehensive old age and health insurance program in 1928 (ibid.).

11. Fine, op. cit., p. 385.

12. Representatives of the AFL-CIO opposed the bill on the grounds that the measure required contributions from workers, and the National Association of Manufacturers opposed

the bill because it levied a payroll tax on employers. See Arthur S. Link and William B. Catton, *The American Epoch: A History of the United States Since the 1880s* (New York: Knopf, 1965), pp. 414–15, 416.

13. Alicia Munnell, *The Future of Social Security* (Washington, D.C.: Brookings Institution, 1977), pp. 1, 26, 43, and 73.

14. John Zalusky, "Shorter Workyears—Earlier Retirement," AFL-CIO *American Federationist*, August 1977.

15. Juanita Kreps, *Lifetime Allocation of Work and Income* (Durham, N.C.: Duke University Press, 1971), pp. 32–33.

16. Munnell, op. cit., p. 78; and *Statistical Abstracts of the United States, 1976*, Bureau of the Census, p. 61.

17. Susanna McBee, "Census Sees More Elderly by Next Century Than Anticipated," Washington *Post*, June 11, 1978, p. A9.

18. Munnell, op. cit., p. 110.

19. Among these adjustments are included reduction of inequitable multibenefits resulting from nonintegrated minimum pension payments from more than one pension plan (ibid., pp. 15 and 51–52), better integration of multiretirement plan coordination (ibid., p. 12), prevention of private pension plans, which are supported by social security minimum benefits (ibid., pp. 22–24), payment of social security benefits to individuals rather than family units (ibid., pp. 48–49), and most importantly the alteration of 1972 Social Security Act Amendments concerning faulty cost-of-living raises (ibid., pp. 30–33 and 101).

20. The number of "dependent" youth under age 20 for every 100 "working age" person between ages 20 and 64 will decline from 64.1 in 1975 to 45.9 in 2000 (ibid., p. 110).

21. Ibid., pp. 77, 86–100.

22. Art Pine, "Social Security Tax Now the Dominant One for Many Households," Washington *Post*, January 24, 1978, pp. A1 and A14. To illustrate, the annual per capita expenditure for social security rose from $67.20 in 1950 to $597.32 in 1975, as measured in constant 1975 dollars. See *Social Indicators 1976*, Office of Federal Statistical Policy and Standards, U.S. Department of Commerce, December 1977, p. 130.

23. While there is doubt that support will persist as taxes rise, survey research indicates that the general public still expresses a commitment to supporting the public retirement system, even if it means higher taxes. See *Current Social Issues: The Public's View*, American Council for Life Insurance, Spring 1977, p. 7; and Rich, op. cit., p. A6.

24. Kreps, op. cit., p. 28; and Harold Sheppard and Sara Rix, *The Graying of Working America* (New York: The Free Press, 1977).

25. Munnell, op. cit., pp. 58–59; James Schulz, Thomas Leavitt, and Leslie Kelly, "Private Pensions Fall Far Short of Preretirement Income Levels," *Monthly Labor Review*, February 1979, p. 31; and Peter Henle, "Recent Trends in Retirement Benefits Related to Earnings," *Monthly Labor Review*, June 1972, pp. 12–20.

26. Figures calculated from data cited from *Statistical Abstracts 1976*, op. cit., 411; and *Social Indicators 1976*, op. cit., p. 455. Relative conditions have improved for the elderly. In 1967 the median income for families headed by persons age 65 and older was 46.2 percent of the median family incomes of families headed by persons aged 24 to 64. See Kreps, op. cit., p. 28.

27. Kreps, op. cit., pp. 30–31. Corresponding data for 1975 are available from *Statistical Abstracts 1976*, op. cit., p. 420.

28. Munnell, op. cit., pp. 5–19, 25–38.

29. *Statistical Abstracts, 1976*, op. cit., pp. 415 and 420. Apparently the incidence of poverty among the aged has declined from about 44 percent in 1967. See Kreps, op. cit., p. 30; and *Social Indicators 1976*, op. cit., p. 409.

30. Figures dealing with "near poor" estimated from data cited from *Facts About Older Americans 1976*, brochure from the Administration on Aging, HEW Publication No. (OHD) 77-20006.

31. *Statistical Abstracts 1976*, op. cit., p. 404.

32. The controversial "earnings test" provision of the 1977 Social Security Act reduces a person's social security benefits one dollar for every two dollars earned in excess of $3,000 a year until the benefit is completely exhausted. See Munnell, op. cit., p. 65. This limitation on earnings is adjusted in accord with inflation and other considerations. For example, it is likely that the limit for tax-free earnings in 1981 will be $4,200. See *1976 Annual Report of the Board of the Federal Old Age and Survivors Insurance and Disability Insurance Trust Fund*, H. Doc. 94–505, 94:2 (Washington, D.C.: U.S. Government Printing Office, 1976), p. 22.

33. Specifically, the nontaxable earnings limit has been increased and social security beneficiaries over age 72 were allowed total benefits regardless of the amount of income earned. See Munnell, op. cit., p. 66.

34. Kreps, op. cit., pp. 13–14.

35. Harold Sheppard, *Research and Development Strategy on Employment-Related Problems of Older Workers* (Washington, D.C.: American Institutes for Research, October 1977), pp. 75–78. Public employment might be especially appropriate in this case. Particularly, semivoluntary programs such as VISTA and the Peace Corps might be adjusted to provide moderate tax-free incomes as well as an opportunity for older persons to apply valuable skills. See Robert Butler, *Why Survive? Being Old in America* (New York: Harper and Row, 1973), pp. 102, 353.

36. Sheppard and Rix, op. cit., p. 73.

37. Jerome A. Mark, "Measurement of Job Performance and Age," *Monthly Labor Review*, December 1956, pp. 1413–14. For an interesting array of antecdotal reports on productive older persons, see "Now, The Revolt of the Old," *Time*, October 10, 1977, pp. 26 and 28.

38. Elizabeth Meier and Elizabeth Kerr, "Capabilities of Middle Aged and Older Workers: A Survey of Literature," *Industrial Gerontology*, Summer 1976, pp. 147–56. For a survey of assessments of the impact of aging on physical and mental capacities with age, see Neugarten, op. cit.

39. Ibid.; Harold Sheppard, op. cit., pp. 87–103; and Sheppard and Rix, op. cit., p. 73.

40. Sheppard and Rix, op. cit., pp. 75–80; and Sheppard, op. cit., pp. 92–94, and 99–101.

41. Indicators of general health are difficult to find or develop. One indicator of "healthy life expectancy" (years of nonbed disability) computed by HEW showed that the expectation of a healthy life increased from 67.2 to 68.2 years between 1958 and 1966. This is a slightly faster growth of years of health than increase of overall life expectancy from 69.5 to 70.2 years for the same time period. Expectation for healthy life for persons over the age of 65 increased from 13.1 to 13.5 years for the same period. See *Toward a Social Report*, U.S. Department of Health, Education and Welfare, January 1968, pp. 3–4. Other evidence suggests that pain-free existence and nonbed disability has declined. See ibid., p. 5; and Fred Best, "Quality of Life Report for Massachusetts," Institute for Man and the Environment, University of Massachusetts, Amherst, June 1975.

42. Munnell, op. cit. p. 79.

43. Lenore A. Epstein and Janet H. Murray, "Employment and Retirement," in Neugarten, op. cit., pp. 354–55; Elizabeth Meier, *Aging in America: Implications for Employment*, Report No. 7, National Council on the Aging, Washington, D.C., 1976, pp. 2–3; and Sheppard, op. cit., pp. 66–67.

44. Raymond G. Kuhlen, "Developmental Changes in Motivation During the Adult Years," in Neugarten, op. cit., pp. 115–36.

45. Most union agreements and many firm personnel policies automatically provide pay increases in accord with seniority as well as merit and cost of living. See Lloyd G. Reynolds, *Labor Economics and Labor Relations*, 5th ed. (Englewood Cliffs, N.J.: Prentice-Hall, 1970), pp. 574–84.

46. Sheppard, op. cit., p. 63.

47. It has been increasingly recognized that set retirement ages are highly desirable to supervisors who wish to be spared the ordeal of terminating senior employees because of

inadequate job performance. It is also argued that retirement in such circumstances preserves the dignity of the older workers. See Sheppard, op. cit., p. 51; William Raspberry, "Mandatory Retirement Makes Sense," Washington *Post*, October 17, 1977.

48. Sumner H. Sliehter, *Union Policies and Industrial Management* (Washington, D.C.: Brookings Institution, 1941), pp. 160–61.

49. Dorothy R. Kittner, "Forced Retirement: How Common is It?" *Monthly Labor Review*, December 1977, pp. 60–61. It should be noted that about 30 million workers are covered under some form of private pension plan. See Alfred M. Skolnik, "Private Pension Plans, 1950–1974," *Social Security Bulletin*, June 1976, p. 3.

50. Available data are not conclusive on the growth of such provisions, but they occur almost totally in firms with private pension plans, which also grew during the 1950s and 1960s. See Fred Slavick, *Compulsory and Flexible Retirement in the American Economy* (Ithaca, N.Y.: Cornell University Press, 1966), pp. 6–7 and 18–19.

51. Munnell, op. cit., pp. 67–68.

52. In the case of social security, the benefit incentives for retirement after age 65 are only slight compared to the benefit penalties for retirement prior to age 65 (ibid., pp. 73–79). In terms of private pensions, the trend appears to be toward a reduction of pension penalties for early retirement coupled with no incentives for later retirement and varying forms of forced retirement by or before age 65 (Skolnik, op. cit., pp. 7–9).

53. Meier, op. cit., p. 8. It should be noted that the UAW now appears to be reversing its push for earlier retirement due to disenchantment of early retirees and resistance from working members. See Martin Nemirow, "Work Sharing: Past, Present and Future," Office of the Assistant Secretary for Policy, Evaluation and Research, U.S. Department of Labor, May 6, 1976, p. 17.

54. Meier, op. cit., pp. 8–9 and 11; Sheppard, op. cit., pp. 163–64.

55. William Bowen and Aldrich Finnegan, *The Economics of Labor Market Participation* (Princeton, N.J.: Princeton University Press, 1969); and Robert J. Havighurst, "Alternative Work Schedules: Implications for Older Workers," *Journal of the College and University Personnel Association* 28, no. 3 (Summer 1977): 61–62.

56. The impact of harsh labor market participation on withdrawal to retirement on the part of older workers is dramatically illustrated by the larger number of minority older workers who choose to accept lower social security benefits in order to retire at age 62 (Sheppard, op. cit., pp. 59–67). This long-run tendency of labor market competition to push vulnerable workers into retirement is further demonstrated by longitudinal studies showing how workers with long-term unemployment and marginal work histories had a greater tendency to retire early. See *The Pre-Retirement Years: A Longitudinal Study of the Labor Market Experience of Men*, Vol. 4, Manpower R&D Monograph 15, U.S. Department of Labor, 1975, pp. 153–97.

57. Meier, op. cit., pp. 6–10.

58. Edna C. Wentworth, "Why Beneficiaries Retire," *Social Security Bulletin*, January 1945, pp. 16–20.

59. Margaret L. Stecker, "Why Do Beneficiaries Retire? Who Among Them Return to Work?" *Social Security Bulletin*, May 1955, p. 3.

60. Erdman Palmore, "Retirement Patterns Among Aged Men: Findings of the 1963 Survey of the Aged," *Social Security Bulletin*, August 1964, p. 9.

61. Virginia Reno, "Why Men Stop Working at or Before Age 65: Findings from the Survey of New Beneficiaries," *Social Security Bulletin*, June 1971, pp. 3–17; and Lenore E. Bixby, "Retirement Patterns in the United States: Research and Policy Interaction," *Social Security Bulletin*, August 1976, pp. 3–19.

62. *Reaching Retirement Age: Findings from a Survey of Newly Entitled Workers, 1968–70*, Social Security Administration, Research Report No. 47, 1976, p. 60.

63. These studies were: Meier, *Aging in America*, op. cit. (data cited from a national random sample of 4,254 respondents, with older age groups oversampled to assure an adequate number of responses from the older population); and Louis Harris, "No Vote on Forced

Retirement," The Harris Survey, Press Release, September 26, 1977 (data cited from a national random sample of 1,491 adults).

64. Although this question did not elaborate whether poor health was to be considered a reason for forced retirement, the context of the question appears to deal with institutional rather than health-related causes of retirement. See *An Index to Available Data from the NCOA/Harris Survey*, National Council on the Aging, Washington, D.C., February 1976.

65. Meier, op. cit., p. 11. These findings were also supported by another national survey that found the percent of those opposing "forced retirement" increasing from 69 to 70 percent between 1976 and 1977 (data courtesy of the American Council for Life Insurance from report *MAP '77*, p. 65).

66. It should be noted that the fact that these responses come from working respondents suggests significant selection effects upon these responses (that is, those who preferred not to work have withdrawn from the labor force).

67. Munnell, op. cit., p. 77.

68. Denis Johnston, "Illustrative Projections of the Labor Force of the United States to 2040" in *Economic Aspects of Population Change*, ed. Elliot Morss and Ritchie Reed, Commission on Population Growth, Washington, D.C.; and Philip Rones, "Older Men—The Choice Between Work and Retirement," *Monthly Labor Review*, November 1978, p. 10.

69. Sheppard and Rix, op. cit., pp. 81–103.

70. Malcolm H. Morrison, "Flexible Distribution of Work and Leisure; Potentials for Aging," unpublished paper, Antioch University, Washington, D.C., 1976, pp. 14–43; and Havighurst, op. cit., pp. 63–64.

71. Leonard Curry, "Kreps Likes Idea of Social Security Retirement at 68," Washington *Star*, July 31, 1977, p. A2; and "Full Social Security at 68, Not 65, Eyed," Washington *Post*, July 31, 1977, p. A3.

7

UNEMPLOYMENT, WORK SHARING, AND THE GROWTH OF LEISURE

In coming years, the tenacious problem of unemployment may catalyze increases of free time and a redistribution of education, work, and leisure over the life cycle. In the United States and other nations, unemployment has been unacceptably high and remarkably persistent. At the same time, there have been growing indications that an increasing portion of those who hold jobs would welcome opportunities to reduce their worktime, even at the cost of foregoing income. These seemingly contradictory trends have stimulated questions as to whether it might be possible to reduce worktime among those who are working in order to create jobs for those who are unemployed.

There are many unresolved questions about the need and viability of sharing work and how it might affect the growth and distribution of leisure for tomorrow's workers. As an exploration of this broad issue, this chapter will discuss the history of work sharing, provide a cursory assessment of the viability of work sharing as a means to combat joblessness, evaluate the likelihood that high unemployment will foster the application of work sharing, and speculate about the impact of work sharing on the growth of leisure.

WORK SHARING IS NOT NEW

Although work sharing has frequently received harsh criticism,[1] it is important to recognize that industrial societies have consistently applied policies to reduce and ration worktime as a means of combating joblessness. The approaches have varied tremendously and have ranged from temporary and permanent reductions of the workweek to systematically removing various sections of the working-age population from the labor force. In a very general sense, there are two basic forms of work sharing. The first type is generally restricted to specific firms and used as a short-term strategy to prevent layoffs and dismissals by temporarily reducing worktime. As an example, employers and employees in a given firm may decide to reduce the workweek and earnings for a short period by 10 percent as an alternative to laying off one-tenth of existing workers. The second type of work sharing seeks to reduce worktime among the employed in order to create jobs for those who are unemployed, thus distributing available work more evenly among a larger number of persons. This second type has been used with the intent of combating unemployment caused by long-term conditions that are likely to persist beyond the periodic downswings of the business cycle.

Worktime reductions to combat unemployment have most commonly occurred in the form of shortened workweeks. During the Great Depression of the 1930s, shortened workweeks were used by many firms with the cooperation of their employees in order to avoid layoffs and impoverishment at a time when there was no unemployment insurance to cushion the lack of earnings for those without work.[2] Over the last 30 years, approximately 30 percent of collective bargaining agreements have had formal provisions for work sharing.[3] However, with the exception of the highly unstable garment industries, these options have rarely been used.[4] Recently, short workweeks were used as an alternative to layoffs by a number of firms within the New York metropolitan area during the dual crises of the 1975 recession and city budget problems.[5]

A variation of reducing workweeks to prevent unemployment known as "short-time compensation" has been in effect in many European nations since the 1920s. This program provides partial unemployment insurance for worktime lost by employees who have taken a reduction in work hours in order to prevent layoffs within a specific firm. As a rough illustration, if a firm were to reduce the workweek and pay levels by 20 percent rather than lay off 20 percent of its employees, those employees working short-time would receive 20 percent of weekly unemployment insurance benefits. In this way, employees on reduced worktime would receive partial compensation for lost earnings and no employees would be disengaged from their jobs.

Germany has one of the best-known and -studied short-time compensation programs. Available data indicate that this program has been an effective short-range tactic for minimizing unemployment. For example, during the peak of the 1975 recession, the average number of workers receiving short-time compensation rose to 773,000 from an average of 292,000 in 1974. Estimates of the impact of short-time on German unemployment have been varied. One of the more sophisticated assessments indicates that short-time reduced employment by about 175,000 in 1975,[6] and that without this program the total registered unemployment may have been as much as one-sixth higher.[7]

Laws have also been enacted by the United States and other nations to permanently reduce and limit the workweek in order to spread employment among a larger number of persons. The major brunt of such efforts within the United States has taken the form of the 1938 Fair Labor Standards Act of 1938. In response to the formidable unemployment of the 1930s depression, a bill was passed defining the standard workweek as 40 hours and mandating payment of an "overtime penalty" of one-and-a-half straight-time wages for all wórktime in excess of 40 hours a week. This act was intended to encourage the hiring of more workers by reducing the workweek and creating disincentives for employers to work employees for excessive hours.

While it is generally recognized that mandatory worktime restriction had some positive impact on employment, available studies suggest that the success of such efforts must be qualified. Since most standard workweeks had already been reduced to about 40 hours prior to 1938,[8] any job creation that can be attributed to the Fair Labor Standards Act came largely from discouraging excess hours. However, this impact has progressively diminished since the 1930s, due to dramatic growth of the nonwage costs of employment such as fringe benefits and contributions to public programs like Social Security.[9] Because these employer expenditures now amount to over 30 percent of base wages or salaries for the average worker,[10] and these costs are relatively fixed for each worker despite the length of his or her worktime, the costs per hour of labor increases as worktime declines (see Table 7.1). Thus the costs of hiring new workers for shorter hours have frequently become greater than payment of higher wages for extra work hours. As a result, the job-creating impact of existing time-and-a-half overtime penalties is now generally considered to be negligible.[11]

In addition to adjustments in the workweek, there have also been an array of less-known work rationing approaches. In response to potential layoffs, firms commonly pursue a progression of cost-cutting policies to avoid loss of their workers. The first of these includes conventional actions such as cessation of hiring with intention of letting attrition reduce labor costs, utilization of workers to build up inventories and undertake nonroutine capital improvements, and release of temporary workers. Following these, a number of worktime adjustments are frequently used as a last resort before layoffs. These include requests that workers retire early, use accumulated vacation time, or take voluntary leaves of absence without pay. Additionally, a number of collective bargaining agreements have negotiated permanent worktime reductions that are specifically designed to share work. Most notably, the electricians' unions of New York City at one time pushed their standard workweek below 30 hours in order to share employment. Another somewhat counterproductive means of sharing work has been the "slowdown." This approach entails a number of informal and formal pace-setting arrangements within workplaces such as peer sanctions against "rate busters" or the classic coffee break. While such dilution of work effort can be explained in terms of employee attempts to "put in minimum effort for pay," it also represents an effort to insure that available work lasts longer.

TABLE 7.1

Dollar Costs per Hour for Fixed Costs of Labor by Variations of Worktime (standard workweek assumed to equal 40 hours)

Weekly Work Hours	1974 National Average Nonwage Compensation[a] ($57.34)	Weekly Fixed Costs of Labor[b]													
		$20	$30	$40	$50	$60	$70	$80	$90	$100	$110	$120	$130	$140	$150
60	.96	.33	.50	.67	.83	1.00	1.17	1.33	1.50	1.67	1.83	2.00	2.17	2.33	2.50
56	1.02	.36	.54	.71	.89	1.07	1.25	1.43	1.61	1.79	1.96	2.14	2.32	2.50	2.68
52	1.10	.38	.58	.77	.96	1.15	1.35	1.54	1.73	1.92	2.11	2.31	2.50	2.69	2.88
48	1.19	.42	.62	.83	1.04	1.25	1.46	1.67	1.87	2.08	2.29	2.50	2.71	2.92	3.12
44	1.30	.45	.68	.91	1.14	1.36	1.59	1.82	2.04	2.27	2.50	2.73	2.95	3.18	3.41
40	1.43	.50	.75	1.00	1.25	1.50	1.75	2.00	2.25	2.50	2.75	3.00	3.25	3.50	3.75
36	1.59	.56	.83	1.11	1.39	1.67	1.94	2.22	2.50	2.78	3.06	3.33	3.61	3.89	4.17

TABLE 7.1 (continued)

Weekly Work Hours	1974 National Average Nonwage Compensation[a] ($57.34)	Weekly Fixed Costs of Labor[b]													
		$20	$30	$40	$50	$60	$70	$80	$90	$100	$110	$120	$130	$140	$150
32	1.79	.63	.94	1.25	1.56	1.88	2.19	2.50	2.81	3.13	3.44	3.75	4.06	4.38	4.69
28	2.05	.71	1.07	1.43	1.79	2.14	2.50	2.86	3.21	3.57	3.93	4.29	4.64	5.00	5.36
24	2.39	.83	1.25	1.67	2.08	2.50	2.92	3.33	3.75	4.17	4.58	5.00	5.42	5.88	6.25
20	2.86	1.00	1.50	2.00	2.50	3.00	3.50	4.00	4.50	5.00	5.50	6.00	6.50	7.00	7.50

Nonwage compensation defined as including life and health insurance, private pensions, social security, paid time off, miscellaneous fringe benefits, and unemployment insurance taxes (*1977 Handbook of Labor Statistics*, p. 237).

Can be viewed to include all nonwage compensation (fringe benefits) as well as costs of supervisorial coordination, record keeping, recruitment, hiring, training, and retraining.

Source: Fred Best, "Individual and Firm Work Time Decisions: Comment," *Work Time and Employment*, Special Report No. 28, National Commission for Employment Policy, Washington, D.C., October 1978, p. 225.

Finally, a number of social policies and norms have become indirect but powerful mechanisms for rationing available work. The most obvious of these has been the encouragement of extended years of schooling during youth and earlier retirement in old age. The reduction of unemployment was one of the commonly noted purposes of the Social Security Act of 1935, as well as private and public retirement policies in subsequent years.[12] Similarly, the expansion of educational facilities and student loan programs in the 1960s and 1970s was frequently viewed by policy makers as a productive and humane way of reducing competition for available jobs. While there are complicating trends for school-aged workers,* earlier retirement appears to have attenuated unemployment. For example, the labor force participation rates for those over age 64 have declined from 27.9 to 13.1 percent between 1948 and 1977.[13] While the purposes of education and retirement policies are too complex to be explained solely in terms of sharing work, they have clearly fostered a reduction in millions of persons who might otherwise be looking for jobs.

An even more subtle form of sharing work by selectively reducing labor force activity of specific groups comes from a number of norms and policies that have discouraged women from working. Of course, the discouragement of women workers is a phenomenon deeply rooted in the nature of traditional sex roles and family patterns and cannot be viewed solely as a work-sharing device. However, in addition to frequently cited norms that "women should not take jobs away from men," it is clear that hiring restrictions and lower wages have discouraged women from participating in the work force. In terms of unemployment, the implications are obvious. In 1977, some 90.2 percent of prime-age men between the ages of 25 and 64 were in the labor force in contrast to only 54.8 percent of women of the same age. Deliberate or subconscious rationing of jobs between the sexes has been an important determinant of the ways work is allocated within most industrial societies,[14] and the ongoing rise of women workers dramatically indicates that our views toward this way of distributing employment must be carefully reexamined.

Clearly, work sharing is not a new idea. Both private and public policies have promoted various ways of sharing and distributing jobs. In many cases, work sharing has been fostered by a number of social forces in conjunction with unemployment; and in many cases the work-sharing implications of many social policies have been secondary but important considerations. The main issue concerning work sharing is not whether or not to use it. Work sharing *is* already a reality. The issues for the future are whether or not work sharing can effectively reduce joblessness, how much (if any) work sharing should be used, and what forms it should take.

---

*Labor force participation rates have increased for persons under age 24, primarily due to the increased work activity of women. However, much of this labor force activity has been in the form of part-year and part-week work.

IS WORK SHARING A VIABLE IDEA?

Recent years have demonstrated what appears to be a renewed interest in work sharing. The idea of short-time compensation to reimburse employees for temporary workweek reductions undertaken to avoid layoffs has been reaffirmed as a key policy in Europe and implemented on a trial basis in the United States and Canada.[15] A growing coalition of labor unions has begun pressing for amendment of the Fair Labor Standards Act in the United States and in other nations in order to reduce the standard workweek to 35 hours and increase overtime pay to twice regular wages as a means of sharing jobs among a larger population on a permanent basis.[16] There has been some discussion, particularly in Europe, of a wide variety of mechanisms to reduce the supply of labor.[17] Finally, some unions have stepped up collective bargaining efforts to reduce worktime in order to share jobs.[18]

In addition to the traditional means of work sharing, a number of novel approaches have been receiving attention. It has been suggested that opportunities for part-time employment should be increased in order to provide more jobs,[19] particularly for the growing portion of the labor force that prefers to work less than full time.[20] Along the same line, the practice of "job splitting," in which two persons hold one full-time job, has been frequently tried to provide opportunities for reduced worktime as well as sharing employment.[21] In a somewhat different vein, there has been some interest in extended vacations, voluntary leaves of absence, and sabbaticals in order to satisfy the desires of workers for leisure as well as shared employment.[22] Finally, the ultimate encapsulation of all these ideas has been the notion of "voluntary time-income tradeoff options" through which employees are given one or more ways to exchange varying amounts of income for more free time. The idea here is that workers desiring more time away from their jobs can exchange earnings for preferred forms of free time (that is, vacations, shorter workdays, and so on) and therefore loosen up worktime to create jobs for others.[23]

Frustration with persistent high unemployment will likely foster interest in a variety of work-sharing proposals, but is the general notion of reducing worktime a viable means of combating joblessness?

Many economists are quick to call work sharing a defeatist strategy based on a faulty "lump of labor" assumption that there is a fixed amount of labor needed within society. They hasten to emphasize that there is a great deal of work that needs to be done, and that there is no fundamental reason why society cannot ultimately create as many jobs as there are willing workers.[24] Certainly no reasonable person would disagree with these basic propositions. However, reasonable persons can and do differ on how fast contemporary industrial societies can and will create jobs, and what means should be used to accomplish this goal. Over recent years the United States and other nations have not created enough jobs for all those who are willing and able to work. Further, the tenacity of inflation has led increasing numbers of economists and policy makers to be wary of stimulating economic growth and job creation by massive government expenditures. As a result, speculations indicate that economic growth and job creation could be considerably below the norms of the past. This emerging acceptance of sluggish economic activity will likely foster consideration of work sharing as a "second best" option for reducing joblessness.

There are others who maintain that the nature of unemployment is changing and that the impact of contemporary unemployment is not severe enough to require extraordinary efforts such as work sharing. Proponents of this view note that the percent of all persons over age 16 who are employed has risen from 55.8 to 57.1 percent between 1967 and 1977 as evidence that the United States is employing a larger portion of its population than ever before.[25] It is also suggested that much unemployment has resulted from increases of women and other "secondary workers" who do not need jobs as badly as males and who cushion the severity of unemployment by providing supplementary earnings for families with jobless men.[26] It is also noted that today's intense competition for jobs is in large part a temporary phenomenon fostered by the initial labor force activity of the post-World War II baby boom generation, a factor that is expected to subside and ultimately create labor shortages as smaller generations follow in their wake.[27] Finally, it is suggested that a significant portion of measured unemployment stems from recipients of public income maintenance funds who are required to register themselves as looking for a job but are in reality either unsuited or unwilling to work.[28]

Without spending time on arguments attesting the extent and hardship of today's unemployment,[29] a case can be made that the very changes that may be reducing the severity of joblessness for some groups may increase the applicability of work sharing. Specifically, the groups (that is, women, young adults, older workers) who are increasing the supply of labor faster than the creation of jobs are demonstrating a preference for shortened worktime and reducing the need to work among "prime-age males." While the rise of women workers and dual-earner families reduces the severity of unemployment for many persons, it also opens the possibility for many full-time workers to work less in order to gain personal leisure and create jobs for the unemployed. Similarly, the fact that women, young adults, and older workers tend to prefer less worktime opens the possibility that more persons in those groups could be employed by the expansion of opportunities for less than what we now consider full-time work.

There are yet other reasons that may make work sharing an inadvisable employment policy. While worktime reductions fitting the changing preferences of today's work force may help create more jobs, it is also likely that such worktime changes might encourage increased labor force participation among those preferring alternative work patterns and therefore further aggravate the unemployment problem. Such a response to reduced work-time would likely be particularly intense among persons such as women with small children, students, and the handicapped who wish to work but cannot do so because of barriers created by prevailing worktime arrangements. At the same time, it is possible that reduced worktime arrangements would eliminate many barriers that keep currently unemployed persons from finding work. Ultimately, whether work sharing would stimulate the entrance of more persons into the labor force than the jobs it creates is a matter of speculation.

Another major reservation expressed about work sharing is that the amount of work created may not equal the amount foregone as worktime reductions. In temporary work sharing used by firms to avoid layoffs, the worktime gained by employees who would otherwise be unemployed appears to equal the worktime reductions of other employees.[30] However, longer-ranged work sharing designed to spread work to the unemployed may not produce equal job time for the worktime that is foregone. This appears to be particularly true in the case of recent proposals to amend the Fair Labor Standards Act so that the standard workweek is reduced to 35 hours and overtime pay is increased to double regular wages. Available studies suggest that this approach would shorten the workweek for some workers, but that organizational constraints would limit the curtailment of overtime and the increased costs of labor to firms might stimulate investment in labor-saving capital that would ultimately nullify employment gains.[31]

For various reasons, other ways of spreading work to create jobs would doubtless suffer from the same problem. One major reason for a less-than-perfect replacement of lost worktime with jobs stems from the previously noted fixed costs of labor such as fringe benefits. Since these costs vary little, if any, with worktime, their price per hour of labor increases as the worktime of employees declines (see Table 7.1). These added costs per hour of labor would encourage firms that have reduced the worktime of their employees to use existing personnel more efficiently, and thus minimize the hiring of new workers. In addition to the impact of these fixed labor costs, it can be expected that most organizations have a number of inefficiencies, and that worktime reductions would provide opportunities for more effective utilization of existing employees rather than new hiring. Ultimately the extent to which reduced worktime is replaced by new jobs will depend on the nature of specific work organizations. Some would have high and others low replacement rates. Clearly, replacement would rarely be total, and the viability of long-run work sharing would therefore have to be assessed by comparing its costs and benefits to other job-creating strategies.

Work sharing is obviously not *the* total solution to the unemployment problem. Like all strategies, it has its particular costs and problems. There are types of unemployment for which it would be, at best, only minimally effective. In cases where individuals or groups are unemployed because they lack necessary skills, work sharing would have low impact. Similarly, in cases where persons remain jobless because the marginal gains of holding a job are only slightly greater than the livelihood afforded by income maintenance programs, work sharing would likely be counterproductive. Clearly, work sharing is only one of many supplementary strategies that might be applied to combat unemployment.

FUTURE UNEMPLOYMENT AND THE DEMAND FOR WORK SHARING

Whether or not work sharing will be necessary or desirable depends in large part on the extent of unemployment in the future. While highly specific forecasting of unemployment is inadvisable, it is possible to make informal speculations based on a number of critical variables. In the broadest sense, unemployment is the result of a surplus of labor over the supply of jobs. The supply of labor and jobs can be simplistically explained by two very general formulations. First, the supply of labor is determined by (1) values toward work and need for income, which influence desire and necessity to work; and (2) the number and quality of available jobs, which determine whether individuals decide that the opportunities for employment make it worth working or hunting for a job. Second, the supply of jobs can generally be attributed to "market demand for goods and services" and the "factors of production," which determine the amount and nature of workers needed to produce the goods and services required by market demand.

In terms of the future supply of labor, the "propensity" or tendency to work is likely to be extremely high. In addition to the ongoing need to earn a livelihood and improve living standards in the face of inflation, there are a number of other factors that may foster an unusually rapid growth of the labor supply.[32] The large post-World War II baby boom generation that crowded the school systems in the 1960s is now swelling the ranks of the labor force and causing competition for work that is likely to remain keen for decades to come (see Figure 7.1). At the same time, the labor force participation rate of working-age women will continue to climb at a rate of about 1 percent a year.[33] Similarly, older persons appear less likely to retire, growing proportions of young persons are seeking jobs to both finance and enrich their education, and minorities who have long borne the brunt of discrimination in the labor market continue to demand a greater share and number of job opportunities.[34] As labor economist Eli Ginzberg has convincingly pointed out, there were some 17 million persons in 1977 who were likely to enter the labor force as the possibilities of finding a job increased.[35]

One conservative indication of the future supply of labor comes from past and projected labor force participation rates (the proportion of the working-age population who are either working or looking for work). In

FIGURE 7.1

Age Groups as Percentage of Total Labor Force, 1960–90

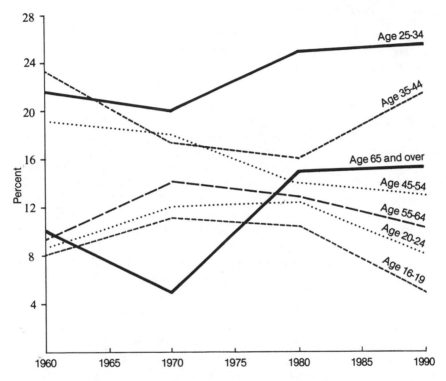

Source: Adapted from Garth L. Mangum, *Employability, Employment and Income* (Salt Lake City: Olympus Publishing Company, 1976), p. 192.

brief overview, the civilian labor force participation rate rose from 60.4 to 63.2 percent between 1970 and 1978,[36] and it is projected to rise to 66.2 percent by 1990 (see Table 7.2).[37] While there has been speculation of future labor shortages, labor force participation is likely to grow more rapidly than these BLS projections.

Given the high propensity to work among the population, an abundance of job opportunities will tend to draw even more persons into the labor force, and vice versa. If jobs are particularly attractive or unattractive, the growth of the labor force will be so much the greater or lesser. In this sense, it is necessary to consider both the prospective supply and quality of jobs in order to assess the nature and extent of future unemployment.

Between 1947 and 1978, the aggregate number of jobs in the U.S.

TABLE 7.2

Actual and Projected Labor Force Participation, 1950–90

Year	Labor Force Participation Rate	Total Civilian Labor Force (000s)	Total Civilian Population (000s)
1950	59.2	62,208	104,995
1960	59.4	69,628	117,245
1970	60.4	82,715	136,995
1975	61.2	92,613	151,268
1978	63.2	100,417	158,942
1985	65.3	113,000	171,900
1990	66.2	119,400	178,967

Source: Figures for 1950, 1960, 1970, and 1975 computed from *1977 Employment and Training Report of the President*, U.S. Department of Labor, p. 135, Table A-7; Figures for 1978 computed from John Bregger and Kathryn Hoyle, "The Employment Situation," U.S. Bureau of Labor Statistics, Press Release 79-181, February 1979, p. 2; and projections for 1985 and 1990 cited from "New Labor Force Projections to 1990: Three Possible Paths," U.S. Bureau of Labor Statistics, News Release No. 78-710, August 1, 1978.

economy has increased at an average rate of about 1.5 percent a year.* While there has been extreme vacillation in recent years, the average rate of job creation has been almost 2 percent a year between 1969 and 1978.† If these trends were to continue, the unemployment problem would be significantly abated in the future. But will the average 1970s job-creation rate persist?

Market demand will be a critical determinant of the supply of jobs because it provides the incentive for employers to retain and hire workers in order to produce saleable goods and services. Although qualifications must be made, the best overall indicator of market demand is the rate of economic growth.[38] Between 1950 and 1975, the average rate of economic growth was about 3.3 percent a year.[39] In cases where unemployment is above 5 percent, the GNP is estimated to require an annual growth rate of 4.5 to 5.0 percent in order to reduce unemployment rates a half a percentage point a year.[40] Base projections from the BLS indicate that the real GNP will grow at an

---

*The measure of job creation used in this discussion is the number of persons employed. While approximately 5 percent of the labor force hold two jobs or more, this portion has remained quite stable over the past several decades, thus allowing the number of employed persons to be used as a reasonable index of job creation. A more precise and interesting index might be the aggregate number of hours worked each year.

† Exceptionally high job creation rates in 1976 and 1977 were in large measure the result of rehiring persons laid off in 1975, 500,000 temporary public service jobs created by countercyclical government programs, and peak business cycle activity, all of which are expected to level off or decline in future years.

average of 3.8 percent a year between 1980 and 1985, and 3.2 percent between 1985 and 1990.[41] Another set of projections from a major study undertaken by the Edison Electric Institute forecast a 3.5 percent annual growth rate between 1980 and 1985.[42] Finally, a review of 22 other economic projections supports this forecast of 3.5 percent growth for the 1980–85 period. While these studies should be viewed with caution,[43] there is a general consensus that economic growth is likely to be sluggish in coming years.

Of course economic growth and market demand do not in themselves create jobs. Whether or not jobs are created is also determined by the importance of labor to the process of production.[44]

It has been suggested that technological advancements and capital investments could increase productivity such that fewer workers are needed and less jobs are created.[45] A Special National Commission explored this issue in the mid-1960s and concluded that technological change may create transitional unemployment by displacing workers from their existing types of work, but that there was no evidence that it was reducing the overall number of jobs in the economy.[46] The Commission's reasoning was that increased productivity will not reduce job creation as long as increased production is passed on to consumers so as to foster the market demand for goods and services that will require the employment of at least the same number of workers. While there has been renewed speculation that automation may cause unemployment,[47] comparison of market demand (real GNP) and productivity (output per labor hour) over past years indicates that productivity has not increased faster than market demand,[48] and thus technological advances have not been a major barrier to aggregate job creation.

Further specification should be made about types of jobs that are being created. In the past, growth of jobs in the service and white-collar sectors have replaced the jobs lost as a result of the ongoing automation of agricultural and manufacturing industries. However, contrary to past speculations of a general upgrading of jobs,[49] available data indicate that an increasing proportion of the jobs generated within the service and white-collar sectors will be menial and low paying.[50] For example, analysis of census data by Marcia Freedman shows that the number of jobs created within industries typified by "low" quality employment increased some 53 percent while the number of jobs in sectors typified by "high" and "medium" quality employment remained constant between 1960 and 1970.[51]

There are three important implications to this trend. First, declining quality of jobs can be expected to dampen the growth of the labor force and thus reduce unemployment. Second, the routine nature of many new jobs, coupled with likely resistance on the part of workers to perform them, may make such jobs vulnerable to increasing automation and reduce the rate of future job creation. Third, the low quality of many new jobs may generate high "frictional unemployment" in which workers are unemployed briefly as they hop from job to job.

Ultimately, there are too many imponderables to allow a concrete projection of unemployment rates in the future. However, existing trends suggest that high propensity to work coupled with sluggish economic growth will be likely to make unemployment a persistent and serious problem for many years to come. No society can remain healthy in the face of the inequities and waste wrought by persistently high unemployment, and such a situation will catalyze an intensive search for new solutions for joblessness.

Traditionally, there have been two principal social policies for combatting unemployment. First, the stimulation of economic growth has provided the primary means of creating needed jobs. Second, a wide range of government programs has been developed to directly create jobs for the unemployed. While these approaches are likely to retain focal importance, they are likely to be limited by the fiscal austerity wrought by inflation. Other approaches will likely be sought. As such, work sharing is likely to receive renewed interest as a means of preventing layoffs and creating jobs.

TRANSFORMING UNEMPLOYMENT TO LEISURE

While there are many proposals for work sharing, it is apparent that many of them may be inapplicable. Available studies indicate that a mandatory reduction of the workweek with an accompanying increase in overtime pay would be inflationary and ultimately cause little job creation due to the unavoidability of much overtime and accelerated replacement of labor with machinery.[52] Application of other proposals to remove persons from the labor force by increasing schooling and retirement years would be exceedingly costly to both individuals and society. Finally, continuation of policies and values that discourage women from labor force participation are neither economically viable nor socially acceptable. In overview, many of the approaches used to ration jobs in the past do not appear to be applicable today.

How then might the notion of work sharing be successfully applied? First, since the workweek has leveled at a generally tolerable 40 hours and expansion of nonwork years in the form of schooling and retirement appears to have reached its limits, there does not appear to be any one form of work reduction that is commonly desired and acceptable to today's workers. Rather, an apparent plurality of work and leisure preferences[53] suggests that an omnibus approach might best be taken to provide a variety of work-sharing options to individuals and firms. Second, all possible efforts should be made to avoid rigidity and insure maximum flexibility for individual accomodations and upward shifts of worktime in response to economic expansion. Third, attention should be given to the development of work-sharing approaches that serve secondary social needs as well as reduce unemployment. As such, work-sharing strategies that also help integrate work with family life, promote desired leisure, increase access to education, and ease transitions to retirement should be given priority.

It is likely that flexible and voluntary approaches to work sharing would be best suited for today's conditions. Rather than mandate work-sharing conditions, social policies might endeavor to remove underlying constraints, such as the extra fixed costs of labor, which prevent temporary or permanent worktime reductions. Of the many work-sharing approaches that might result from such a neutralization of constraints, the notion of "voluntary time-income tradeoff options" would appear to provide the greatest flexibility and job-creation potential while also meeting secondary social purposes. For example, if ways could have been found to encourage or allow 30 percent of the 1977 U.S. labor force to freely trade an average of 12 percent of their annual income for desired free time, and only half of this foregone time became jobs for the unemployed, it would have been possible to create about 2 million new full-time jobs. While far from a total solution for the unemployment problem, this would be a significant contribution that would simultaneously produce many secondary social benefits.

The thrust for work sharing has had profound impact on work and leisure time in the past and may exhibit similar influences in the future. In conjunction with other social forces, efforts to spread employment played a critical role in shortening the workweek and expanding time for schooling and retirement. In the future, drives toward work sharing will likely be a major cause of worktime reductions and increased worklife flexibility. However, in contrast to past efforts that tended to foster a monolithic 40-hour workweek and a somewhat rigid education-work-retirement lockstep, interest in sharing work combined with other social goals can be expected to catalyze a wide variety of work and leisure options ranging from part-time work to sabbatical leaves. Whether such future work-sharing efforts prove to be an effective way of saving and creating jobs remains to be seen. Until proven otherwise, there is reason to hope that these new approaches to work sharing have the potential to transform the wasted time of unemployment to the valued commodity of leisure.

Unemployment and the prospect of work sharing is only one of the several forces that are altering the fabric of industrial societies and increasing the plausibility of more flexible life patterns. For a growing number of individuals, every stage of the life cycle appears to hold an increasing need for more flexibility in scheduling the activities of education, work, and leisure.

While the reasons supporting more flexible life scheduling appear compelling, there are two important obstacles that require consideration in assessing the probability of such change. Although there are indications that the institutions of education and retirement are changing in ways conducive to flexible life schedules, there are serious questions as to whether work organizations can or will make corresponding adaptations. Organizational constraints such as the need for coordination, technological rigidities, seasonal business cycles, pursuit of cost efficiencies, needs for personnel continuity, and a host of other complications provide major obstructions. Even for individuals with great interest in more flexibility, occupational responsibilities and the problems of maintaining personal influence in organizations present additional problems. There is also the question of whether the general population is developing conscious preferences that are supportive of flexible life scheduling. For only when the desire for more flexible patterns becomes embedded into the general consciousness and given form through discussion and action will major institutions be stimulated to explore the viability of the major changes that will be necessary.

NOTES

1. Work sharing has often been criticized as an advisable policy on the grounds that it does not create jobs but only shares the hardships of unemployment, reduces political pressures to create more jobs, conflicts with seniority rights, is unacceptable to both workers and employers, and is a "defeatist" response to joblessness. See Lloyd G. Reynolds, *Labor Economics and Labor Relations* (Englewood Cliffs, N.J.: Prentice-Hall, 1970), pp. 46–50 and 576–83; Paul Samuelson, *Economics*, 8th ed. (New York: McGraw-Hill, 1970), pp. 552–53; and *1963 Manpower Report of the President*, U.S. Department of Labor, p. xxi.

2. J. W. Fagan, "Work Sharing During a Depression," uncited published article; and Sar A. Levitan, *Reducing Work Time as a Means to Combat Unemployment* (Kalamazoo, Mich.: Upjohn Institute, 1964), pp. 1–2.

3. *Characteristics of Major Collective Bargaining Agreements*, July 1, 1974, U.S. Department of Labor, Bureau of Labor Statistics, Bulletin 1888, 1975. For further background on collective bargaining agreements with provisions for work sharing, see Robert Platt, "Layoff, Recall and Work Sharing Procedures," *Monthly Labor Review*, December 1956, pp. 1385–93.

4. Peter Henle, *Work Sharing as an Alternative to Layoffs*, Congressional Research Service, Library of Congress, July 19, 1976, pp. 10–14; and Reynolds, op. cit., pp. 576–79.

5. Henle, op. cit., pp. 15–21; Edith F. Lynton, "Alternatives to Layoffs," Conference Report prepared for the New York City Commission on Human Rights, April 1975, pp. 31–49; and Richard Beleous and Sar Levitan, *Shorter Hours, Shorter Weeks: Spreading the Work to Reduce Unemployment* (Baltimore: Johns Hopkins University Press, 1977), pp. 66–73.

6. Interpretation of study provided by Beatrice Reubens from *Mitteilungen aus der Arbeitsmarkt-und Berufsforschung*, No. 1 (1977), p. 8.

7. "Short-Time Work Compensation," *What's New in Labor and Social Policy*, Federal Republic of Germany, Embassy to the United States, April–May 1976, p. 7.

8. John D. Owen, "Hours of Work in the Long-Run: Trends, Explanations, Scenarios and Implications," in *Work Time and Employment*, Special Report No. 28, National Commission for Employment Policy, Washington, D.C., 1979.

9. Joseph Garbarino, "Fringe Benefits and Overtime as Barriers to Expanding Employment," *Industrial and Labor Relations Review*, April 1964, pp. 426–42; and Robert L. Clark, *Adjusting Hours to Increase Jobs: An Analysis of the Options*, Special Report No. 15, National Commission for Employment Policy, Washington, D.C., September 1977.

10. *1977 Handbook of Labor Statistics*, U.S. Department of Labor, p. 237; R. A. Hart and P. J. Sloane, "Working Hours and the Distribution of Work," Conference on Collective

Bargaining and Government Policies (Paris: Organisation for Economic Co-operation and Development, July 1978), p. 13; and U.S. Chamber of Commerce, *Employee Benefits 1975*, Washington, D.C., 1976.

11. Joyce Nussbaum and Donald Wise, "The Overtime Pay Premium and Employment," in *Work Time and Employment*, op. cit.; and Ronald Ehrenberg, "The Impact of the Overtime Premium on Employment and Hours in the U.S. Industry," *Western Economic Journal*, June 1971.

12. Arthur S. Link and William B. Catton, *The American Epoch: A History of the United States Since the 1880's* (New York: Knopf, 1965), pp. 414-15; William F. Leuchtenburg, *Franklin Roosevelt and the New Deal* (New York: Harper and Row, 1963), pp. 103-06; and Juanita Kreps, *Lifetime Allocation of Work and Income* (Durham, N.C.: Duke University Press, 1971), pp. 73-75.

13. *1978 Employment and Training Report of the President*, U.S. Department of Labor, 1978, p. 186.

14. Laurie Werner, "Where are Working Women Now?: Update from Eli Ginzberg," *Working Women*, December 1978, pp. 32-35.

15. *Jobs for the Hard to Employ: New Directions for Public-Private Partnership* (Washington, D.C.: Committee for Economic Development, January 1978), pp. 73-75 and 77; Fred Best et al., *Short-Week Compensation: An Approach to Saving Jobs and Skills*, Office of the Assistant Secretary for Policy, Evaulation and Research, U.S. Department of Labor, April 1979, Chapter 1; and "Work Sharing in Canada," Prepared for the Manpower and Employment Conference, Australia, by the Department of Employment and Immigration, Ottawa, Canada, April 1978.

16. "Unions Campaign to Shrink Work Time," *Business Week*, April 24, 1978, p. 30; Jerry Flint, "Unions Meet Resistance in Trying to Cut Workweek," New York *Times*, April 16, 1978; and Clayton Fritchey, "Pushing for a Shorter Workweek," Washington *Post*, May 20, 1978, p. A15.

17. *Wales T.U.C. Fourth Annual Report*, Report of Conference, Wales Trade Union Council, Cardiff, 1977, pp. 99-102; "Objectives and Effects of Work Sharing," Directorate General, Employment and Social Affairs, Commission of the European Communities, November 1977; Hart and Sloane, op. cit.; Jean Ross-Skinner, "Europe Gambles on Work Sharing," *Dun's Review*, September 1978, pp. 114-22; Christian Tyler, "Union's Crusade for the Shorter Working Week," *Financial Times* (London), June 2, 1978, Editorial page; and "Measures to Alleviate Unemployment in the Medium Term: Work Sharing," *Department of Employment Gazette* (Great Britain), April 1978, pp. 400-02.

18. "Paid Personal Holidays," *Solidarity*, October 21, 1977, pp. 6-10.

19. Stanley Nollen, "Whither Alternative Work Schedules?" unpublished paper, School of Business Administration, Georgetown University, Washington, D.C., November 1978, p. 14.

20. William V. Deuterman and Scott C. Brown, "Voluntary Part-Time Workers: A Growing Part of the Labor Force," *Monthly Labor Review*, June 1978, pp. 3-10.

21. "Jobs: Two for the Price of One," *Time*, May 3, 1976.

22. Jule Sugarman. "The Decennial Sabbatical," *The CUPA Journal* 28, No. 3 (Summer 1977): 47-52; and Robert Rosenberg, "A Pilot Project for Extended Leaves." Working Paper No. 10, Senate Office of Research, California State Senate, Sacramento, December 1976.

23. James Mills, "Leisure Sharing: Its Time Has Come," *State Government*, Spring 1979, pp. 75-79; and *Leisure Sharing*, Hearings of the Select Committee on Investment Priorities and Objectives, California State Senate, San Francisco, November 1, 1977, pp. 41-49 and 128-35.

24. Samuelson, op. cit., pp. 552-55; and Reynolds, op. cit., pp. 46-50 and 576-83.

25. Alfred Malabee, Jr., "More and More People Seek and Find Jobs Even Though the Unemployment Rate Stays High," *Wall Street Journal*, January 18, 1978.

26. "Unemployment: Rate Remains High But Some Hardship is Alleviated," *Commerce America*, March 15, 1976, pp. 2-4.

27. Michael Wachter, "The Demographic Impact on Unemployment: Past Experience and Outlook for the Future," *Demographic Trends and Full Employment*, Special Report No. 12, National Commission for Employment Policy, Washington, D.C., December 1976, pp. 27–100.

28. Kenneth W. Clarkson and Roger E. Meiners, *Inflated Unemployment Statistics: The Effects of Welfare Work Registration Requirements*, Law and Economics Center, University of Miami, Coral Gables, March 1977.

29. Most specifically, it is noted that "discouraged workers" who have withdrawn from an active job search because of harsh labor market competition account for additional "hidden unemployment" (Alfred J. Tella, "Labor Force Sensitivity to Employment by Age, Race and Sex," *Industrial Relations*, February 1965, pp. 69–83; and Paul O. Flaim, "Discouraged Workers and Changes in Unemployment," *Monthly Labor Review*, March 1973, pp. 8–16); and that aggregate unemployment rates downplay the acute hardships of minorities, women, youth, and other groups ("Taking the Measure of Unemployment," New York *Times*, January 12, 1978, Editorial page; William Raspberry, "Fighting Joblessness: Two Uncommon Views," Washington *Post*, September 9, 1977, p. A27; and Jacob Mincer, "Determine Who Are the 'Hidden Unemployed,'" *Monthly Labor Review*, March 1973, pp. 27–30).

30. Lynton, op. cit., pp. 31–49; and Gunter Schmid, *Selective Employment Policy in West Germany: Some Evidence of Its Development and Impact*, International Institute of Management, Berlin, July 1978, pp. 14 and 31.

31. Nussbaum and Wise, op. cit.; and Michael Wachter and Jeffrey Perloff, "Work Sharing, Unemployment and Economic Growth Rates," in *Work Time and Employment*, op. cit.

32. In addition to the factors noted below, it has been estimated that the United States has within its borders between 6 and 8 million illegal immigrants, most of whom are of working age. Estimates of illegal immigrants are subject to error, but most are low rather than high. It is estimated that about 800,000 illegal aliens are entering the United States annually. In 1976, the Immigration and Naturalization Service apprehended some 875,915 illegal entrants compared to 110,000 in 1965. See John D. Juss and Melanie J. Wirken, "Illegal Immigration: The Hidden Population Bomb," *The Futurist*, April 1977, pp. 114–20. Also see *Illegal Aliens: An Assessment of the Issues*, National Council on Employment Policy, Washington, D.C., October 1976; and *The Illegal Alien and the Economy*, Economic Development Council of New York, April 1977.

33. Ralph Smith, "Women in the Labor Force in 1990," Preliminary Draft, The Urban Institute, Washington, D.C., August 1978, pp. 1–98.

34. Although the labor force participation rate of minorities is lower than that of nonminorities, a number of studies has indicated that minority labor force participation will increase rapidly as the opportunities for employment rise. See Alfred Tella, op. cit., pp. 69–83; and Paul O. Flaim, op. cit., pp. 9–16.

35. Eli Ginzberg, "The Job Problem," *Scientific American*, November 1977, pp. 43–51. The likely validity of Ginzberg's estimate is supported by the hordes of job seekers who swarmed New York City Employment Offices looking for jobs to repair damage resulting from the 1977 "blackout" and other similar incidents. See Stanley Brezenoff, "110,000 Applications, 55,000 Jobs for Youths," New York *Times*, June 17, 1978.

36. *1977 Employment and Training Report of the President*, U.S. Department of Labor, 1977, p. 135, Table A-7; and Bureau of Labor Statistics, "Employment Situation," February 1979, Press Release 79-181, p. 2.

37. "New Labor Force Projections to 1990: Three Possible Paths," U.S. Bureau of Labor Statistics, News Release No. 78-710, August 1, 1978.

38. Of course, the size of the total U.S. population must be considered, so that economic growth is viewed on a per capita basis. For discussion, see Howard Bowen and Garth Mangum, eds., *Automation and Economic Progress* (Englewood Cliffs, N.J.: Prentice-Hall, 1966), pp. 11–12.

39. Growth of real GNP was 3.3 percent per year between 1950 and 1975, 2.9 percent per

year between 191Q and 1975, and 2.6 percent between 1965 and 1975. See *Statistical Abstracts of the United States, 1976*, Bureau of the Census, p. 395.

40. This assumption is based on the conditions of the late 1970s in which unemployment rates are high and increased utilization of labor does not approach optimal productivity nor cause undue inflation. See "Statement of Ray Marshall, Secretary of Labor," before Joint Economic Committee, U.S. Congress, February 10, 1978, p. 6.

41. Norman Saunders, "The U.S. Economy in 1990: Two Projections for Growth," *Monthly Labor Review*, December 1978, pp. 36–46. It should be noted that BLS projections have generally been high. See Thomas Mooney and John Tschetter, "Revised Industry Projections to 1985," *Monthly Labor Review*, November 1976, p. 4; and Charles Bowman and Terry Morian, "Revised Projections of the U.S. Economy to 1980 and 1985," *Monthly Labor Review*, March 1978, pp. 9–12.

42. The figures cited were for moderate growth projections for the real GNP. High projections were at a rate of 4.8 percent between 1975 and 1980, and 4.0 percent between 1980 and 1985. Low projections were 4.15 percent between 1975 and 1980, and 2.21 percent between 1980 and 1985. See Edison Electric Institute, *Economic Growth in the Future: The Growth Debate in National and Global Perspective* (New York: McGraw-Hill, 1976), pp. 121, 151, and 175.

43. Gary Fromm, "Forecasts of Long-Run Economic Growth," *U.S. Economic Growth from 1976 to 1986: Prospects, Problems and Patterns*, Joint Economic Committee, U.S. Congress, December 15, 1976, pp. 1–37.

44. Samuelson, op. cit., p. 40.

45. *The Triple Revolution*, Statement of the Ad Hoc Committee on the Triple Revolution, Santa Barbara, Calif., March 22, 1964; and Robert Theobald, *The Guaranteed Income* (Garden City, N.Y.: Doubleday, 1967).

46. Report of the National Commission on Technology, Automation and Economic Progress, *Technology and the American Economy*, Vol. 1, February 1966.

47. Wassily Leontief, "Work Sharing, Unemployment and Economic Growth: Comment," in *Work Time and Employment*, op. cit.; and Wassily Leontief, "Newer and Newer and Newer Technology with Little Unemployment," New York *Times*, March 6, 1979, Editorial page.

48. Edward F. Denison, "The Puzzling Drop in Productivity," *The Brookings Bulletin* 15, no. 2 (1978), pp. 10–12.

49. Burton Clark, *Educating the Expert Society* (San Francisco: Chandler, 1962); and more recently Daniel Bell, *The Coming of the Post-Industrial Society* (New York: Basic Books, 1973), pp. 134–38 and 212–65.

50. Ginzberg, "The Job Problem," op. cit., pp. 48–50; and Fred Best and Barry Stern, "Education, Work and Leisure—Must They Come in that Order?" *Monthly Labor Review*, July 1977, pp. 4–6.

51. Marcia Freedman, *Labor Markets: Segments and Shelters* (New York: Allanheld, Osmun, 1976), p. 75.

52. Nussbaum and Wise, op. cit.

53. Fred Best, "Preferences on Worklife Scheduling and Work-Leisure Tradeoffs," *Monthly Labor Review*, June 1978, pp. 31–37; and Best, "Individual and Firm Work Time Decisions," op. cit.

PART III

THE EMERGING CONSENSUS FOR NEW LIFE PATTERNS

We had always expected one of the beneficent results of economic affluence to be a tranquil and harmonious manner of life. What has happened is the exact opposite. The pace is quickening, and our lives in fact are becoming steadily more hectic. We had long expressed hopes that the elimination of material cares would clear the way for a broad cultural advancement. The tendency is rather the reverse. The cause of these and similar modern anomalies lies in a circumstance that has been entirely ignored, namely the increasing scarcity of time. The limited availability of time and the increasing claims made on it mean that affluence is only partial.

Staffan Linder
The Harried Leisure Class

8

TIME AS A
SCARCE COMMODITY

Every era has its own aspirations and priorities, and there are indications that late twentieth century American society will place greater emphasis upon the value of time. Over the last several centuries, the dominant values of Western civilization have shifted from a concern with basic survival to the pursuit of affluence. In times past, when survival and the day-to-day agreeability of life were linked closely to the achievement of basic material welfare, it was understandable that basic economic concerns were of primary importance. Today there is ample economic well-being and opportunity to engender thoughts about the value of the allotted time of our lives and how we use it. Time, which is the ultimate measure of our existence, is likely to be increasingly recognized as a scarce commodity in the same way as conventional economic goods and services.[1] To be sure, the problems of producing the goods and services necessary for survival and material comfort will not disappear. However, a growing number of persons in late industrial societies can be expected to seek new balances between work-and nonworktime.

One broad indicator of changing perceptions of the value of time relative to material wealth comes from a national survey of the American public conducted in May 1977. This survey found that a majority of 79 to 17 percent believed the nation desires to place greater emphasis on "teaching people how to live with basic essentials" rather than "reaching higher standards of living." Responses to another question revealed that a 76 to 17 percent majority expressed a preference for "learning to get pleasure out of nonmaterial experiences" rather than "satisfying our needs for more goods and services." Finally, another slightly less lop-sided majority of 63 to 29 percent felt that the country would be better served if more attention were put on "learning to appreciate human values more than material values" as opposed to "finding ways to create more jobs for producing more goods."[2]

These and other responses suggest that American society may wish to give less importance to materialistic endeavors and shift concern toward gaining more free time and using time for more fulfilling purposes. Findings such as these suggest the evolution of a general value system that would be highly supportive to more flexible life patterns. They also raise important questions about the degree of importance that is likely to be placed on time, and the specific ways in which people may seek to realign work- and nonworktime.

While there are abundant statistics on worktime trends and numerous studies of how groups with varying social characteristics respond to available worktime options, there is unfortunately little data concerning how persons might prefer to balance work and leisure if they had free choice on such matters. If persons could do as they liked, how much income-earning worktime might they exchange for more free time? What types of free time would they prefer most? How do time-income tradeoff preferences vary among groups broken down by family cycle stage, sex, socioeconomic position, and other social characteristics?

This part of the book will examine the issue of what people might prefer concerning worktime by the analysis of data from two exploratory surveys on worktime preferences. To set the stage, this chapter will review theoretical literature and existing data on time-income tradeoff choices.

THEORIES ON THE VALUE OF TIME

The nature of worker preferences and choices concerning the balance of work and leisure has been the subject of speculation since the beginning of economics, and more recently other social sciences.[3] Through the eighteenth century, it was assumed that increased wages would diminish the labor supply because workers would work "just so much and no more as may maintain them in that mean condition to which they have become accustomed."[4] Around the turn of the nineteenth century, Adam Smith, J. B. Say, and other non-Mercantilist thinkers proposed the contrary notion that higher wages would induce longer and harder work effort.[5] Thomas Malthus, however, continued to advocate the belief that most workers would be content with subsistence and would cease working when incomes rose beyond that level.[6]

W. S. Jevons, who agreed with Malthus, also observed that the "irksomeness" of work was an important determinant of time-income preferences. Laborers performing disagreeable and onerous work would be expected to be less willing to increase their work efforts than would professionals pursuing more pleasant careers.[7] Correspondingly, Alfred Marshall noted that any increase in worktime induced by higher wages would also heighten fatigue and thus increase the value of leisure time to the worker.[8] By the late nineteenth century, economists began to integrate the host of contradictory forces that simultaneously motivate workers to both seek and avoid work.[9] Finally, A. C. Pigou applied the concept of marginal utility to this issue and postulated that the value of each additional unit of income would decline as workers earned greater earnings.[10] With this the circle came full round, and economists theorized that increased remuneration would increase the supply of labor, but that the financial discretion gained by larger incomes coupled with the increased fatigue accompanying longer hours would ultimately limit the amount of time that a person would work at a given wage.

Current economic theory has postulated two counterposing principles that determine how individuals come to make choices between earned income and time. The first principle, called the "income effect," is the tendency to forego earnings for time as income increases. Thus, a worker who finds it necessary to work 60 hours a week when paid $4 an hour might find it desirable to work less if the pay rate were increased to $6 an hour. The second principle, called the "substitution effect," is the tendency to work more as the rate of pay increases. Thus, an individual unwilling to work no more than 40 hours a week at $4 an hour might be readily willing to work 60 hours a week if paid $8 an hour.[11] These theoretical concepts provide a helpful framework for thinking about choices between work and free time. Nonetheless, they must be integrated with empirical data and the perspectives of other disciplines in order to more fully explore the complex social forces that determine the values and preferences that influence worktime decisions.

THE GROWING DESIRE FOR LEISURE

Over the last several decades it has been commonly assumed that the American worker is not overly anxious to exchange income-earning work time for more free time.[12] Considering that there have been no major reductions in the workweek in the last three decades, this is an understandable point of view. Unfortunately, most conclusions of this type have been restricted to limited scheduling options and the time frame of workdays and workweeks. Recently there has been cause to suspect that more flexibility in scheduling work and free time over both short- and long-range time frames may be an important factor in determining worker tradeoff preferences between time and income. If this is true, evolving time-income tradeoff preferences could conceivably alter the proportions of work and free time and usher forth a major realignment in the planning and scheduling of work over total "lifetimes."

The task of generalizing the emerging time-income tradeoff preferences of the American worker is something akin to the age-old fable of the five blind people trying to describe an elephant. One, holding the tail, said the elephant was long and skinny; another, touching the foot, reported that it was like a fleshy tree trunk; and so on. Just as with the blind persons in the story, each of the types of data available for study purposes, if used in isolation, lacks the scope and accuracy that is necessary for the development of an accurate overview of time-income preferences in the United States. However, we can utilize the different forms at our disposal in such a way that allows the strength of one data source to compensate for the weaknesses of another.

Three types of data will be used to make a preliminary evaluation of American preferences for free time as opposed to income: (1) behavioral data such as work hours, voluntary part-time work, vacation days in union contracts, and the like, which reflect real choices or tradeoffs that people make when confronted with institutional worktime options; between different kinds of work benefits; (2) attitude surveys dealing with life priorities, the causes of job satisfaction, and the level and types of concerns expressed over time; and (3) consumer expenditure data from the U.S. Departments of Labor and Commerce, including data on recreational and "time saving" expenditures, which reflect the level of discretion among consumers. These three types of data will be used to describe income-time tradeoff issues and trends that may evolve in the future.

Worktime and Collective Bargaining Trends

Behavioral data can tell us what people have chosen to do in the past and suggest what they are likely to do in the future, but they may not reveal the options of tomorrow that today are little known or not yet created. With this limitation in mind, behavioral data can be quite useful in assessing American tradeoff preferences between income and free time.

There is a general consensus that U.S. society has foregone significant portions of economic growth for more free time over the last century.[13] However, available estimates of these tradeoffs indicate that the proportion of economic growth foregone for time (as measured primarily in the form of reduced workweeks) has declined steadily. Prior to 1920 it was estimated that reductions of the workweek took about half of the growth in output per labor hour, with the proportion forfeited for reduced hours declining to 40 percent between 1920 and 1950.[14] Between 1940 and 1960, the proportion of increased productivity given up for gains of leisure declined still further to an estimated 11 percent, and it has been figured that only 8 percent of real economic growth was forfeited for free time in the 1960s.[15]

Time series data compiled by the Bureau of Labor Statistics help elaborate and qualify the nature of past American time-income tradeoff behaviors. These indicators can be classified into two broad categories: indicators that show the amount of time devoted to work, primarily workweek hours; indicators that suggest changing desires for free time, most notably provisions in collective bargaining agreements.

One indicator of the time devoted to work can be found in the changing length of the workweek. The average workweek has declined from more than 53 hours in the 1870s to about 39 hours in 1977.[16] However, since the late 1940s the trend toward a shorter workweek has slowed markedly. Indeed, the growing number of women and students who tend to work part-time has disguised somewhat the fact that over the last 25 years the average male nonstudent workweek has remained about 43 hours, a figure significantly higher than today's overall 39-hour average.[17]

In recent years there have been a number of efforts to alter the 5-day, 40-hour format; most notably the 4-day, 40-hour workweek. Despite the presence of these alternatives, the 5-day or more workweek remained the pattern of 98 percent of full-time U.S. workers in 1974.[18] Futhermore, few of these modified workweeks entail shorter work hours.

It is noteworthy that the proportions of full-time employees (those working over 35 hours a week) working over 40 hours declined from 44 percent in 1955 to 37 percent in 1978, and those working less than 40 hours increased from 7 percent to 9 percent.[19] Nonetheless, the trend has clearly been down the middle, with the proportion of workers putting in a 40-hour workweek increasing from 49 percent to 55 percent during the same time span (see Table 8.1). Up to the recent United Auto Worker's agreement for shorter workweeks,[20] there has been little growth of union interest in shorter workdays or weeks.[21]

Other indications of income-time tradeoff preferences come from a review of data concerning voluntary part-time workers and "moonlight" workers with second jobs. The proportion of the labor force who work part-time hours (less than 35 hours a week) has increased from 15.4 percent in 1954 to 22.1 percent in 1977.[22] In addition to emphasizing that all part-time is not "voluntary,"[23] the use of part-time work as an indication of time-income preferences must be done with a recognition that a large portion of the part-time workers can be attributed to the entry or reentry of married women and student workers into the labor force. While these new entrants or reentrants are moving from no or little work to more work, therefore indicating a preference for income as opposed to free time, it is also true that they are choosing to work fewer hours per week than the labor force norm, thus indicating a desire to reserve substantial free time for themselves while they are working.

Economic fluctuations and changes in the composition of the labor force limit the use of the percentage of "moonlighters," or persons with two or more jobs, as an indicator of time-income tradeoff preferences. Since 1956 this figure percentage has vacillated between 4.5 and 5.7 percent and, if anything, is declining. This downward tendency may suggest that individuals are seeking shorter work hours, or, at least, are willing to let other family members work so that they do not have to work so much.[24]

While the average workweek and workday have not declined significantly during the last few decades, increases in the length of vacations suggest an increasing desire for more free time at the expense of income.

TABLE 8.1

Percentage Distribution of Hours Worked by Full-Time Employees, Selected Years, 1955–78

Year	Number of Full-Time Workers	Total Percent	Weekly Hours of Work				
			35–39	40	41–48	49–59	59 and Over
1955	51,008	100	7	49	21	23*	
1960	52,723	100	7	52	17	23*	
1965	56,528	100	8	51	17	12	11
1970	58,360	100	9	53	15	12	11
1975	61,335	100	10	55	13	11	10
1976	61,596	100.0	9.3	55.9	13.9	11.6	9.3
1977	63,892	100.0	9.3	54.5	14.3	12.1	9.7
1978	67,335	100.0	9.3	54.5	14.3	12.7	9.7

*Data for 1955 and 1960 not broken down for workweeks over 49 hours.

Sources: Geoffry Moore and Janice Hedges, "Trends in Labor and Leisure," Monthly Labor Review, February 1971, Reprint 2714; John Owen, "Work Time: The Traditional Workweek and Its Alternatives," prospective chapter of the 1979 Employment and Training Report of the President, U.S. Department of Labor; and figures for 1976 through 1978 provided courtesy of Robert Bednarzik, Office of Current Employment Analysis, Bureau of Labor Statistics, U.S. Department of Labor.

Available figures indicate that the length of the average worker's vacation has increased from 1.3 weeks in 1960 to 1.7 weeks in 1969 and suggest that this trend has continued up to the present.[25] A review of collective bargaining proposals and agreements further indicates that more free time is being pursued in the forms of longer "lumps" of time, such as vacations and three-day weekends. As one example, a review of selected collective bargaining agreements found that 67 percent of 1,314 agreements negotiated in 1949 provided for maximum vacations of two weeks or less. In contrast, 97 percent of 1,008 agreements negotiated in 1973 provided over two weeks' maximum vacation and 47 percent for maximum vacations of five weeks or more (see Figure 8.1).[26] More recent data for 1978 show that some 69 percent of agreements provide maximum yearly vacations of five or six weeks.[27] Of course, such vacation benefits are not distributed equally. For example, more than one-fourth of U.S. workers received no paid vacation in 1973.[28]

In sum, available data on actual worktime behaviors show a constant trend toward reducing time given to work and a shift toward new forms of scheduling free time. There has been some reduction in average workdays and workweeks, but this form of shortening worktime has been due primarily to changes in the composition of the labor force. Increasingly, growth of free time appears to be veering toward extended periods away from work rather than reduced workweeks or workdays.

Attitudes Toward Work Time

Many scholars of worktime have suggested that the relative stability of today's worktime trends indicates that workers are satisfied with current conditions and have no pressing interest in foregoing current or potential earnings for more free time. One indication of the popularity of current worktime arrangements comes from a 1971 panel study of employed men who were "heads of families." While this study found that only one-third were free to vary their work hours; the vast majority reported themselves satisfied with their worktime conditions, and those who were dissatisfied generally wanted more work.[29] Further, other studies of grievances arising under collective bargaining agreements, as well as frequent observations that most workers freely choose overtime work, suggest that a significant portion of workers place a high value on long hours.[30] While the issue is not without debate, such studies have led many scholars to conclude that workers are satisfied with the current workweek and even willing to work longer hours.[31]

In considering the above studies, it is important to recognize that personal worktime behaviors and preferences are determined by forces beyond individual control. A large degree of how persons behave and think concerning worktime is determined by job opportunities and the scheduling flexibility of available jobs. The *supply* of work and income is a powerful

FIGURE 8.1

Maximum Vacation Allowances in Selected Collective Bargaining Agreements, Selected Years, 1949–73

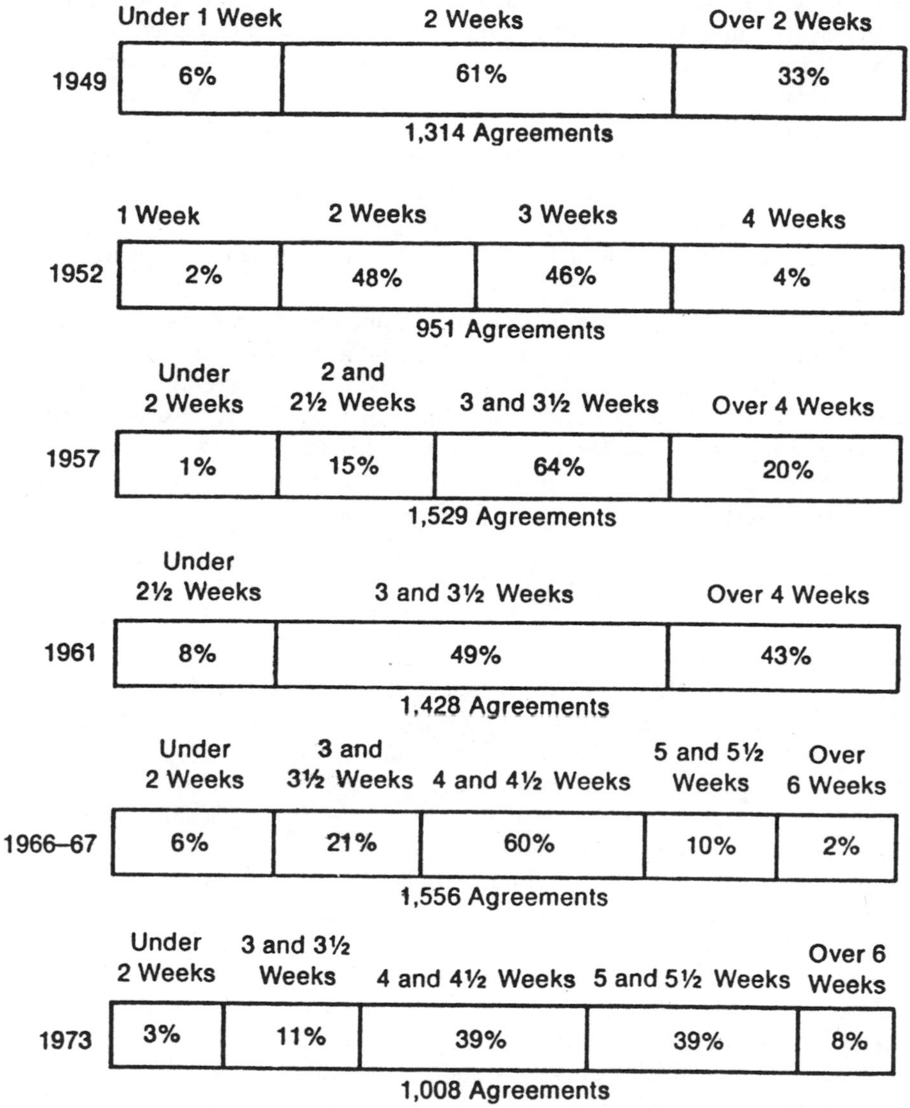

1949	Under 1 Week	2 Weeks	Over 2 Weeks
	6%	61%	33%

1,314 Agreements

1952	1 Week	2 Weeks	3 Weeks	4 Weeks
	2%	48%	46%	4%

951 Agreements

1957	Under 2 Weeks	2 and 2½ Weeks	3 and 3½ Weeks	Over 4 Weeks
	1%	15%	64%	20%

1,529 Agreements

1961	Under 2½ Weeks	3 and 3½ Weeks	Over 4 Weeks
	8%	49%	43%

1,428 Agreements

1966–67	Under 2 Weeks	3 and 3½ Weeks	4 and 4½ Weeks	5 and 5½ Weeks	Over 6 Weeks
	6%	21%	60%	10%	2%

1,556 Agreements

1973	Under 2 Weeks	3 and 3½ Weeks	4 and 4½ Weeks	5 and 5½ Weeks	Over 6 Weeks
	3%	11%	39%	39%	8%

1,008 Agreements

Source: Bureau of Labor Statistics, *Paid Vacation and Holiday Provisions*, bulletin 1425–9, chart I (Washington, D.C; U.S. Government Printing Office, 1969); *Charactistics of Agreements Covering 1000 or More Workers*, July 1, 1973, bulletin 1822, table 49 (Washington, D.C.: U.S. Government Printing Office, 1974).

determinant of worktime and labor force participation, as are institutional factors such as overtime, retirement laws, and other organizational constraints and policies.[32] While some workers have considerable choice concerning the amount of time they work, the vast majority of the labor force confront situations in which the time spent on the job is largely out of their control, being determined more by employers' preferences than their own. These constraints not only limit the decisions of individuals between income and time but may even dull the imagination and awareness of alternative worktime arrangements among many employees.

Attitude surveys have the potential of revealing worker preferences toward time and income free of institutional constraints and personal habits. Not only can such surveys create options that are generally out of range to most persons, but they can also breach issues that might not otherwise be even considered. At the same time, survey research has notable limitations. Perhaps the greatest limitation is that they do not necessarily predict behavior. Opinion and attitude studies may indicate the wishes and concerns of a population, but a serious question remains as to whether these same respondents will act upon these concerns. A second limitation of attitude studies is that respondents infrequently are allowed to express the strength of their preferences by being forced to make hard tradeoffs between desirable commodities or benefits. This problem, of course, can be reduced by phrasing questions in tradeoff terms. A third limitation is that available attitude studies frequently lack continuity between samples and questions over time. Similar questions and similar samples may have been used from time to time, but the comparability is rarely perfect. Despite these limitations, attitude surveys are useful in pinpointing specific issues in the minds of people.

Several kinds of attitudinal data are reviewed. They include:

Tradeoff preferences between income and free time: To what extent are people willing to sacrifice income in order to gain more free time?

Overall life priorities: What life priorities do people have and how do these reveal income-time tradeoff preferences?

Sources of job satisfaction and dissatisfaction: What are the causes of satisfaction and dissatisfaction on the job, and how do these factors indicate income-time tradeoff preferences?

Importance and nature of desire for free time: Has the concern over free time increased or decreased over past years and do shifts of concern in this area suggest a changing tradeoff preference between income and free time?

Some highlights of the findings of these types of attitudinal studies are noted below.

Time-Income Tradeoff Preferences

Unfortunately, few studies focus directly upon income-time tradeoff preferences. A study by Katona, Strumpel, and Zahn in 1966 posed the following question to a random sample of 1,322 respondents: "Some people would like to work more hours a week if they could and be paid for it. Others would prefer to work fewer hours per week even if they earned less. How do you feel about this?" The sample responded that 34 percent would work more, 10 percent less, and 56 percent would keep their current hours.[33] Breakdowns of these results indicated that age and, to a lesser degree, level of earnings affected this choice between income and time. The overall responses to this survey suggest that most workers are satisfied with their current balance between income-earning worktime and free time. Further, any desire to alter this balance would appear to tilt in the direction of working longer to earn more.

Three more limited studies of relatively small, nonrandom samples suggest somewhat different tradeoff preferences. These studies posed a number of equally costly benefit options (a 2 percent pay raise, or the equivalent in terms of more paid vacation, earlier retirement, shorter workdays, and so on) to their respective samples. The tradeoff options provided in one 1967 study conducted by Nealey and Goodale were ranked by 197 predominantly male factory workers in the following order:

Additional vacation of one week per year with pay
Five Fridays off per year with pay
Five weeks off every five years with pay
Four-day workweek of 9 hours and 45 minutes each day
Two percent annual pay increase
Earlier retirement by accumulating 5 days per year.
Five day workweek of 7-hour and 50-minute days.[34]

A similar but more costly set of options (5 percent pay raise, 2.5 weeks' added vacation, and so on) ranked by Chapman and Ottemann's 1975 sample of 149 clerical and operative employees from a public utility company revealed roughly the same preferences.[35] A third study conducted by Best and Wright in 1976 found similar results.[36] When the results of these three studies were disaggregated by age, sex, job title, and number of children, the idea of foregoing income for more time was found to be more popular among women, younger and pre-retirement workers, white-collar employees, and respondents with few or no dependent children.

A comparison of the results of the latter three studies with the Katona et al. study indicates that the extent of the tradeoff that people are willing to make between income and time is largely dependent on the range of choices. Apparently, the number of people who are willing to sacrifice income for time increases when there are a number of options for the scheduling of potential free-time gains.

Life Priorities

A number of open-ended questions posed to nationally representative samples by Albert Cantril and Charles Roll requested respondents to list their personal hopes and fears.[37] In the list of hopes, "better standard of living" was listed by 38 percent, 40 percent, and 29 percent for the corresponding years 1959, 1964, and 1971. In contrast, "having more leisure time" was listed by only 11 percent, 5 percent, and 6 percent in the same corresponding years.[38]

These and other studies of life priorities found U.S. respondents listing material wealth about four times more often than leisure, and that concern over both were declining.[39]

Sources of Job Satisfaction and Dissatisfaction

A review of attitudinal studies of factors causing job satisfaction and dissatisfaction provides some insight into the time-income tradeoff preferences of American workers. One rank-order consolidation of 19 different job satisfaction studies conducted between 1957 and 1973 showed that "income" was on the average ranked third and "free time and good hours" ranked twelfth out of 17 job characteristics.[40]

Importance and Nature of Desire for Free Time

Trend data concerning the importance of different job attributes to the general population are sparse but useful. Providing some rather short-range, yet valuable, national indicators of changing income-time tradeoff preferences are two similar studies done by Gurin et al.[41] and Converse and Robinson;[42] two successive "quality of employment surveys" conducted for the Department of Labor in 1969–70 and 1972–73;[43] and two studies of the value placed on various job characteristics conducted by the National Opinion Research Center during 1973, 1974, and 1975.[44] These studies suggest that the order of priority between income and free time has not changed, but the gap between them may be narrowing. The studies also indicated that the desire for free time among workers has been increasing. The evidence is mixed, however, about whether workers would be willing to give up some of their income in order to get more free time. For example, a series of Gallup Polls indicates that the proportion of persons favoring the "reduction of the workweek from 40 to 35 hours" increased slightly between 1953 and 1965, but a substantial proportion, about half, continually opposed corresponding reductions in pay.[45]

More recent national surveys conducted by the National Opinion Research Center suggest that willingness to trade income for time is responsive to fluctuation in the economy—the willingness to make such tradeoffs is greater when the economy is booming and decreases during recessions. Although the findings were only marginally reliable from a statistical point of view, the percentage of persons ranking "shorter working hours" among the top three of five job characteristics increased from 27.9 percent in 1973 to 30.3 percent in 1974 but declined to 25.2 percent in the recession year of 1976.[46] Similarly, the percentage ranking income among the top three of five job characteristics went from 72.5 percent and 70.2 percent in 1973 and 1974 to 75.3 percent in 1976.

Four recent surveys indicate that the scheduling of work and free time may be a powerful determinant of income-time tradeoff preferences. Although the data are statistically nonsignificant, two "quality of employment" surveys found that 29.5 percent of the workers surveyed cited "inconvenient or excessive hours" as a problem in 1969 compared to 33.6 percent in 1977.[47] Further analysis of these data suggests that work-scheduling problems represent over half the discontent with "inconvenient or excessive hours."[48] An Opinion Research Corporation study of 318 employees from 22 firms found that 81 percent of the employees favored the 4-day, 40-hour workweek and that the major reasons for favoring the plan were related to the increase of "lump" free time made available in the form of three-day weekends.[49] This observation was also supported by a recent study of 59 corporations applying flexible work schedules.[50] Finally, a Roper Organization study of a nationally representative sample of 2,000 workers found that the option of two-three months' leave every five years was the job benefit most desired out of 15 job benefits being negotiated at that time (See Table 8.2).[51]

While none of the above survey studies measures directly the ways in which increases of free time are preferred, they do suggest that increases of free time are preferred in "lump" amounts and that such extended time off is often preferred over income or other material benefits. With due regard to the limitations of the attitude data cited in this report, it is possible to make four generalizations. First, while most respondents preferred income over free time by a substantial margin, the American public desires both. An overview of the data suggests that three units of income are preferred for every unit of free time worth one unit of income.[52] Second, the gap of preference between income and free time appears to be closing as free time gradually becomes more important relative to income. This generalization does not appear to hold, however, during periods of economic slowdown. Third, the tradeoff between income and time is not a simple two-option choice, but rather a choice made within the context of numerous other values, most notably those associated with the "quality of work." Fourth, the priority given to income as opposed to free time may be strongly influenced by the ways in which potential free time gains are scheduled.[53]

Consumer Expenditure Trends

Data concerning consumer expenditures can provide some indication of

TABLE 8.2

Percentage of Worker Groups Who Have and Desire Different Job Benefits

	The Affluent		College-Educated		Executives/Professionals		Blue-Collar Workers		Union Members		White-Collar Workers		Women		Nonwhites	
	Have	Want	Have	Want	Have	Want	Have	Want	Have	Want	Have	Want	Have	Want	Have	Want
Pension plan collectable on retirement	51	6	48	7	47	10	46	8	64	7	34	6	35	8	48	9
Pension plan, part before retirement	27	19	35	18	30	16	22	24	30	22	26	26	17	26	13	24
Health insurance plan	87	10	75	12	84	10	70	13	81	3	72	13	68	18	74	15
Life insurance plan	73	8	64	12	61	9	55	10	72	4	60	6	49	9	55	11
Dental care insurance plan	21	26	14	29	12	14	19	21	27	24	10	23	10	18	15	14
Legal services plan	14	8	10	13	17	11	10	10	12	10	7	7	8	7	8	10
Pension after 30 years	29	16	33	15	29	16	33	19	50	21	23	21	21	16	34	24
Flexible working hours	39	13	36	13	33	16	21	10	18	10	33	12	25	13	23	17
Four-day week	7	21	3	13	5	13	4	22	2	27	4	18	3	14	2	19
Employee cafeteria	33	4	31	5	42	3	19	10	21	12	23	6	30	7	26	19
Overtime not required	50	5	35	5	28	3	39	8	41	8	46	3	43	5	32	17
Air conditioning	61	3	56	2	65	3	27	8	24	9	68	8	60	8	39	6
Stock options	21	8	14	7	17	8	11	5	12	9	10	11	14	7	9	13
Option of 2–3 months leave every 5 years	7	39	11	33	12	30	6	27	8	36	10	22	7	22	4	23
None of these (volunteered)	1	7	2	9	3	10	8	5	2	3	12	4	15	5	9	—

Note: Data cited from a national representative sample of 2,000 persons over age 18 conducted in January 1974. Respondents were asked to identify a preset list of job benefits that they currently had and those that they desired most in the future.

Source: Table cited from *Work: Desires, Discontents and Satisfaction: A Closer Look at Three Studies,* Special Report, The Roper Organization, New York, June 1974.

the tradeoff preferences between income and free time.[54] However, inasmuch as people have widely different motives for purchasing the things they do, considerable caution must be exercised in interpreting these data. Consumer expenditure data must be used as "indicators" rather than as pinpoint measures and tests. Only when these data are fit into a configuration including behavioral and attitudinal data can the interpretations of this last section be made with a fair degree of confidence. With this caveat in mind, this section explores the income-time tradeoff issue by testing three propositions:

Proposition 1: An increase in the portion of personal expenditures on "recreational" goods and services suggests that consumers may also desire more free time for "recreational" activities.

Proposition 2: An increase in the proportion of expenditures for "inexpensive" recreation suggests that the demand for income may be declining relative to the demand for free time.

Proposition 3: An increase in the proportion of expenditures spent on "time saving" items suggests that consumers are willing to exchange income for more free time.

It is important to note that each of these propositions has two parts. The front end is relatively factual, the back end is interpretive. Put differently, the initial premises of these propositions are easily measured and tested, while the interpretive implications are more diffuse and speculative.

The first proposition deals with the proportion of consumer budgets expended on recreation as an indicator of preferences for free time as opposed to income. Whether one uses the periodic consumer expenditure surveys or the yearly National Product Accounts, it can be said that the proportion of expenditures going to recreational goods and services has increased slowly but steadily over the last few decades. For example, National Accounts data show an increase from 5.4 percent in 1945 to 6.7 percent in 1975, and figures adjusted to compensate for the real dollar value of different goods and services show an even greater increase from 6.0 percent in 1966 to 7.9 percent in 1973.[55] Interpretation of these data is precarious, but it is reasonable to assume that increasing purchases of recreational goods and services may indicate a parallel growth in the desire for free time in order to use these purchases.

The second proposition evaluates the difficult question of whether the cost of recreation per unit of time is increasing, thereby also increasing the income requirements needed to participate in recreational activities. A complex juggling of available time-budget studies and adjusted dollar costs of different forms of recreation shows that the unit costs of recreational expenditures, like all expenditures, have been increasing.[56] However, there is no evidence that consumers are moving toward the most expensive of available recreational goods and services. Although today's consumer seems to be purchasing the more expensive forms of recreation (TV sets and sport equipment), available data suggest that these cost relatively little per hour of involvement and hence constitute "inexpensive" types of recreation. While the data used in this particular analysis can be interpreted in a number of ways, it is plausible that Americans need more time as opposed to money to fully utilize the leisure resources available to them.

The last proposition deals with whether or not expenditures on "time saving" goods and services (kitchen appliances, domestic servants, cleaning services) indicate a growing concern for more time as opposed to income. A series of consumer goods and services was isolated as "indicators" of expenditures made "in large part" for the purpose of saving time.[57] In brief, real dollar figures based on National Accounts, which are adjusted to compensate for relative price changes (Consumer Price Index), show that there is no significant change in the proportion of expenditures given to "time savers" between 1963 and 1974. If "time saver" expenditures are to be taken as an indicator of income-time tradeoff preferences,[58] these indicators support the status quo.

In general, analysis of consumer data concerning recreational expenditures, cost per hour of recreation, and "time saving" purchases suggests no major changes in the desire to trade off income for more free time.

MAJOR FACTORS DETERMINING TIME-INCOME TRADEOFFS

This and prior chapters have isolated a host of factors that influence individual time-income tradeoff preferences. While efforts have been made throughout this volume to interrelate these factors, no overarching formula or theoretical framework will be presented to explain and predict worktime preferences. Nonetheless, it is possible to draw upon available data to create a number of working propositions to guide thought on this topic.

Impact of Social Characteristics on Tradeoff Preferences

Time-income tradeoff preferences are likely to vary in accord with the unique impacts of a number of major social characteristics:

Income levels: Increases in earnings resulting from higher pay rates or longer workhours will lead to declining value for each additional unit of income while the relative value of additional nonworktime will increase. On the other hand, increased pay rates will encourage longer work hours because the reward for each unit of worktime is higher. Aside from cases in which earnings are extremely low, higher income levels are likely to increase the value of nonworktime relative to earnings.

Educational attainment: Added education may increase the capacity to use discretionary time and thus foster desire for more nonworktime. At the same time, education is an investment toward greater earning levels, thus fostering longer hours as an attempt to maximize returns for years of schooling. As educational attainment rises, it can be generally expected that the desire to maximize school investment will be balanced with leisure appreciation, with the quality of one's work proving to be a major determinant of this balance.

Occupation and quality of work: Work that is personally viewed as unpleasant is likely to encourage the minimization of worktime, while work that is viewed as pleasant will tend to encourage longer worktime.

Family cycle stage: Dependent children are likely to have a major impact on worktime preferences. Single persons and couples without children are likely to have the temporal and financial discretion to place high value on nonworktime relative to income. Parents with children are likely to have pressing financial pressures due to child raising and other household expenses while also experiencing a scarcity of time for family and personal matters. As such, family units with children will commonly have conflicting needs for added income and nonwork time, which are likely to be resolved in favor of income. Parents with matured and independent children will once again have the financial and temporal discretion to choose more freely between time and earnings.

Sex roles and family structure: The working status of spouses and parents and their views toward sex roles may influence worktime preferences. Traditional families in which the husband works on a paying job and the wife keeps house will probably place greater premium on income relative to time; while nontraditional families in which both spouses work and assume home chores may have greater financial discretion and scarcity of time leading to a greater premium for time relative to earnings.

Sex: Sex is likely to have a conflicting and changing impact on time-income tradeoff preferences. Traditional tendencies for women to stay at home and care for children can be expected to foster a strong interest in time relative to earnings among women. Tendencies of men to be the sole family income earners are likely to cause them to be cautious about exchanging income for time and perhaps prone to work longer for more pay. However, if sex and family roles become more flexible, these differences between sexes concerning worktime preferences are likely to decline.

Age: Age may be a major determinant of worktime preferences during youth and old age. However, it is likely that other variables such as family cycle stage and socioeconomic grouping will dominate age as a determinant of time-income preferences during the middle years of life. While many young persons may need income-earning work to meet living and discretionary expenses, frequent access to nonemployment income from parents and educational assistance programs, deferment of employment due to school enrollment, peer group acceptance of low earnings, and lack of health barriers to many forms of inexpensive recreation can be expected to minimize the value of earnings relative to time. For workers near retirement, personal discretion caused by senior pay levels and independent offspring coupled with declining physical stamina may increase preferences for time over money, while the need to save for retirement and future health care may foster a desire for income over time. For all older persons, the extra costs of retirement brought about by longer life expectancy and inflation may increase an interest for less than full-time employment as opposed to full retirement.

Impact of Scheduling on Tradeoff Preferences

The diversity of factors influencing time-income tradeoffs can be expected to foster a plurality of preferences concerning the scheduling of potential free time. Different individuals will place greater and lesser premium on alternative forms of time off the job, and an increase in the variety of ways potential free time might be scheduled may increase willingness to forego earnings for time.

Impact of Structural Changes on Tradeoff Preferences

Future willingness to forego earnings for time is likely to be significantly influenced by long-term structural trends. First, the increase of women workers, who tend to work shorter hours, can be expected to shift the composition of the labor force away from traditional male dominance and in doing so give rise to a greater incidence of less than "full time" work. Second, the ongoing movement of the occupational structure away from manufacturing and toward white-collar and service jobs will likely increase institutional adaptability for other than "standardized" worktime arrangements. These changes can be expected to liberalize worktime options and foster a general shift toward exchanging earnings for time.

While available data on worktime issues provide a general sense of evolving preferences, they also raise as many questions as they answer. How much existing or potential income would workers be willing to exchange for more free time? What are the preferred forms of free time? What are the most desired ways of scheduling existing amounts of worktime? What types of workers prefer changes in their worktime conditions, and what types do not?

NOTES

1. For further discussion of the rising importance of time, see Daniel Bell, *The Coming of Post-Industrial Society* (New York: Basic Books, 1973), pp. 456–74; Staffan Linder, *The Har-*

ried Leisure Class (New York: Columbia University Press, 1970); and Gilbert Ghez and Gary Becker, *The Allocation of Time and Goods Over the Life Cycle* (New York: Columbia University Press, 1975).

2. Interviews for this survey were conducted between March 26 and April 2, 1977. The questions were answered by a nationally representative sample of 1,502 respondents. See Louis Harris, "Quality Wins Over Quantity," The Harris Survey, Press Release, May 23, 1977.

3. A large measure of this summary of past labor economics theory is attributed to Juanita Kreps, "Some Time Dimensions of Manpower Policy," in *Jobs for Americans*, ed. Eli Ginzberg (Englewood Cliffs, N.J.: Prentice-Hall, 1975), pp. 184–205.

4. Josiah Child, *A New Discourse on Trade*, 6th ed., p. 12, quoted from Paul Douglas, *The Theory of Wages* (New York: Macmillan, 1934), p. 210.

5. Edgar Furniss, *The Position of the Laborer in a System of Nationalism* (New York, 1920), Chapters 6 and 7; Lupo Brentano, *Hours and Wages in Relation to Production* (New York, 1894), pp. 2–7; and Adam Smith, *An Inquiry into the Wealth of Nations* (New York: Modern Library Edition, 1937), pp. 81–82; and J. B. Say, *Traité d'economic politique* (Paris, 1841), Book II, Chapter 7, Section 4.

6. Thomas Malthus, *An Essay on the Principles of Population* (London, 1826), pp. 339–48, 368, 379, and 424.

7. W. S. Jevons, *The Theory of Political Economy*, 5th ed. (Edinburgh, 1864), pp. 142–44, 328, 330, and 339–48.

8. Alfred Marshall, *Principles of Economics*, Variorium ed. (London, 1961), pp. 140–43, 526–629, 680–96, and 720–74.

9. S. J. Chapman, "Hours of Work," *Economic Journal* 19 (1909): 354–73.

10. A. C. Pigou, *A Study of Public Finance* (London, 1929), pp. 83–84; and *The Economics of Stationary States* (London, 1935), pp. 163–64.

11. Paul Samuelson, *Economics*, 8th ed. (New York: McGraw-Hill, 1970), pp. 415–17.

12. This section is an abridged summary and updating of a 150–page report prepared for the Office of the Assistant Secretary for Education. See Fred Best, "Changing Values Toward Material Wealth and Leisure in the United States," U.S. Department of Health, Education and Welfare, Contract No. POO-75-0221, January 1976. This report is summarized in Fred Best, Phillip Bosserman, and Barry Stern, "Income-Time Tradeoff Preferences of U.S. Workers: A Review of Literature and Indicators," *Leisure Sciences* 2, no. 2 (July 1979): 119–41.

13. H. C. Lewis, "Hours of Work and Hours of Leisure," *Proceedings of Ninth Annual Meeting of Industrial Relations Research Association* (Cleveland, 1957); and Gordon Winston, "An International Comparison of Income and Hours of Work," *Review of Economics and Statistics* 48, no. 1 (1966): 28–39.

14. Clark Kerr, "Discussion," *American Economic Review*, May 1956, p. 219.

15. Peter Henle, "Recent Growth of Paid Leisure for U.S. Workers," *Monthly Labor Review*, March 1962, p. 256; and Geoffrey Moore and Janice Hedges, "Trends in Labor and Leisure," *Monthly Labor Review*, February 1971, p. 11.

16. Janice Niepert Hedges and Geoffrey Moore, op. cit., pp. 4–6; and *Employment and Earnings*, U.S. Bureau of Labor Statistics, January 1971, Table 27.

17. John D. Owen, "Workweeks and Leisure: An Analysis of Trends, 1948–1975," *Monthly Labor Review*, August 1976, pp. 3–8.

18. Janice Hedges, "How Many Days Make a Workweek?" *Monthly Labor Review*, April 1975, pp. 30–31.

19. Hedges and Moore, op. cit., p. 6; 1976–78 figures from U.S. Bureau of Labor Statistics.

20. United Auto Workers Public Relations Department, *Summary of Tentative Agreement Between U.A.W. and Ford Motor Company*, October 1976.

21. U.S. Bureau of Labor Statistics, *Hours, Overtime and Weekend Work*, Bulletin 1425–15 (Washington, D.C., 1974); and Edward Lawler and Edward Levin, "Union Officers' Perspectives of Members' Pay Preferences," *Industrial and Labor Relations Review*, July 1968, p. 514. Some survey studies comparing the priorities of union leaders with rank-and-file

members suggest a latent desire for more free time than may manifest itself in future bargaining. See Public Opinion Index, *Current Union Demands: Who Speaks for Labor?* (Princeton, N.J.: Opinion Research Corporation, October 15, 1967), pp. 2–3.

22. William V. Deuterman and Scott C. Brown, "Voluntary Part-Time Workers: A Growing Part of the Labor Force," *Monthly Labor Review*, June 1978, p. 5.

23. Voluntary part-time work increased from 11.7 to 13.8 percent between 1964 and 1975. See BLS, *Hours, Overtime and Weekend Work*, op. cit., 1974. For further discussion, see Fred Best, "Changing Values," op. cit., p. 24.

24. *1976 Employment and Training Report of the President*, Table B-13.

25. Moore and Hedges, op. cit., p. 5; and Robert P. Quinn and Graham L. Staines, *The 1977 Quality of Employment Survey* (Descriptive Statistics and Comparisons to 1969 and 1973 Studies) (Ann Arbor: Institute for Social Research, University of Michigan, 1978), Table 5.9.

26. U.S. Bureau of Labor Statistics, *Characteristics of Agreements Covering 1,000 Workers or More*, Bulletin 1822, 1974, Table 49, p. 47 and p. 12. It should be noted that maximum paid vacation data refer mostly to employees with seniority. Regrettably, figures on the average length of paid vacation of all U.S. workers are of questionable accuracy.

27. "Collective Bargaining Negotiations and Contracts," *Daily Labor Report*, October 18, 1978, pp. F1–F3.

28. BLS *Characteristics of Agreements*, op. cit.

29. Jonathan Dickinson, "Labor Supply of Family Members," in *Five Thousand American Families—Patterns of Economic Progress*, James Morgan et al. (Ann Arbor: Institute for Social Research, University of Michigan, 1974), Vol. 1, pp. 177–250.

30. Sar A. Levitan and Richard S. Belous, *Shorter Hours, Shorter Weeks: Spreading the Work to Reduce Unemployment* (Baltimore: Johns Hopkins University Press, 1977), p. 32.

31. Lloyd Reynolds, *Labor Economics and Labor Relations*, 5th ed. (Englewood Cliffs, N.J.: Prentice-Hall, 1970), p. 48; Edward Kalachek, "Workers and the Hours Decision," *Work Time and Employment*, Special Report No. 28, National Commission for Employment Policy, Washington, D.C., 1979.

32. Winston's comparative study of 31 nations found that increasing scarcity of work, as indicated by unemployment rates, was the most important variable other than income causing a decline of worktime. See Winston, op. cit. Other similar studies have found that labor force participation has declined with the rise of unemployment, particularly around youth, women, and older persons. See William Bowen and Aldrich Finnegan, *The Economics of Labor Market Participation* (Princeton, N.J.: Princeton University Press, 1969). As a parenthetical note, it has been suggested that the constraints of economic decline and unemployment have been more responsible for reduced workweeks than human preferences for more free time during times of plenty. Thus, comparative research by Juanita Kreps suggests that labor demands in a tight labor market do affect worktime and scheduling. See Juanita Kreps, *The Lifetime Allocation of Work and Income* (Durham, N.C.: Duke University Press, 1970), pp. 51–75.

33. George Katona, Burkhard Strumpel, and Ernest Zahn, *Aspirations and Affluence* (New York: McGraw-Hill, 1971), pp. 129–33 and 220.

34. S. M. Nealey and J. G. Goodale, "Workers Preferences Among Time-Off Benefits and Pay," *Journal of Applied Psychology* 5, no. 4 (1967): 354–61.

35. Brad L. Chapman and Robert Ottemann, "Employee Preference for Various Compensation and Fringe Benefit Options," *The Personnel Administrator*, November 1975, pp. 30–36.

36. Fred Best and James Wright, "The Effect of Scheduling on Time-Income Tradeoffs." *Social Forces* 57, no. 1 (September 1978): 136–53.

37. Albert Cantril and Charles Roll, *Hopes and Fears of the American People* (New York: Universe Books, 1972), pp. 10 and 19.

38. The same question posed to respondents from different nations suggests that cultural factors can affect time-income tradeoff preferences equally as much as economic wealth. For example, a survey of Poland with an average income of $468 in 1964 (compared to $2,160 for the United States) found 21 percent of the respondents citing "leisure time" as a personal hope.

See Hadley Cantril, *The Pattern of Human Concerns* (New Brunswick, N.J.: Rutgers University Press, 1965).

39. Public Opinion Index, *The American People: How Satisfied are They?* 27, no. 20 (October 31, 1975) (Princeton, N.J.: Opinion Research Corporation).

40. Best, "Changing Values," op. cit., pp. 67–69; and Best, Bosserman, and Stern, op. cit., pp. 130–32.

41. G. Gurin, J. Veroff, and S. Feld, *Americans View Their Mental Health* (New York: Basic Books, 1960).

42. Philip Converse and John Robinson, *Measures of Occupational Attitudes and Occupational Characteristics* (Ann Arbor: Survey Research Center, University of Michigan, February 1969), pp. 54–55.

43. Robert Quinn and Linda Shepard, *The 1972–73 Quality of Employment Survey* (Ann Arbor: Institute for Social Research, University of Michigan, 1974), pp. 66–68.

44. Garth Taylor, "Value Placed on Various Job Characteristics." Unpublished report, National Opinion Research Center, April 1975.

45. George Gallup, *The Gallup Poll* (New York: Random House, 1972), pp. 1189–90, 1305, 1593, 1781, and 1924.

46. Taylor, op. cit.

47. Quinn and Shepard, op. cit., pp. 137–38; and Graham L. Staines and Robert P. Quinn, "American Workers Evaluate the Quality of their Jobs," *Monthly Labor Review*, January 1979, pp. 8–9.

48. Quinn and Shepard, op. cit., p. 13.

49. Public Opinion Index, *The Effects of a Shorter Workweek on Employees' Job Attitudes and Leisure Activities* (Princeton, N.J.: Opinion Research Corporation, February 1973).

50. Virginia Martin and Jo Hartley, *Hours of Work When Workers Can Choose* (Washington, D.C.: Business and Professional Women's Foundation, 1975).

51. The Roper Organization, *Work: Desires, Discontents and Satisfactions: A Closer Look at Three Studies* (New York, June 1974).

52. Archibald Evans, *Flexibility in Working Life* (Paris: Organisation for Economic Co-operation and Development, 1973), pp. 13–14; John Owen, "Workweeks and Leisure: An Analysis of Trends, 1948–1975," *Monthly Labor Review*, August 1976, pp. 3–8; Lionel Robbins, "On the Elasticity of Income in Terms of Effort," *Economica*, June 1930, pp. 123–29; Gary Becker, "A Theory of the Allocation of Time," *Economic Journal*, September 1965, pp. 493–517; Juanita Kreps and Joseph Spengler, "The Leisure Component of Economic Growth," in *Report of the National Commission on Technology, Automation and Economic Progress*, Appendix, Vol. II: *The Employment Impact of Technological Change* (Washington, D.C.: U.S. Government Printing Office, 1966); and Juanita Kreps, "Some Time Dimensions of Employment Policy," op. cit., p. 192. Additionally, exploratory survey research suggests that this 3 to 1 preference ratio holds up for small increments or reductions of income. See Best and Wright, op. cit.

53. Robert Quinn, *Job Satisfaction: Is There a Trend?*, U.S. Department of Labor, Manpower Research Monograph No. 30, 1974, pp. 33–35; and Janice Hedges, "New Patterns of Working Time," *Monthly Labor Review*, February 1973, pp. 3–8.

54. Two sources of data will be used. The first includes seven Consumer Expenditure Surveys conducted on a national scale at approximately ten-year intervals since 1901. While these surveys are roughly comparable, changing economic conditions and methods of research have created a number of discontinuities between them. See *How American Buying Habits Change* (Washington, D.C.: U.S. Government Printing Office, 1959), pp. 27–56; and Michael Carlson, "The 1972–73 Consumer Expenditure Survey," *Monthly Labor Review*, December 1972, p. 10. The second group of data is from the U.S. National Income and Product Accounts, which have been computed in relatively consistent fashion by the U.S. Department of Commerce since 1929. These accounts, which also provide the basis for measuring the GNP, are

computed from a number of cash flow and productivity records accumulated by a number of government agencies. See U.S. Department of Commerce, *Survey of Current Business*, July 1974, pp. 11 and 24.

55. Max Kaplan estimates that goods and services partially used for recreation might bring "the total expenditures for recreation . . . by Americans . . . up to one-fifth of our total consuming expenditures." See Max Kaplan, *Leisure: Theory and Policy* (New York: John Wiley, 1975), p. 123.

56. Best, "Changing Values," op. cit., pp. 123–37.

57. Sebastian deGrazia, *Of Time, Work and Leisure* (Garden City, N.Y.: Doubleday, 1968), pp. 57–85; and Alvin Toffler, *Future Shock* (New York: Random House, 1970), pp. 219–34.

58. It should be noted that "time saving" expenditures may not save time because they increase the possibilities for accomplishing more. See Katherine Walker, "Homemaking Still Takes Time," *Journal of Home Economics*, October 1969, pp. 621–24. However, the possibility that consumers think that such expenditures save time suggests their viability as an indicator of time-income tradeoff preferences.

9

THE DESIRE TO EXCHANGE
EARNINGS FOR LEISURE

In recent years, the commonly held view that American workers are not interested in exchanging income for more free time has come to be questioned. As this book has noted in previous chapters, there are signs that a number of social changes may be fostering a desire on the part of a growing portion of persons to work less than what we now consider to be "full time." Among the most important of these changes has been the rise of working women, many of whom are mothers who prefer less than full-time jobs and flexible work scheduling in order to jointly pursue careers and child rearing activities. Along with working women has come the rise of dual-earner families and fewer children, which tends to increase family income and reduce financial needs, thus allowing men to reduce their worktime and earnings. At the same time there has been increasing interest in part-time and part-year work among the younger student population and older workers near or past retirement age. In addition, persistently high levels of unemployment have increased interest in sharing available worktime, not only to spread available jobs among more persons, but also to share the limited number of desirable positions among an increasingly skilled work force. Finally, there are indications that American values may be moving away from materialistic goals in favor of concern with the quality of life. While these social changes are not likely to cause massive reduction of worktime, they may tilt American society toward growing concern with worktime issues.

TWO EXPLORATORY SURVEYS ON WORKTIME

Two exploratory survey studies conducted in 1976 and 1978 provide striking evidence that workers may desire major changes in the amount and scheduling of work and nonwork activities. The 1976 study was based on a technically nonrepresentative but highly diverse sample of 791 county

employees in California; the 1978 study was based on a nationally representative sample of 1,566 persons over 17 years of age.[1] While these studies had
many overlapping questions, the national survey will provide the bulk of
data concerning time-income tradeoff preferences, and the smaller county
survey will provide the basis for analysis of work and free time scheduling
preferences.

The data for the nonrepresentative study were collected during September 1976 from selected groups of employees of Alameda County, California.
The respondents were requested to complete a questionnaire on worktime
issues at a prearranged time during work hours at or near their places of
work. The survey was administered in a way that minimized interaction
effects between respondents on each other's views and resulted in a response
rate of nearly 100 percent of all employees present within groups selected for
study. The sample of 791 respondents was collected from a population of
about 10,000 county employees with the goal of approximating as closely as
possible the demographic characteristics of the U.S. labor force. While the
resulting sample was skewed toward women, upper-middle-range income
groups, white-collar workers, and the more highly educated (see Table A.1
in the Appendix), it was both diverse and large enough to both allow
analysis of preference variations among different groups and speculations
about the preferences of American workers.

The second survey of a national sample was conducted during the last
two weeks of August 1978 by Louis Harris and Associates. The study
entailed 22 questions concerning worktime fielded with questions contracted
by other clients of the survey firm. Because the issues under consideration
were viewed as being somewhat complex, particular efforts were made to
design the questions for maximum simplicity and clarity. The questions were
presented to respondents on flip cards and placed at the beginning of the
survey in order to minimize respondent fatigue. Some 1,566 respondents
were interviewed from all states except Alaska and Hawaii so as to
guarantee responses representative of the total noninstitutionalized civilian
population over 17 years of age. Responses were collected through person-
to-person interviews with respondents at their place of residence.

Comparison of the characteristics of the 955 respondents from the
national survey who reported themselves as holding a job with recent data
on the employed labor force indicates that this subsample is generally
representative of the U.S. working population (see Table A.1). However,
two important qualifications must be made. First, breakdowns of a subsample composed of employed workers reveal that the sample underrepresents
women and clerical occupations while overrepresenting men and the skilled
trades.* Second, data collection at place of residence tends to bias the

---

*This bias can likely be explained as resulting from sampling procedures in which survey
interviewers ask for the "head of the household" when both spouses are present. In the case of
dual-earner families, the man is still commonly viewed as the "head," thus creating a bias in the
data collection process in favor of men and the trades.

sample in favor of more sedentary as opposed to active persons.* Since more active persons and women are thought to be more prone to exchange income for time, it can be expected that any sampling biases in this direction would represent a conservative picture of national preferences toward foregoing income for more free time.

While a randomly selected sample of 1,566 persons can be reasonably accurate in representing the views of the U.S. population, it is important to recognize that all such surveys have defined ranges of error. These ranges of error and the probability that survey responses may vary within these ranges can be statistically elaborated. As a general guideline for analysis, it can be said that it is highly unlikely that the actual responses of the total population under study will vary more than three percentage points more or less than the responses from a randomly selected sample of around 1,600. However, this margin of error increases as sample or subsample size declines. In the case of the subsample of 955 employed workers used in much of the following analysis, the range of error is generally within four percentage points. In the case of a subsample of 100 respondents, it is reasonable to expect the responses of the total population could vary as much as 12 percentage points from that of the survey data.

Both these surveys indicate that American workers may be interested in foregoing substantial portions of current and potential income for time. However, the ways in which potential gains of free time are scheduled proved to be a major determinant of tradeoff preferences. While the data confirmed the common view that the majority of workers are satisfied with the length of today's average workweek, the survey also indicated a wide diversity of worktime preferences and a strong interest in gaining extended time away from work such as vacations and sabbatical leaves. If individuals were somehow allowed to choose the preferences revealed by this survey, worktime conditions would be markedly different from those prevailing today.

GENERAL TIME-INCOME TRADEOFF CHOICES

The first question posed to respondents of the national study dealt with whether they would prefer to work longer hours at their present pay level and earn proportionally more, work the same hours and earn the same, or work less and earn less. In response, 60.7 percent of a subsample of 949 employed respondents reported that they would choose to work the same hours and earn the same. Some 28.0 percent said they would like to work more and earn more, and 11.3 percent said they would work less and earn less (see Table A.2).

These responses closely paralleled those from a previously mentioned

---

*While this would presumably lead to a smaller proportion of younger respondents than would be found in the population, this bias does not appear to any notable extent in the sample.

survey question fielded to a representative sample of the U.S. population in 1966. As formerly noted, responses to this identical question showed that 56 percent wished to work the same and earn the same, 34 percent wished to work and earn more, and 10 percent wished to work and earn less.[2] Comparison of this 1966 data with the 1978 responses suggests that the desire to forego income for leisure has remained virtually constant over the last decade, with the vast majority expressing satisfaction with the current workweek.

The 1978 responses to this general tradeoff question were remarkably constant among groups broken down by selected social characteristics (see Table A.2). Most notably, willingness to reduce hours increased with total family income. Similarly, desire to work and earn more declined with age and education. Breakdowns by other social characteristics such as occupation, sex, and age of youngest child surprisingly revealed little variation of responses. Multivariate analysis* indicated that race, socioeconomic standing,† and age were the strongest predictors of general tradeoff preferences, while weekly hours, family cycle stage,† sex, and union affiliation had relatively low impact. Similar analyses run for subgroups broken down by sex and age of youngest child suggested that sex and family cycle stage should not be discounted as notable determinants of time-income exchange preferences (see Table A.3).

TRADING POTENTIAL INCOME FOR TIME

Responses from employed workers to additional time-income tradeoff questions entailing options for scheduling potential gains of free time reveal

---

*In order to assess the relative strength of several predictor variables on the variation of one dependent variable while simultaneously controlling the impact of the numerous predictor variables, multiple regression techniques will be used from time to time. The general nature of the findings will be summarized in the text, and statistical tables will be provided in the Appendix.

†In order to consolidate the combined influence of educational attainment, occupation, and total family income, a composite variable (SES) was constructed giving equal weighting to its three components. Construction of this variable is outlined as follows: Variables were recorded by use of computer programming so that points for various values of education, occupation, and family income were assigned. Points for educational attainment were: 1 = some graduate school; 2 = four-year college degree; 3 = some college; 4 = high school degree; and 5 = some high school or less. Points for occupation were: 1 = professional or managerial; 2 = clerical, sales, and skilled labor; 3 = services; 4 = operatives and unskilled labor; and 5 = farmworkers. Points for family income were: 1 = $25,000 and over; 2 = $20,000 to $24,999; 3 = $15,000 to $19,999; 4 = $10,000 to $14,999; and 5 = under $10,000. Totals from adding up the scores for all these variables were classified into socioeconomic groups so that scores of 13 to 15 = lower class; 10 to 12 = lower-middle class; 6 to 9 = middle class; and under 6 = upper middle class plus.

‡A detailed series of computerized selection procedures were used to construct a composite family cycle stage (FACYCLE) variable from marital status, number of dependents, and age of youngest child. The categories of this composite variable were single, couples without children, parents with young children, and parents with older or independent children.

far different preferences than those revealed by the first question. The second group of questions presented the respondents with five equally costly options: a pay raise of 2 percent, 10 minutes taken off each workday, 50 minutes taken off one workday a week (presumably Friday), five additional days of paid annual vacation, and earlier retirement by seven workdays a year. Respondents were asked to give their first, second, third, and fourth choices between these options.

The responses to these questions show that the pay raise was chosen most by a plurality of 35.5 percent of working respondents. However, the remaining 64.5 percent chose one of the alternative forms of free time. Most notably, additional days of paid vacation proved to be particularly popular, with 25.7 percent selecting this option. The 50-minute reduction of one workday a week and earlier retirement were also in demand, being chosen by 17.1 and 18.6 percent respectively (see Table A.4). The 10-minute shortening of each workday was notably unpopular, receiving only 3.2 percent of the first choices. To some degree, the low popularity of this option can likely be attributed to the negligible value of such small reductions of the workday. Presumably, those interested in shorter workdays might prefer to make larger exchanges of income for significant gains of daily free time (an issue that will be explored later).[3]

The second and subsequent choices among 2 percent tradeoffs reveal some interesting patterns (see Table A.4). Most particularly, the percent of respondents selecting income for their second choice is surprisingly low. Looking to the choices among the free-time options, it is noteworthy that added vacation time was remarkably popular among the second and third choices. Indeed, if the first and second choices were averaged, added vacation time alone would receive more choices than the pay raise.

Foremost among the observations to be made about these 2 percent tradeoff responses is the tremendous importance of scheduling on choices between income and time. First, some forms of free time, most notably vacations, are extremely popular. Presumably, opportunities to exchange earnings for such forms of leisure would be likely to encourage a substantial portion of the American work force to make time-income tradeoffs. Second, the responses to these 2 percent exchanges suggest that there is considerable diversity of preferences within the American work force concerning the types of free time that are most desirable to individuals. Although some forms of potential free time such as vacations are most popular, a number of persons would clearly choose other forms of free time as their personal first choices.

Breakdowns of these 2 percent tradeoff choices by a number of social characteristics reveal some variation of preferences, but a general consistency of the overall pattern (see Table A.4). Respondents broken down by occupations show that workers employed in the most toilsome and lower-paying occupations are more likely to choose the pay raise over time, suggesting that less pleasant work may create a desire to work less but that financial needs prevail against such desires. The proportion of workers choosing the pay raise declines as education rises, with most of this reduced interest in pay shifting to preferences for longer vacations. This indicates that well-educated persons, who presumably work long hours to reap returns on educational investments,[4] may have the resources and occupational discretions to pursue extended leaves from work. Among those with lower than average incomes, the pay raise was preferred more frequently over gains of free time. Those at all the higher levels of earning were less likely to choose the pay raise. While there was some moderate variation of tradeoff preferences according to family cycle characteristics, the impact of these variables was surprisingly small and erratic. Contrary to expectations, time-income choices varied little between single-earner and dual-earner families (an issue that will be discussed more thoroughly later). Age proved to have a fluctuating relationship with tradeoff preferences. Specifically, young respondents, who presumably had pressing financial needs, and older workers, who presumably are saving for retirement, expressed strong interest in pay over time. Finally, women surprisingly were slightly more prone to choose the pay raise over added free time.

As a slight digression, a point might be made about common assumptions concerning tradeoff preferences. An earlier exploratory survey using a 2 percent tradeoff question identical to the one used in the national survey also asked respondents how they thought their coworkers (who also took the survey) would choose among the options. Comparison of the results from these two questions showed that respondents tended to think that their coworkers were far less willing to exchange earnings for time than their direct personal responses revealed.[5] As such, it is possible that we commonly assume that the interest in trading income for leisure is a good deal less than it is in reality.

Another series of questions explored worker interest in exchanging all or part of a potential pay increase for alternative forms of free time. Each question was a paired choice between all or part of a 10 percent pay raise and varying amounts of five forms of free time, which included shorter workdays, reduced workweeks, added vacation time, sabbaticals (extended leaves with pay every seven years), and earlier retirement. The respondents were asked to choose their preference among the total pay raise, 60 percent of the pay raise and some free time, 30 percent of the pay raise and more free time, or forfeiture of the total pay raise for a maximum amount of the specified form of free time.

The responses to these five paired tradeoff questions reveal marked differences in the amount of potential income gains that workers would be willing to forego for alternative forms of free time. At the baseline, 73.2 percent would not give up any part of a 10 percent raise for a shorter workday, 56.5 percent would give up no part of the raise for a reduced workweek, a smaller 34.4 and 34.7 percent would not forego any raise for longer vacations or a sabbatical, and 48.6 percent would not give up potential gains in earnings for earlier retirement (see Table 9.1). Clearly, more persons would forego some portion of a raise for vacation time and sabbatical leaves. Earlier retirement was valued third, reduced workweeks fourth, and the shorter workday last.

It is interesting to turn the tables around and examine the proportion of respondents claiming themselves willing to forego *all* of a pay raise for various forms of free time. Curiously, the proportions are reasonably high and roughly equal among all tradeoff options other than that concerning the shorter workday. The vacation option still leads, with 29.4 percent choosing to forego the total pay raise for an additional 25 workdays of paid vacation. The proportion willing to give up all of the pay raise for a workweek reduced by four hours, a 30-week paid sabbatical, or earlier retirement by 25 working days for each future year worked was essentially equal at about 23 percent. Once again, the shorter workday came in as a poor last, with only 14.1 percent willing to give up a total 10 percent pay raise for 48 minutes off work each day.

It is noteworthy that the proportion of respondents who were willing to forego all of a pay raise for a shorter workday or reduced workweek was greater than the proportion willing to make lesser exchanges. While this does not in any way alter previous observations that these forms of free time tend to be less popular than others, it once again leads one to speculate that persons who value shorter workdays and reduced workweeks may be willing to make substantial exchanges of earnings for these types of leisure rather than deal with small incremental reductions.

Although most of the tradeoff patterns observed for the total sample hold within subsamples broken down by major social characteristics, some attention is merited for the occasional variations (see Tables A.5, A.6, A.7, and A.8). For all the responses to these questions, there was little or only slightly moderate variation of tradeoff choices by socioeconomic group (a composite variable incorporating education, family income, and occupation). Aside from a statistically questionable observation that women may wish to exchange more potential income for shorter workdays and reduced workweeks, their preferences were almost identical to those of men concerning vacations, sabbaticals, and earlier retirement. The tendency to forfeit any portion of a raise for free time appears to decline markedly with age, particularly in the case of the tradeoff dealing with earlier retirement. This suggests that older workers may be more concerned with saving for retirement than hastening the date of retirement. There appear to be erratic and uninterpretable variations according to family cycle stage. Finally, respondents in dual-earner families appear to be less willing to forego potential earnings for time than do working respondents with a housekeeping spouse. While this observation can be interpreted with the speculation that working spouses originally sought employment to meet pressing

TABLE 9.1

Stated Worker Preferences toward Exchanging All or Portions of a 10 Percent Pay Raise for Alternative Forms of Free Time (percentage breakdown)

Value of Tradeoff	Reduced Workday Vs. Raise	Reduced Workweek Vs. Raise	Added Vacation Vs. Raise	Sabbatical Vs. Raise	Earlier Retirement Vs. Raise
No part of raise for free time	73.2	56.5	34.4	34.7	48.6
40% of raise for free time	6.7	15.4	31.8	34.2	19.3
70% of raise for free time	4.9	5.3	4.5	8.1	8.3
100% of raise for free time	14.1	22.8	29.4	23.0	23.7
Total percent	100.0	100.0	100.0	100.0	100.0
Total respondents	950	952	954	949	952

Questions:

Workday. Which one of the following choices would you select? (A) 10 percent pay raise and no shorter workday; (B) 6 percent pay raise and a 19-minute reduction of the workday; (C) 3 percent pay raise and a 34-minute reduction of each workday; (D) No pay raise and a 48-minute reduction of each workday.

Workweek. Which one of the following choices between a pay raise and a shorter workweek would you select? (A) 10 percent pay raise and no reduction of each workweek; (B) 6 percent pay raise and a 1.6-hour reduction of each workweek; (C) 3 percent pay raise and a 2.8-hour reduction of each workweek; (D) No pay raise and a 4-hour reduction of each workweek

Vacation. Which one of the following choices between a pay raise and a longer paid vacation would you select? (A) 10 percent pay raise and no added vacation time; (B) 6 percent pay raise and 10 workdays of added vacation; (C) 3 percent pay raise and 17.5 workdays added vacation; (D) No pay raise and 25 workdays added vacation.

Sabbatical. What is your choice between a pay raise and an extended leave with pay from work after six years of work? (A) 10 percent pay raise and no leave time; (B) 6 percent pay raise and 12 workweeks (60 workdays) paid leave; (C) 3 percent pay raise and 21 workweeks (105 workdays) paid leave; (D) No pay raise and 30 workweeks (150 workdays) paid leave.

Earlier Retirement. What is your choice between a pay raise and earlier retirement? (A) 10 percent pay raise and no change in retirement plan; (B) 6 percent pay raise and 10 workdays earlier retirement for each future year of work; (C) 3 percent pay raise and 17.5 workdays earlier retirement for each future year of work; (D) No pay raise and 25 workdays earlier retirement for each future year of work.

Source: Data cited from results of a national random survey conducted in August 1978 (Fred Best, *Exchanging Earnings for Leisure*, Special Research Monograph, Office of Research and Development, Employment and Training Administration, U.S. Department of Labor, Washington, D.C., 1980).

financial needs, the impact of spouse employment needs more detailed analysis.

An overview of the American worker's interest in foregoing future raises for more free time can be gained from the use of a special composite variable designed to show the maximum portion of pay increases that respondents are willing to give up for any of the five forms of free time studied in this section.* For example, if a respondent would forego only 40 percent of his or her pay raise for four of the five available types of potential free time, and 100 percent for a reduced workweek, that individual could be said to have a maximum tradeoff preference of 100 percent of the raise for one of the five types of free time. If similar computations are made for all respondents in accord with the ways they answered the five questions on time-pay raise tradeoffs, it is possible to compute a variable that estimates the overall maximum portion of a raise that would be forfeited if workers could choose the type of free time they individually preferred.†

Computations of the maximum portion of the 10 percent pay raise that workers would forego for more free time reveal a surprisingly high desire for free time. In overview, only 15.6 percent would give no part of their raise, 25.4 percent would give 40 percent of their raise, 11.6 percent would forego 70 percent of their raise, and a remarkable 48.9 percent would trade the total raise for more free time (see Table A.9). Analysis of sample subgroups indicates that the advancement of age brings a declining tendency to trade potential income for time, nonwhites are less likely than whites to forego portions of a raise for time, clerical workers stand out among the occupations as particularly willing to give up pay raises for time, and willingness to take smaller raises in trade for time surprisingly increases along with the number of household dependents. Aside from these variations, the general responses for the total sample remain almost monolithic when the data are broken down by selected social characteristics (see Table A.9).

Some speculative computations can demonstrate how actualization of expressed preferences for exchanging portions of pay raises for time could dramatically alter worktime conditions within the United States. If American workers were willing and able to make the kinds of exchanges indicated by the 10 percent potential tradeoff responses three times over the next 12 years, the total number of hours worked each year by the average worker

---

*It should be noted that such a computation of maximum tradeoff preferences does not necessarily measure the true maximum income that a person might forego for time. For example, a person might be willing to give up 70 percent of his or her pay raise for a reduced workweek but still prefer to forfeit the remaining 30 percent of the raise for added vacation time.

†A composite variable (MAXTRD1) was developed to estimate the maximum portion of a pay raise that respondents might forfeit for more free time. This variable used a series of computer IF statements to systematically isolate the one or more tradeoffs among the five raise-time questions that had the highest exchange of potential income for time.

would decline from 1,910 hours in 1978[6] to 1,517 hours in 1990.* This would mean that the average worker might have a 6-hour workday, or a 30-hour workweek, or a 10-week paid vacation each year, or a 62-week sabbatical every six years, or 3 months' earlier retirement for every future year worked, or some combination of these options. Presumably, the bulk of such free-time gains would be preferred in the form of vacations and sabbaticals, with lesser amounts of potential income gains foregone for earlier retirement, reduced workweeks, and shorter workdays.

Of course, the extent and nature of the potential tradeoff preferences suggested by the survey data might not stay constant over the next several years. Social changes could shift time-income tradeoff preferences toward greater or lesser exchanges. More important, major gains in the forms of leisure, which are now most popular, may alter the utility of continued reductions of worktime. For example, widespread attainment of eight weeks' annual vacation might greatly attenuate interest in further vacation gains, thus causing an overall reduction in the desire to forego potential income for time or a realignment of interests toward other forms of free time such as the reduced workweek. Regardless of the long-range possibilities, it must be said that the stated survey responses dealing with potential time-income tradeoffs suggest that American workers may be willing to forego major portions of future economic growth for more free time.

TRADING CURRENT INCOME FOR TIME

Up to this point, this book has focused on the exchange of potential gains in income for time. However, it is also plausible that current earnings might be traded for more time. To explore this dimension of the time-income tradeoff issue, another series of questions pitted current income in paired choices against varying amounts of the same five forms of free time used in the previous potential tradeoff questions. However, unlike the previous series, the degree of possible exchange varied from question to question. The reason for this is that the maximum portion of current income that respondents may give up for time may vary among different types of potential free time. For example, it is quite plausible that workers may wish to trade as much as 50 percent of current earnings for a drastically reduced

---

*The average maximum proportion of a 10 percent pay raise that survey respondents would forego for any of five forms of free time was computed to be 65.6 percent, which was equal in value to 131.2 hours of added free time each year for the average worker. This sum of 131.2 hours was subtracted from the average 1978 workyear of 1,910 hours to obtain 1,778.9 hours. This was once again reduced by the time value of 65.6 percent of a 10 percent raise to obtain 1,663.3 hours a year, which was reduced a third time in similar fashion to obtain 1,555.2 hours of work a year. Thus, three exchanges of 65.6 percent of a 10 percent pay raise over one 12-year time period would lead to a reduction of 354.8 hours of work each year.

workweek or workday but almost unthinkable that many would forego half of their current income for a six-year sabbatical every six years.

As in the case of the exchanges between a pay raise and various forms of free time, tradeoff preferences dealing with current earnings varied considerably in accord with the type of free time to be gained. In every paired choice, the majority of respondents were unwilling to give up any of their current pay for each of the five types of potential free time. Specifically, only 23.0 percent would trade some income for a shorter workday, 26.2 percent would forfeit earnings for a reduced workweek, 42.2 percent would give up pay for more paid vacation, 42.1 percent would exchange some income for a sabbatical leave, and 36.0 percent would forego earnings for earlier retirement (see Table 9.2).

Although responses to questions concerning current tradeoffs are not directly comparable, there are very slight indications that the maximum portion of income that respondents may be willing to forego for time varies according to the form of potential free time. For example, some 3.1 percent of respondents would give up 30 or 50 percent of their earnings for a significantly shorter workday, and 2.5 percent would give up to 40 to 50 percent for a greatly reduced workweek. In contrast, 2.0 percent would give up as much as 33 percent of current income for more vacation, 4.8 percent selected the maximum option of 15 percent of earnings for a sabbatical leave, and 4.4 percent chose the maximum 20 percent exchange for earlier retirement (see Table 9.2). While interpretation of this data is highly speculative, there is some reason to suggest that shorter workdays and reduced workweeks elicit a willingness to exchange larger portions of income than other forms of free time. However, these differences are not dramatic and this topic requires further research.

Breakdowns of current tradeoff responses dealing with shorter workdays are particularly interesting because they deal with the type of free time most likely to ease the time pressures of the growing number of dual-earner families. A table breaking down responses to this question by family cycle and sex role characteristics provides somewhat puzzling results (see Table A.10). There was little variation according to sex; respondents with no children were more willing to exchange income for shorter workdays than those with children; and respondents in dual-earner families were, as expected, more willing to give up money for reductions of the workday than workers in single-earner families.

The impact of changing family patterns on the desire to trade income for shorter workdays can best be evaluated by examining married respondents broken down by age of youngest child, work activity of spouse, and sex (see Table 9.3). While the preference for money over time increased during the early and middle child raising years, the desire to exchange income for shorter workdays did not differ appreciably between married men from either dual-earner or single-earner households. Although it might be ex-

TABLE 9.2

Stated Worker Preferences toward Exchanging Portions of Current Income for Alternative Forms of Free Time (percentage breakdown)

Value of Tradeoff	Shorter Workday Vs. Pay	Reduced Workweek Vs. Pay	Added Vacation Vs. Pay	Sabbatical Leave Vs. Pay	Earlier Retirement Vs. Pay
Nothing for time	77.0	73.8	57.8	57.9	64.0
2% of pay for time	8.7	11.6	23.2	24.4	17.6
5% of pay for time	5.8	—	8.5	8.0	8.1
10% of pay for time	—	7.6	6.2	4.8	5.9
12% of pay for time	5.5	—	—	—	—
15% of pay for time	—	—	—	4.8	—
20% of pay for time	—	4.5	2.2	—	4.4
30% of pay for time	1.6	—	—	—	—
33% of pay for time	—	—	2.0	—	—
40% of pay for time	—	.9	—	—	—
50% of pay for time	1.5	1.6	—	—	—
Total percent	100.0	100.0	100.0	100.0	100.0
Total respondents	954	953	952	951	951

Questions:

Workday. What is the largest portion of your current yearly income that you would be willing to give up for shorter workdays? (A) Nothing; (B) 2 percent ($1/50$) of your income for 10 minutes off each workday; (C) 5 percent ($1/20$) of your income for 25 minutes off each workday; (D) 12 percent ($1/8$) of your income for 1 hour off each workday; (E) 30 percent of your income for 2 hours off each workday; (F) 50 percent ($1/2$) of your income for 4 hours off each workday.

Workweek. What is the largest portion of your current yearly income that you would be willing to give up for shorter workweeks? (A) Nothing; (B) 2 percent ($1/50$) of your income for 50 minutes off 1 workday a week; (C) 10 percent ($1/10$) of your income for 4 hours off 1 workday a week; (D) 20 percent ($1/5$) of your income for 1 full workday off each week; (E) 40 percent ($4/10$) of your income for 2 full workdays off each week; (F) 50 percent ($1/2$) of your income for 2 full workdays off each week.

Vacation. What is the largest portion of your current yearly income that you would be willing to give up for more paid vacation time? (A) Nothing; (B) 2 percent ($1/50$) of your income for 5 workdays added paid vacation each year; (C) 5 percent ($1/20$) of your income for 12.5 workdays added paid vacation each year; (D) 10 percent ($1/10$) of your income for 25 workdays added paid vacation each year; (E) 20 percent ($1/5$) of your income for 50 workdays addec paid vacation each year; (F) 33 percent ($1/3$) of your income for 87.5 workdays (17.5 workweeks) added paid vacation each year.

Sabbatical. What is the largest portion of your current yearly income that you would be willing to give up in exchange for an extended leave without pay every seventh year? (A) Nothing; (B) 2 percent ($1/50$) of your yearly income for 7 workweeks' paid leave after six years of work; (C) 5 percent ($1/20$) of your income for 17.5 workweeks' paid leave after six years of work; (D) 10 percent ($1/10$) of your income for 35 workweeks' paid leave after six years of work; (E) 15 percent ($3/20$) of your income for 52 workweeks' (1 workyear) paid leave after six years of work.

Earlier Retirement. What is the largest portion of your current yearly income that you would be willing to give up in exchange for earlier retirement? (A) Nothing; (B) 2 percent ($1/50$) of your income for earlier retirement at a rate of 5 workdays for every year worked until retirement; (C) 5 percent ($1/20$) of your income for earlier retirement at a rate of 12.5 workdays for every year worked until retirement; (D) 10 percent ($1/10$) of your income for earlier retirement at a rate of 25 workdays for every year worked until retirement; (E) 20 percent ($1/5$) of your income for earlier retirement at a rate of 50 workdays for every year worked until retirement.

Note: Column spaces are frequently blank for many tradeoff options because questions dealing with different forms of free time did not always have parallel exchange options.

Source: Data cited from results of a national random survey conducted in August 1978 (Fred Best, *Exchanging Earnings for Leisure*, Special Research Monograph, Office of Research and Development, Employment and Training Administration, U.S. Department of Labor, Washington, D.C., 1980).

TABLE 9.3

Worker Preferences toward Exchanging Current Income for Shorter Workdays by Sex, Major Activity of Spouse, and Age of Youngest Child (percentage breakdown)

Tradeoff Preferences by Sex	Not Married				Working Spouse			
	No Child	Youngest Child Under 6	Youngest Child 6–14	Youngest Child Over 14	No Child	Youngest Child Under 6	Youngest Child 6–14	Youngest Child Over 14
Men								
Nothing	70.0	88.9	100.0	60.0	77.3	87.0	79.2	81.5
2% of pay for 10 min. off	8.7	11.1	0	40.0	6.1	2.2	9.1	11.1
5% of pay for 25 min. off	8.7		0	0	1.5	2.2	6.5	0
12% of pay for 1 hour off	7.8		0	0	10.6	4.4	3.9	3.7
30% of pay for 2½ hrs. off	1.0		0	0	0	4.3	0	0
50% of pay for 4 hrs. off	2.9		0	0	4.5	0	1.3	3.7
Total percent	100.0	100.0	100.0	100.0	100.0	100.0	100.0	100.0
Number of respondents	(103)	(9)	(15)	(5)	(66)	(46)	(77)	(27)
Women								
Nothing	76.4	90.0	63.2	80.0	75.0	71.7	63.1	82.1
2% of pay for 10 min. off	5.6	10.0	26.3	10.0	5.0	7.5	16.9	10.7
5% of pay for 25 min. off	8.3	0	5.3	0	5.0	11.3	7.7	3.6
12% of pay for 1 hour off	4.2	0	5.3	10.0	5.0	5.7	7.7	3.6
30% of pay for 2½ hrs. off	2.8	0	0	0	7.5	1.9	4.6	0
50% of pay for 4 hrs. off	2.8	0	0	0	2.5	1.9	0	0
Total percent	100.0	100.0	100.0	100.0	100.0	100.0	100.0	100.0
Number of respondents	(72)	(10)	(19)	(10)	(40)	(53)	(65)	(28)

	Spouse Keeps House or Other			
Tradeoff Preferences by Sex	No Child	Youngest Child Under 6	Youngest Child 6–14	Youngest Child Over 14
Men				
Nothing	75.8	87.5	73.8	86.1
2% of pay for 10 min. off	10.6	5.6	8.2	5.6
5% of pay for 25 min. off	6.1	4.2	8.2	5.6
12% of pay for 1 hour off	6.1	1.4	6.6	2.8
30% of pay for 2½ hrs. off	1.5	1.4	0	0
50% of pay for 4 hrs. off	0	0	3.3	0
Total percent	100.0	100.0	100.0	100.0
Number of respondents	(66)	(72)	(61)	(36)
Women				
Nothing	76.9	83.3	100.0	33.3
2% of pay for 10 min. off	76.9	0	0	33.3
5% of pay for 25 min. off	7.7	0	0	0
12% of pay for 1 hour off	0	16.7	0	0
30% of pay for 2½ hrs. off	0	0	0	0
50% of pay for 4 hrs. off	0	0	0	0
Total percent	100.0	100.0	100.0	100.0
Number of respondents	(13)	(6)	(6)	(3)

Question: What is the largest portion of your current yearly income that you would be willing to give up for shorter workdays? (A) Nothing; (B) 2 percent ($\frac{1}{50}$) of your income for 10 minutes off each workday; (C) 5 percent ($\frac{1}{20}$) of you income for 25 minutes off each workday; (D) 12 percent ($\frac{1}{8}$) for 1 hour off each workday; (E) 30 percent ($\frac{1}{3}$) of your income for 2.5 hours off each workday; (F) 50 percent ($\frac{1}{2}$) of your income for 4 hours off each workday.

Source: Data cited from results of national random survey conducted in August 1978 (Fred Best, *Exchanging Earnings for Leisure,* Special Research Monograph, Office of Research and Development, Employment and Training Administration, U.S. Department of Labor, Washington, D.C., 1980).

pected that higher financial discretion within dual-earner families might encourage greater tradeoffs, it is possible that resistance about sharing household responsibilities coupled with the low popularity of this form of free time might nullify willingness to forego income for shorter workdays. Contrary to the responses of men, working women from dual-earner households demonstrated an increased interest in foregoing income for shorter workdays during the early and middle stages of the child raising cycle. Interestingly, women in this group who had school-aged children between ages 6 and 14 were more prone to make tradeoffs for the shorter workday than those with pre-school children under 6 years of age. Presumably, these responses can be attributed to the fact that many women tend to withdraw completely from the labor force during the early child raising years unless they have full-time career commitments or pressing financial needs. Thus, the women returning to the work force after the youngest child reaches school age might be expected to prefer work hours that coincide with the school schedules of their children.

Aside from the impact of family cycle and sex-role factors, willingness to forego income for shorter workdays varied little by other social characteristics (see Table A.10). There was some variation by age, but this can likely be explained primarily by family cycle factors. Multivariate analysis controlling for the impact of seven key variables confirmed the prominence of the family cycle as the strongest predictor of shorter workday tradeoff preferences and indicated that the relative influence of other variables in order of impact to be length of workweek, age, race, socioeconomic group, sex, and union affiliation (see Table A.11).

As already noted, the desire to trade current income for a reduced workweek was low but still higher than interest in the shorter workday. These preferences varied little by major social characteristics. Respondents in professional occupations, who typically work long hours, had more than average interest in the reduced workweek. As might be expected, willingness to exchange income for a reduced workweek increased as the reported length of respondents' workweek rose. Finally, worker interest in a reduced workweek declined with age (see Table A.12).

Willingness to exchange earnings for vacation is particularly interesting because this form of free time, along with sabbaticals, clearly proved to be the most popular of potential gains of leisure. As previously noted, some 42.1 percent of the working sample reported that they would forego 2 percent or more of their current income for more paid vacation, and some 10.4 percent stated a willingness to exchange 10 percent or more of earnings for significant gains in vacation time.

While responses to the income-vacation tradeoff question varied somewhat by social characteristics, the basic pattern of responses held for all major social groups (see Table A.13). Among occupational groups, operatives, service workers, and laborers evidenced stronger than average desire for more vacation; while managers, skilled laborers, and farm workers had less than average interest. Interestingly, a relatively large 10.2 percent of service workers would trade 20 or 33 percent of their pay for greatly extended vacations. The desire for more vacation rose slightly along with education and income. Conversely, interest in forfeiting earnings for vacation declined slightly as the number of dependents rose, and fell considerably with the rise of weekly work hours and age. In the case of age, it is likely that older workers already have the long vacations that accompany seniority job status.

Contrary to claims that women prefer shorter workdays and weeks while men prefer extended time away from work, women exhibited a significantly larger interest in foregoing earnings for vacation than did men. Further, the desire for vacation relative to earnings was higher for respondents from dual-earner families than for those from single-earner households; and the value of vacation curiously declined with increases in the age of youngest child.

The fact that vacations were valued highly by women and respondents at the peak of family cycle responsibilities raises an interesting question. If longer vacations and the forfeiture of income for such free time would be of little help in relieving the financial and time pressures of home care and child raising, why do those who are most affected by such family needs exhibit high desires to exchange income for vacation time? The most plausible answer lies with the distinctions that are often made between "leisure" and "nonmarket work." Concisely stated, all time off the job is not used for the recreational and self-enriching activities that one commonly associates with "leisure." Much nonjob time is spent on "nonmarket work" such as paying bills, cleaning house, and preparing meals—for which no monetary payment is received.[7] For the most part, the shorter workday that many persons claim is necessary for family well-being falls into the category of nonmarket work, while vacation probably approaches the category of pure leisure. In view of this distinction, it is plausible to suggest that many persons of both sexes evidence a stronger desire for vacation over shorter workdays and weeks, not because such time is necessary or good for their families, but because they simply want real leisure. Indeed, this may be particularly true of dual-earner families confronting the peak demands of child raising. Such persons are pushed and battered in an almost ceaseless treadmill of job and family duties, and it is not surprising that they are willing to make significant monetary and nonmonetary tradeoffs to escape for some extended period to a different pace of life.

Multivariate analysis on the total sample and selected subsamples further confirms the impact of selected social characteristics on income-vacation choices. Most notably, age consistently appears as the major predictor among seven variables, further suggesting that the long vacations accompanying job seniority are likely to reduce the utility of additional vacation time. For the total sample, the predictors in order of impact on vacation-income choices were age, family cycle stage, length of workweek, socioeconomic group, union affiliation, sex, and race. Among a subsample of men, family cycle stage, age, and race were the leading predictors in order of impact—with the advancement of the family cycle stage reducing the desire for vacation. Among a subsample of women, age had the greatest influence as a predictor, followed by current length of the workweek and socioeconomic group. Analysis within subsamples broken down by presence and age of children was not always statistically reliable, but it reaffirmed the importance of age, socioeconomic group, and length of workweek as influential determinants of income-vacation exchange preferences. While most of these computations were statistically reliable, the variation of tradeoff preferences explained by the seven selected predictor variables was modest. For the most part, the results serve only to confirm the importance of age and the overall progression of the family cycle stage* as factors that reduce willingness to forego earnings for vacation time.

The desire to exchange some portion of current pay for a sabbatical (extended leave with pay every six years) was almost identical to the vacation income tradeoff preferences. Some 42.1 percent of the sample were willing to forego 2 percent or more of their current earnings for both added vacation time and sabbatical leaves. Breakdowns by social characteristics were only slightly different from those concerning vacation time (see Table A.14). Indeed, the only notable differences were that farmers, respondents in the highest income bracket (over $34,999), and those who were widowed or divorced were more favorably disposed toward sabbaticals than vacations. It is also interesting, but statistically insignificant, that those workers over age 64 were less disposed to the sabbatical than other age groups—presumably because they were on the verge of retirement and therefore had little interest in extended time away from work.

The popularity of the sabbatical is something of a surprise. The concept is hardly known, let alone practiced, outside of academia. Thus it must appear as rather strange and exotic to the average American. For this reason, it is noteworthy that so many workers stated a willingness to forego income for this type of free time. Of course, there are many appealing aspects to the sabbatical. With the possible exception of extremely long vacations, the sabbatical represents a form of free time that allows people to accomplish things that might otherwise be very difficult or impossible. In short, it provides an opportunity for a prolonged and total break from daily and yearly routines. Such prolonged leaves could be used for any of a number of purposes, including returning to full-time school, care of young children, entrepreneurial business efforts, initiation of a new career, construction of a house, or simply a period to reassess one's life. Additionally,

---

*It should be noted that the composite family cycle stage variable (FACYCLE) was used as an independent variable because it allowed the consolidation of marital status, age of youngest child, and number of dependents into a roughly ordinal progression of stages. However, the rise and decline of child care responsibilities incorporated into this variable give it a curvilinear nature that makes it, at best, marginally acceptable as an independent variable.

the almost total absence of sabbaticals within American society may give this form of free time extremely high utility when compared to other types of worktime reductions. Correspondingly, there may be something of a novelty appeal to the concept, which could decline if the idea receives more discussion and application in the future. In any event, the popularity of the sabbatical in the face of its almost total absence must be viewed as another indication that the worktime preferences of many Americans are significantly at variance with reality.

The willingness of working respondents to forego current income for earlier retirement was reasonably high, with 36.0 percent choosing to give up some earnings for this option. As might be expected, respondents within the more physically demanding occupations (operatives, service workers, and skilled laborers) were more prone to make this exchange than persons in other occupations. Men were also more prone than women to make tradeoffs for earlier retirement, as were persons who worked long weekly hours and those with lower levels of education. Notably, interest in early retirement declined with the advancement of age. Otherwise, income-retirement tradeoff preferences varied little when respondents were broken down by union affiliation, age of children, work activity of spouse, and race (see Table A.15). However, it must be emphasized that these responses may be biased by self-selection factors. Specifically, persons over age 50 who wish to retire early may already have done so, thus leaving a disproportionate number of respondents who do not value earlier retirement in the subsample of older workers. Clearly, the issue of early retirement preferences must be examined with other types of samples.

As in the case of the previously discussed pay raise tradeoffs, an overview of the maximum amount of current income that American workers may exchange for time can be approximated by the computation of a composite variable that shows the highest percentage of earnings that each respondent will give up for any of the five forms of free time that were studied. Thus, if a respondent states a willingness to forego 15 percent of current pay for a sabbatical and less than that amount for all other forms of free time, he or she would be recorded as having a maximum tradeoff preference of 15 percent.* Such computations were made for all working respondents, then summarized to create a distribution of maximum tradeoff choices.†

---

*As in the case of estimating maximum exchanges of potential pay raises for time, computation of maximum tradeoff preferences does not necessarily measure the true maximum income that a person might forego for time. For example, a person might be willing to give up 10 percent of his or her pay for a reduced workweek but still prefer to forfeit another 10 percent of current income for added vacation time, thus leading to a total trade of 20 percent of income for time.

†A composite variable (MAXTRD2) was developed to estimate the maximum portion of current income that respondents might forfeit for more free time. This variable used a series of

The computation of maximum tradeoff choices indicates that a majority of American workers may be willing to exchange some portion of their current income for some form of free time. Some 59.4 percent of the respondents expressed a desire to forego at least 2 percent of their earnings for more free time. More specifically, 23.6 percent would give up 2 percent of earnings for time, 9.7 percent would forego 5 percent, 10 percent would trade 10 percent, and 16 percent would exchange between 12 and 50 percent of their income for some type of work-time reduction (see Table A.16). This distribution of maximum tradeoff choices remained remarkably constant among groups broken down by occupation, education, union affiliation, number of children, and age of youngest child. The tendency to forego earnings for time increased among respondents reporting the higher levels of family income and working long hours each week. Women were far more likely than men to make tradeoffs, particularly if they were in dual-earner families. Nonwhite and older respondents were less likely to favor exchanges for time.

More detailed breakdowns of maximum current income tradeoff choices by family cycle and sex role characteristics support prior observations about the impact of these factors on the desire for all types of free time (see Table A.17). With minor exceptions, both men and women in dual-earner households were far more likely to forfeit current earnings for time than their counterparts in single-earner families. Further, considerably more men in dual-earner families were willing to forego income for time during the prechild and young child stages of the family; and an extremely large portion of women in dual-earner families were willing to make similar tradeoffs. Finally, men in dual-earner households were willing to make larger exchanges of income for time than men in single-earner families; and women in dual-earner families were willing to make even larger exchanges. All in all, these breakdowns of maximum tradeoff choices by family characteristics lend support to the previously stated hypothesis that the financial discretions and time pressures of dual-earner families increase the value of time relative to income for purposes of meeting family responsibilities as well as meeting needs for leisure-oriented time such as vacations.

Speculative computations using maximum tradeoff choices indicate that the average U.S. worker would forego some 4.7 percent of his or her current earnings for more free time. In terms of yearly worktime estimates, this would mean that the average worker's total annual worktime would decline from the current 1978 level of 1,910 hours to some 1,821 hours. This would give the average worker a 7.5-hour workday, or a 37-hour workweek, or about 11.5 added days of paid vacation, or almost 9 weeks' sabbatical leave every six years, or 11.5 days' earlier retirement for every year worked in

---

computer IF statements to systematically isolate the one or more responses to the five paired current income-time tradeoff questions that elicited the highest exchange of income for time.

the future, or some combination of the above. If these tradeoffs came in preferred forms, most would likely take the form of added vacation and sabbaticals.

While these computations of average tradeoff preferences can serve to illustrate differences between stated worktime preferences and existing conditions, it is important to note that the use of averages is a poor way of viewing desired worktime arrangements. One of the major trends in worktime is an increasing plurality of preferences. Indeed, it is probably true that a large portion of today's labor force is quite satisfied with most dimensions of their worktime conditions. At the same time, this survey indicates that another large portion wishes to work less than what is currently called full time and is willing to forego current and potential earnings to do so. While actual tradeoff behavior is not likely to be as great as that evidenced by the survey responses reported in this study, the magnitude of these survey preferences for more free time suggests that American society has not only slipped behind in the task of providing the growth of free time desired by today's work force but has also failed to provide the most preferred forms of free time.

NOTES

1. Chapters 9 and 10 provide abridged versions of two longer studies prepared for the U.S. Department of Labor and National Commission for Employment Policy. See Fred Best, "Time-Income Tradeoff and Work Scheduling Preferences: A Report on an Exploratory Survey Study of Alameda County Employees in California," unpublished report prepared for the Office of the Assistant Secretary for Policy, Evaluation and Research, U.S. Department of Labor, October 1977, Contract No. 41-USC-252; and Fred Best, "Exchanging Earnings for Leisure: Findings of an Exploratory National Survey on Work Time Preferences," draft paper prepared with joint sponsorship of the National Commission for Employment Policy and the Office of Research and Development, Employment and Training Administration, U.S. Department of Labor (Interagency Agreement No. 20-11-78-36), January 15, 1979.

2. George Katona, Burkhard Strumpel, and Ernest Zahn, *Aspirations and Affluence* (New York: McGraw-Hill, 1971), pp. 129–33 and 230.

3. Other exploratory surveys with an identical 2 percent tradeoff question with scheduling options and a 2 percent question of the same nature found that an increase of available reduction in the workday elicited a significantly greater exchange of potential income for time. See Best, "Time-Income Tradeoff and Work Scheduling Preferences," op. cit., pp. 34–36; Fred Best, "Preferences on Worklife Scheduling and Work-Leisure Tradeoffs," *Monthly Labor Review*, June 1978, p. 33; and Fred Best and James D. Wright, "Effects of Work Scheduling on Time-Income Tradeoffs," *Social Forces* 57, no. 1 (September 1978): 142–45.

4. Harold Wilensky, "The Uneven Distribution of Leisure Time," *Social Problems*, Summer 1961; and John D. Owen, "Hours of Work in the Long Run," *Work Time and Employment*, Special Report No. 28, National Commission for Employment Policy, Washington, D.C., October 1978, pp. 46–52.

5. Best, "Preferences on Worklife Scheduling and Work-Leisure Tradeoffs," op. cit., pp. 32–33; and Best, "Time-Income Tradeoff and Work Scheduling Preferences," op. cit., pp. 10–13.

6. It is estimated that the average U.S. employee has a 39-hour workweek, with about two weeks' annual vacation, and five holidays each year. The average workweek was estimated by interpolation of May 1978 data showing the distribution of weekly workhours among the work force. See John Owen, "Worktime: The Traditional Workweek and Its Alternatives," draft chapter, *1979 Employment and Training Report of the President*, U.S. Department of Labor, p. 3 (data cited from *Employment and Earnings*, June 1978). Vacation and holiday figures were roughly estimated on the basis of a 1977 survey on working conditions, allowing extra days for nonpaid vacation and holidays. See Robert Quinn and Graham Staines, *The 1977 Quality of Employment Survey: Descriptive Statistics* (Ann Arbor: Institute for Social Research, University of Michigan, 1978), Table 5.9.

7. Gary Becker, "A Theory of the Allocation of Time," *Economic Journal*, September 1965, pp. 493–517; Edward Kalachek, "Workers and the Hours Decision," *Work Time and Employment* (Washington, D.C.: National Commission for Employment Policy, 1979), p. 176; and Juanita Kreps, "Some Time Dimensions of Manpower Policy," in *Jobs for Americans*, ed. Eli Ginzberg (Englewood Cliffs, N.J.: Prentice-Hall, 1976), pp. 197 202.

10

WORK AND LIFE SCHEDULING PREFERENCES

The observed effects of work and free-time scheduling on time-income tradeoff preferences raise questions about the ways in which workers may prefer to schedule existing amounts of work over both short- and long-run time frames. Particularly, how would workers prefer to allocate current proportions of work and free time over days, weeks, years, and total lifespans?

SCHEDULING WORK OVER DAYS, WEEKS, AND YEARS

Most current discussions concerning the scheduling of fixed amounts of worktime have focused upon the idea of "flexitime" or sliding work hours. In a nutshell, the notion of daily flexitime entails an agreement that workers can arrive and depart from their places of work as they wish, as long as they work a set number of hours each day and are on the job during "core hours," generally set during the peak hours of the mid-workday. Through such arrangements, workers are given considerable individual flexibility in setting their workday schedules.

Data from the 1976 survey of county employees provide some insight into worker preferences concerning the scheduling of work over days and and longer periods. It is not surprising that most respondents from this study "favored" or "strongly favored" this idea: 48.6 percent strongly favored flexitime, 24.3 percent favored, 9.8 percent were indifferent, and 17.3 percent disfavored or strongly disfavored the idea. Women tended to favor flexitime more than men, and the desire for flexitime declined markedly with the rise of age, and rose for respondents with young children.* However, there was

---

*Multiple regression of 11 independent variables on preferences toward flexitime confirmed that age, stated sex role flexibility, and expectation of changing occupation were the

very little variation of these preferences according to other social characteristics. Of particular interest; respondents in managerial occupations were *not* distinguished as having more than average opposition to flexitime (see Table A.18).

Respondents were also asked to express their first, second, and third choices between four alternative ways of scheduling a 40-hour workweek. The options were 6.5 hours' work per day for 6 days a week, 8-hour workdays for 5 days a week, 10-hour workdays for 4 days a week, and 13.5-hour workdays for 3 days a week. For first choice, 55.3 percent of the sample chose the 10-hour workday for 4 days, 32.2 percent chose the currently prevalent 8-hour workday for 5 days, 11.0 percent chose the 13.5-hour workday for 3 days, and a paltry 1.5 percent chose to work 6 hours a day for 6 days a week. There were notable differences in the strength of first-choice preferences according to age, number of children, education, and other major social characteristics (see Table A.19). Of the second choices, 39.8 percent went to the 5-day workweek, 35.9 percent to the 4-day workweek, 18.4 percent to the 3-day workweek, and 6.0 percent to the 6-day workweek. All in all, the responses support the alleged popularity of the "4 day-40 hour" workweek,[1] and the hypothesis that there is a desire to reschedule existing quantities of worktime in ways that allow more extended free time.

Further support for the notion that workers may prefer extended time away from work as opposed to other forms of free time comes from questions concerning the scheduling of 2,000 work hours (40 hours per week average) over an entire year. The respondents were asked to indicate their first, second, and third choices between the following options for scheduling the workyear: fifty 40-hour workweeks with 2 weeks' annual vacation; forty-four 45-hour workweeks with 8 weeks' annual vacation; or forty 50-hour workweeks with 12 weeks' annual vacation. For first choice, 49.4 percent chose the 44 workweeks per year with 8 weeks' vacation, 32.0 percent chose the 40 workweek year with 12 weeks' vacation, and 18.6 percent chose the currently common 50-workweek year with 2 weeks' vacation (see Table A.20). There were noteworthy variations of first choices within groups broken down by some key social characteristics, but not by sex or income. Preferences for the more compressed workyears with longer vacations declined with age and number of children and increased with the rise of socioeconomic status and educational attainment (see Table A.20).* For

---

variables with greatest impact on views toward flexitime, in respective order. In order of impact, the other variables—sex, degree of past life changes, family cycle stage, length of workweek, socioeconomic status, expected number of children, degree of financial worry, and expectation of returning to full-time school—accounted for slightly over 16 percent of the variation of preferences toward flexitime (adjusted $R^2 = .1618$ at .01 significance).

* Multiple regression of 11 independent variables on workyear scheduling preferences indicated that strength of impact declined in the following order: age, socioeconomic status, sex, sex role flexibility, degree of past life changes, degree of financial worry, length of workweek, expectation of returning to full-time school, family cycle stage, expected number of

second choice, 46.5 percent chose the 44-workweek year, 30.3 percent the 50-workweek year, and 23.2 percent the 40-workweek year. A full 81.4 percent expressed first preference for one of the two options that allowed extended free time at the cost of more lengthy workweeks. This suggests that an enlargement of the time frame under consideration reveals preferences different from the way existing amounts of work and free time are scheduled over prolonged stretches of time.

VIEWS TOWARD THE SCHEDULING OF SCHOOL AND RETIREMENT

Data from both the county and national surveys have strongly suggested that a large number of workers would prefer more free time during the workyears of their lives and more flexibility in scheduling the time given to their jobs. But what about the nonworkyears of the life cycle? How do people feel about the historic trend toward increasing nonwork time at the extremes of the life cycle in the form of schooling for the young and retirement for those in the later stage of life? Two questions were fielded in the 1978 national survey to make a preliminary exploration of this issue.[2] One deals with work during the school years, and the other with work during retirement years. The questions are extremely general, somewhat ambiguous, and will leave many issues unresolved. However, the responses do provide a rough indication that current trends concerning the distribution of work over the total life cycle may become a pressing policy issue of the future.

The question dealing with work and schooling asked respondents whether they thought it best for young persons to go straight through their formal education in youth (with the exception of summers) before starting career-oriented work involvements; or if it would be better for young persons to alternate periods of school enrollment with significant amounts of work for a longer portion of life before undertaking a predominant career involvement. The responses of workers were almost equally divided, with 51.3 percent choosing the more flexible cyclic pattern of work and education, and 48.7 choosing the more linear pattern of consecutive schooling before work (see Table A.21). Responses for the total sample of workers and nonworkers combined were essentially the same.[3]

For both the total sample and subsample of workers, the choices between these two school-work scheduling options remained essentially equal when responses were broken down by major social characteristics (see Table A.21). One exception was that those in professional occupations, who are presumably concerned with repeatedly updating their skills, had a

children, and expectation of changing occupation. These variables explained only 7 percent of the variation in workyear scheduling preferences (adjusted $R^2 = .0695$ at .01 significance).

moderately larger preference for the cyclic school-work schedule. Preferences for the more linear schedule grew with the number of children and age of youngest child. Preferences remained equally divided as age increased among workers, but preferences for the cyclic school-work option were moderately greater among young persons from the total population. Most likely, this discrepancy can be attributed to the fact that more younger persons are enrolled in school, and students tend to strongly favor the cyclic education-work scheduling option.

The school-work scheduling preference question was only one of many that might have been used to assess the desire to intermingle more work activity into the school years of youth. Although responses to this question leave many issues open, they do indicate that the American population and work force is equally divided on the point of whether schooling should take place in consecutive years of formal training as opposed to a more flexible approach involving considerable work activity for both financial and educational purposes. While the data collected by this study are very limited concerning the relationship between education and work, it is reasonable to hypothesize that the preferences of half the sample for flexible school-work scheduling in youth coupled with interest expressed for more free time during the traditional workyears could indicate that a significant portion of the American public may also be interested in various "lifelong learning" activities well beyond the traditional school years of youth.

A second question dealing with the lifetime distribution of work asked respondents the extent of work activity they would prefer at age 65. In response, 23.1 percent of the working population said they did not want to work at all, 44.9 reported they would like to work part week all year (allowing for vacations), 10.4 percent chose to work full time for only part of the year, 9.1 expressed an interest in continuing to work full time, and 12.5 percent were not sure of their preferences (see Table A.22). General responses to this question by the total sample of employed and nonemployed persons were virtually the same.[4]

As might be expected from the results of other research,[5] worker responses to this retirement-age worktime question varied according to major social characteristics (see Table A.22). Those in the more physically demanding occupations were more prone to choose no work at age 65; respondents from professional occupations, whose jobs were not physically taxing but likely to provide generous pensions, were only slightly less than average in their disposition to cease work totally; and those in service and clerical occupations, who might be expected to have more part-time job opportunities,[6] were moderately more disposed to less than full-time employment. Those with higher levels of education, who could be expected to have higher paying and less physical jobs as well as high "leisure competency," had notably high interest in both part-week and part-year work. Union members, who could be assumed to have better private pension coverage as well as more physically demanding jobs, were more prone to full withdrawal from work activities. The proportion of respondents choosing no work at all grew only slightly with the rise of earnings, which was something of a surprise because one might expect persons with higher incomes to best affotd total free time. Retirement-age worktime preferences varied only moderately with erratic patterns among respondents from dual-earner and single-earner households. Increase in the age of youngest child, which indicates a decline in financial dependents, was associated with increased preference for total labor force withdrawal. Nonwhite respondents, who generally have poorer than average health in old age as well as lower pensions and declining employment opportunities, still expressed a higher interest in full retirement than whites. Finally, increasing age among working respondents was accompanied by declining interest in full retirement and less indecision about choices. However, the fact that many older workers wishing to retire will have done so requires that a more detailed analysis be made of the impact of age.

Breakdowns of retirement-age work preferences within the total sample of workers and nonworkers indicate two notable differences from the response patterns of the working respondents.[7] Particularly important, the previously observed impact of age is strongly reversed. Among the total population sample, the desire for full retirement increases dramatically with age. However, it is important to observe that the desire for full retirement among the total sample is still less than 50 percent, and that about half of those respondents reported to be fully retired at the time of the survey preferred some work activity. The second distinction between the total sample and that of the workers was that the desire for full withdrawal from work declined only slightly with the rise of income suggesting that factors other than the financial ability to retire are important in the work withdrawal decision. More detailed breakdowns among the total sample over age 50 indicated much the same patterns as those observed for the total sample (see Table A.23).

Retirement-age work choices, along with the time-income tradeoff preferences reported in Chapter 9 broken down by age and the response to questions dealing with the exchange of earnings for earlier retirement, indicate that there is a wide diversity of desires toward worktime conditions during the later stages of life. In terms of social policy, these data provide a clear mandate for the encouragement of a wide variety of worktime options for the older population.

What was said about retirement-age work preferences appears to follow also for the worktime choices of those in mid-life and the traditional school years. While many persons appear to prefer the segregation of education, work, and leisure into three stages of life, there appears to be at least an equal number of persons who would choose more flexibility in the lifetime scheduling of these activities. Aside from the humanistic benefits that might be accrued by adjusting public and private-sector policies to maximize individual choice in these matters, the future economic costs of pensions and problems associated with prolonged schooling may foster an increasing necessity to consider the viability of increasing overall life-scheduling flexibility. If future conditions do require consideration of such changes, the American public is likely to be reasonably receptive.

LIFE-SCHEDULING PREFERENCES

Exploratory survey data concerning time-income tradeoffs and the scheduling of school and retirement invite curiosity about how persons might wish to schedule existing amounts of education, work, and leisure over their total lifespans. In order to roughly assess worker desires concerning overall life patterns, the 1976 study of Alameda County employees presented respondents with three major life-scheduling alternatives. These admittedly nonexclusive alternatives were: the currently prevalent "linear life plan" in which most persons proceed straight from continuous years of schooling in youth to an extended period of work in middle years and then to retirement in old age; a "moderate cyclic plan" in which years for school in youth are unchanged but the years now given to retirement in old age are reduced and redistributed into the middle years of life for extended periods of leisure; and the "full cyclic plan" in which years spent in school during youth and retirement in old age are reduced and redistributed into the mid-years for extended periods away from work for continued education or personal leisure. Respondents were asked to rank these three alternative life patterns by first, second, and third choice.

The response to these "lifetime" scheduling questions suggests a strong desire for life patterns significantly different from those that are now dominant. In a nutshell, 46.3 percent of the respondents stated their first choice to be the "full cyclic plan," 33.0 percent chose the "moderate cyclic plan," and 20.7 percent chose the currently predominant "linear life plan." A full 79.3 percent preferred one of the two "cyclic" plans as their first choice (see Table 10.1). Second choices were roughly the same order as the first choices.

Respondents were also asked to choose the lifeplan they believed to be best for overall societal well being, and the lifeplan they felt their coworkers would prefer. Some 80.6 percent felt that one of the two "cyclic plans" would be best for society in general, with 48.6 percent selecting the "full cyclic plan." In terms of the respondents' views of coworker preferences, some 29.8 percent thought that their peers would choose the "linear plan" and only 26.7 percent thought their peers would select the "full cyclic plan." These responses suggest that respondents felt that their coworkers had a stronger preference for the status quo than was indeed the case (see Table 10.1).

Preferences toward lifeplan options were remarkably constant among groups broken down by major social characteristics. The only noteworthy

TABLE 10.1

Worker Preferences and Views of Peer Preferences among Alternative Lifeplans (percentage breakdowns)

Lifeplan Preferences	First Choice	Second Choice	Third Choice	Respondent Views of Others' Choice	Lifeplan Best for Societal Well Being
Linear lifeplan	20.7	19.3	60.3	29.8	19.5
Moderate cyclic lifeplan	33.0	56.1	10.8	43.5	32.0
Full cyclic lifeplan	46.3	24.6	29.0	26.7	48.6
Total percent	100.0	100.0	100.0	100.0	100.0
Number of respondents	709	688	687	727	727

Question: The basic text of the life scheduling preference question was as follows: "Below you will find three alternative ways of scheduling work, education, and free-time periods throughout entire lifetimes. Please read each carefully.

(A) *Straight Progression from School to Work to Retirement*: A life pattern in which all schooling and prework training is accomplished in youth or early adulthood, where one works full-time with limited annual vacations during middle adult years, and enters full time retirement sometime after age 60. Thus school education is restricted to youth, work to middle adulthood, and free-time to old age. (Diagram provided on questionnaire.)

(B) *Most Schooling in Youth with Several Rotations between Work and Free Time throughout the Remainder of Life*: A life pattern in which most schooling and prework training is accomplished in youth or early adulthood, where one primarily works full time during middle adulthood but with extended periods away from work (for example six months) every five or six years, and increases the proportion of free time in later years until complete retirement in late 60s. Thus maximum retirement would be exchanged for extended free time periods in mid-life. (Diagram provided on questionnaire.)

(C) *Basic Schooling in Early Youth with Continous Rotations between Education, Work, and Free Time throughout the Remainder of Life*: A life pattern in which basic education in essential skills (reading, math, and so on) ends early, where most persons leave school periodically, starting in mid-teens, for limited periods of work, and then finish high school and other education in the course of lifelong rotations between work, school, and free time. Thus time spent for education in youth and time spent for retirement in later years would be reduced in exchange for extended periods of education and free time during the middle years of life. (Diagram provided on questionnaire.)

Which life pattern do you personally prefer most? ( ) Which do you prefer second? ( )"

Source: Fred Best, "Time-Income Tradeoff and Work Scheduling Preferences," unpublished report prepared for the Office of the Assistant Secretary for Policy, Evaluation and Research, U.S. Department of Labor (Contract No. 41-USC-252), Washington, D.C., October 1977, pp. 107 and 109.

variations occurred according to age, number of dependent children, degree of past life changes,* educational attainment, and socioeconomic status.† Preferences for the more "cyclic" lifeplans increased moderately as age declined, number of children dropped, education increased, socioeconomic status increased, and degree of major life changes increased. Also, women were more prone than men to favor the more cyclic patterns (see Table A.24).

In addition to choosing among alternative lifeplans, respondents were asked to state their preferences for a number of secondary questions about lifetime scheduling of education, work, and leisure. These questions dealt with expectation of returning to full-time school, desire for flexible school scheduling, expectation of changing occupation, desire to change job or occupation, sex-role flexibility, relative importance of on- and off-job time, and desire for work after retirement age. Responses to questions concerning these issues both supported previously stated desires for more flexible and cyclic life patterns and generally had high statistical correlation with lifeplan choices (see Table A.25) and each other. Special note should be made of some of these secondary indicators of life scheduling preferences.

---

*Degree of past life changes were measured by a composite variable dealing with the number of jobs of last seven years, past occupational changes, and time taken off from work for personal interests. This variable classified the backgrounds of respondents into four categories: very linear, moderately linear, moderately flexible, and very flexible. Classification was made on an accumulative point system based upon four variables: stability-change of occupation (v44 recoded so that current occupation same as seven years ago = 1 and current occupation different from primary activity seven years ago = 2); number of jobs in last five years (v45 recoded so that one or two jobs = 1 and three or more jobs = 2); continuity of formal education (v57 recoded so that continuous from ninth grade = 1, finished final stage after one or two six-month to one-year absences = 2, finished final stage after one- to four-year absence = 3, and finished final stage after over four-year absence = 4); and extended time taken off work (v60 recoded so that no time = 1, up to four weeks = 2, five to ten weeks = 3, over ten weeks = 4). Points totaled from all the above variables were used to classify respondents into one of four life-change history categories as follows: very linear (1–5 points), moderately linear (6–7 points), moderately flexible (8–9 points), and very flexible (10–12 points).

†The composite socioeconomic status variable was developed by totaling points assigned to value categories of income, educational attainment, and occupation. Total family income was given points as follows: $0–$9999 (5pts), $10,000–$14,999 (4pts), $15,000–$19,999 (3pts), $20,000–$29,999 (2pts), and $30,000 plus (1pt). Educational attainment was given points as follows: none to some high school (5pts), completed high school (4pts), high school and trade school or some college (3pts), completed four-year college and some graduate study (2pts), and completed advanced degree (1pt). Occupational categories were given points as follows: nonfarm labor (5pts), operatives (4pts), service (3pts), clerical and crafts (2pts), and professional and managerial (1pt). Points for these three variables were totaled for each respondent. Respondents were categorized into socioeconomic grouping according to point totals as follows: lower class (13–15 points), lower-middle class (10–12 points), middle class (6–9 points), and upper middle class (3–5 points). As might be expected, measures of association between the composite socioeconomic variable and its component variables are high.

Expectation of Returning to School: Some 30.2 percent of the sample thought that it was very likely that they would return to full-time school, and 48.8 percent thought it possible. Expectation of returning to school was one of the most prominent predictors of the desire for more flexible life scheduling.

Desire for School Scheduling Flexibility: When asked to choose between the desirability of completing all formal schooling during youth before starting a continuous career, or attendance in school during youth to obtain basic skills followed by ongoing rotation between work and education into mid-life, 59.8 percent of the Alameda County sample chose the more flexible rotational way of scheduling education. It should be emphasized that choice of school scheduling was the strongest predictor of life scheduling preferences, underscoring the importance of educational plans to lifeplan preferences (see Table A.25).

Expectation of Changing Job or Occupation: Some 35.8 percent thought it very likely that they would change their occupation, and 42.7 thought it possible.[8] These expectations were also closely associated with life-scheduling preferences.

Willingness to Rotate Quality Jobs: Widespread pursuit of more cyclic and flexible life patterns could cause persons to share and rotate better quality jobs among those qualified to perform them. Some 50 percent of the respondents expressed a desire to rotate the limited numbers of quality jobs among qualified persons; 12 percent opposed this idea, and 38 percent expressed mixed feeling about it. Somewhat surprisingly, there was only a moderate relationship between preferences toward job rotation and alternative life-scheduling options.

Importance of On- and Off-Job Activities: Responses to a question about the relative importance of on- and off-job time support the speculation that persons placing greater importance on their off-job time would be more likely to favor cyclic life schedules that provided more free time during mid-life. Of the sample, 29 percent stated that their off-job activities were more important than their on-job activities, 34 percent were neutral, and 36 percent said that their on-job activities were more important. In terms of life scheduling, those placing more importance on off-job activities were moderately more likely to prefer one of the two cyclic life patterns.

Workyear Scheduling Preferences: Choices among alternative ways of scheduling a fixed amount of work over a year's time (which were reviewed previously) were moderately related to lifetime scheduling preferences. In overview, those preferring more compressed workyears with longer workweeks and longer vacations also tended to choose the more cyclic lifeplans.

Choices between Pay Raise, Better Quality Work, and Longer Vacations: When presented with a "forced choice" question among a 10 percent pay raise, better quality of work, and five weeks' added vacation with pay, 28 percent selected the pay raise, 28 percent chose better quality work, and 44 percent selected longer vacations. When lifeplan preferences were broken down by these choices, those stating a desire for longer vacations also tended to have the greatest desire for the cyclic life patterns. Those stating a desire for a better quality of work were the second most prone to choose cyclic lifeplans, and those choosing the pay raise the least prone.

Graduated Time-Income Tradeoff Preferences: Preferences for the more cyclic lifeplans rose as the stated willingness to forego current income for more vacation time increased. Specifically, approximately 95 percent of those willing to forego 10 percent or more of their present earnings for more vacation also chose one of the two cyclic lifeplans.

Sex-Role Flexibility: When respondents were asked whether or not they favored or opposed the idea that "women should work more in paying jobs and men should devote more time to child rearing and housekeeping," some 33.8 percent opposed the idea, 28.3 were neutral, and 37.9 favored the idea. Desire for life-scheduling flexibility dramatically increased among respondents indicating the most sex-role flexibility. This interrelation supports frequently expressed hypotheses that changes in family life will influence worktime preferences.[9]

Desire for Work after Retirement Age: Some 53.7 percent of the Alameda sample wanted to work after reaching retirement age, but an overwhelming 91 percent of those wishing to work want only part-time work. Some 28.6 percent did not want to work after retirement age, and 17.7 percent were not sure of their preferences. While postretirement-age work preferences were not highly correlated with other life-scheduling preferences, they are conceptually supportive of the general desire for more flexible scheduling of work over the total life cycle.

There were notable relationships not only between lifeplan choices and secondary indicators of life-scheduling preferences, but also among the secondary indicators themselves (see Table A.26). These crisscrossing relationships suggest that there may be a group of values and aspirations growing out of the specific conditions of late-twentieth century American society that may be fostering a general set of values and preferences favorable to major increases in life-scheduling flexibility.

Multivariate analysis of respondent characteristics and perceptions most strongly associated with overall life-scheduling preferences provides further insight. Two different analyses using slightly differing groups of predictor variables revealed that interest in mid-life schooling, degree of past life changes, and sex-role flexibility were the strongest predictors of desire for flexible life patterns. Somewhat less important, family cycle stage*

---

*A composite family cycle stage variable (FACYCLE) was developed to categorize respondents into the major family developmental stages. These stages were single (never married and no children), married couple (no children), new nest (married couple with oldest child under ten years), old nest (married couple with oldest child over ten years), empty nest (married couple with children who are no longer dependent), single parent (one parent with dependent children), and survivor (widow or widower without dependent children).

The FACYCLE variable was computed on the basis of five component variables: age (v31 proved to be a relatively strong predictor of preferences for more linear life patterns. In approximate order of impact, less important predictors included sex, socioeconomic status, degree of financial worry, age, expectation of changing occupations, and others. Similar multivariate analysis for subsamples showed that family cycle stage had a considerably greater impact on the lifeplan preferences of women than men (see Table A.27).

In sum, responses to major lifeplan options and a number of questions concerning life-scheduling preferences indicate that a large number of today's workers may have a strong desire for more flexibility in the scheduling of education, work, and leisure over their entire lifespans. More particularly, responses from a number of varied survey questions indicate that most workers tend to feel that education should not be restricted to youth and early adulthood, that there should be more time for leisure and educational pursuits during mid-life, and that it may be desirable to pursue some measure of work activity after retirement age.

READY FOR A CHANGE OF OUR LIFETIMES?

What do the results of this exploratory survey research show? Technically, they show us that a representative and nonrepresentative group of American workers say that they would exchange income for time if the options for more free time matched personal needs; and that they would favor the rescheduling of existing amounts of worktime to allow for more extended free time and a general increase in worktime scheduling flexibility ranging from the workday to the worklife. Realistically, we can expect that the actual behavior of workers may be considerably more conservative when it comes to actually foregoing income for more free time. However, the few cases where employees have actually been given options similar to those provided in this survey indicate that the actual willingness to make time-income tradeoffs may be surprisingly similar to stated preferences.[10]

The desire for more leisure during mid-life and flexibility in scheduling life's major activities indicated by national and exploratory survey studies will have to be more rigorously assessed by further research. In the meantime, it can only be said that available data strongly suggest the emergence of new aspirations for major alterations in prevailing life patterns. This, of course, raises the question of what type of institutional changes might be made to allow and encourage such life-pattern changes.

---

without recoding); marital status (v37 recoded so that never married = 1, married = 2, and separated-widowed-divorced = 3); number of children (v39 recoded so that none = 1 and one or more = 2); number of dependent children (v40 recoded so that none = 0, one = 2, and two or more = 3); and age of first or oldest child (v72 recoded so that child under ten years of age = 1 and child over ten years of age = 2).

NOTES

1. Public Opinion Index, *The Effects of a Shorter Workweek on Employees' Job Attitudes and Leisure Activities* (Princeton, N.J.: Opinion Research Corporation, 1973); Riva Poor, *4-Days, 40 Hours* (Cambridge, Mass.: Bursk and Poor, 1970); and Virginia Martin and Jo Hartley, *Hours of Work When Workers Can Choose* (Washington, D.C.: Business and Professional Women's Foundation, 1975).

2. Identical questions were fielded in the 1976 survey of Alameda County employees, but only the 1978 national data concerning these questions will be analyzed in this section. For responses from the 1976 county study, see Fred Best, "Time-Income Tradeoff and Work Scheduling Preferences," unpublished report prepared for the Office of the Assistant Secretary for Policy, Evaluation and Research, U.S. Department of Labor (Contract No. 41–USC–252), October 1977, pp. 110–17.

3. Fred Best, "Exchanging Earnings for Leisure: Findings of an Exploratory National Survey on Work Time Preferences," prepared for the National Commission for Employment Policy and the Office of Research and Development, Employment and Development Administration, U.S. Department of Labor, January 1979, Table 17A, Appendix IV.

4. Ibid., Table 18, p. 131.

5. An excellent survey of this research can be obtained from Philip L. Rones, "Older Men—The Choice Between Work and Retirement," *Monthly Labor Review*, November 1978, pp. 3–10.

6. Ibid; and William Deutermann and Scott Brown, "Voluntary Part-time Workers: A Growing Part of the Labor Force," *Monthly Labor Review*, June 1978, pp. 8–10.

7. Best, "Exchanging Earnings for Leisure," op cit., Table 18, p. 131.

8. These responses compare well to national survey data on the desire to change jobs and occupations. See Robert Quinn and Linda Shepard, *The 1972-73 Quality of Employment Survey* (Ann Arbor: Institute for Social Research, University of Michigan, 1974), p. 54.

9. For a more detailed analysis of this relationship, see Fred Best, "Changing Sex Roles and Worklife Flexibility," *Psychology of Women Quarterly*, Fall 1980.

10. A voluntary time-income tradeoff options plan put into effect by Santa Clara County, California, offered employees the choice of exchanging 5 percent of current earnings for 10.5 days' vacation, 10 percent of earnings for 21 days' vacation, or 20 percent of earnings for two 21-day vacations. During the first year, 18 percent of all county employees requested one of these options. Requests for the second year are lower, but there are indications that middle management supervisors are discouraging participation in the plan. See "Statement by Dan McCorquodale," in *Leisure Sharing*, Hearings of the Select Committee on Investment Priorities and Objectives, California State Senate, Sacramento, November 1, 1977, pp. 41–49; Requests for more part-time work during the week also suggest high willingness to exchange earnings for time. See "Statement of Carol Lobes," in ibid, pp. 174–85. It can be hypothesized that an increase in the forms of free time available will increase the number of persons willing to exchange income for time.

PART IV

GETTING FROM HERE TO THERE

With the change of circumstances, institutions must advance also to keep pace with the times. We might as well require a man to wear still the coat which fitted him when a boy as civilized society to remain ever under the regimen of their barbarous ancestors.

Thomas Jefferson

11

THE PROSPECTS FOR INSTITUTIONAL CHANGE

Several years ago the New York *Times* News Service carried an interesting story that reported on the activities of an unusual man who had spent much of his recent past moving from one low-paying, undesirable job to another. Through a series of firings, layoffs, and spells of unemployment, he traveled from Ontario to Atlanta and worked as a farmhand, ditchdigger, dishwasher, quick-service counterman, and garbage collector. But what, you may ask, is so noteworthy about this? Society has always had its underdogs, transient "job hoppers," and outcasts; those who could not "fit in" and were destined to some shadowy existence at the border lines of what most of us consider mainstream society.

But there is more to this story. This particular transient is better known as Dr. John Coleman, a past president of Pennsylvania's respected Haverford College, current head of the Edna Clark Foundation, and widely reputed author and labor economist. As a college president, Coleman repeatedly voiced concern about how school sheltered and separated students and faculty from a vast realm of experience and knowledge lying beyond the ivy-covered walls of academe. Finally, at the age of 51, he put himself where his advice had been, took a long-overdue sabbatical, and, with the exception of returning periodically to chair the board meetings of the Federal Reserve Bank of Philadelphia, thrust himself into a series of escapades that one might expect of a John Steinbeck rather than a college president.[1]

Coleman's adventures provide us with a novel and perhaps inspirational story of one individual who was able to snap the ties of conventional life patterns. For many of us, this tale may captivate our imagination and even bring forth a wave of daydreams. Yet at the same time, it is easy to disregard Coleman's self-chosen odyssey as the isolated and atypical act of a person whom some might see as a courageous eccentric and others as a total fool.

The case of John Coleman is indeed a rather dramatic and highly unusual story, but numerous other individuals have also found ways to alter the scheduling and activities of their lives. From time to time, newspaper articles carry stories of successful corporate executives who make decisions to leave their high-paying positions in order to tour the world or set up an apple farm in Virginia.[2] One hears numerous stories of military officers, who retire on pensions at age 40, take a year off, then start lucrative second careers.[3] Other more daring efforts at mid-life career change are familiar to all of us, as are persons who voluntarily work part time or take extra leaves of absence at their own expense to gain "minisabbaticals" every year.[4] Then there are the somewhat shady reports of persons who have used prolonged unemployment insurance or disability benefits as a means of financing a personal sabbatical.[5] There can be little doubt that a fair number of individuals have taken it upon themselves to use their wits and the resources available to them to forge life schedules that match their particular needs and aspirations. However, it must be recognized that these pioneer efforts at alternative life patterns are often highly costly to the individual, occasionally illegal, and certainly still a rarity. Nonetheless, there is cause to think that pressures will continue to mount for more life-scheduling flexibility.

THE PROBLEMS OF INSTITUTIONAL ADAPTABILITY

While our society can sustain a good number of life-scheduling mavericks, any broadly based movement toward more flexible lives will require major adjustments of our principal social institutions. Indications are that the institutions of education, retirement, and the family are well on the way toward such adjustments. However, it must be emphasized that the key to any major changes in the ways we schedule our lives will ultimately be determined by the constraints and options of organizations concerned with work activities.

The list of problems that must be overcome if work organizations are to allow more life-scheduling flexibility seems overwhelming. Indeed, practical administrators and scholars of complex organizations would justly express grave reservations about the feasibility of such changes. Foremost among these reservations would be the problems of coordination and communication that would be created by individualized work scheduling. Tasks depending upon cooperation among many workers would become more difficult with employees working a variety of daily, weekly, or yearly schedules. Predictability could decline, continuity of effort may become erratic, and communication or the simple arrangement of a meeting could become a major ordeal. Many organizational functions that are now mechanical could become cumbersome and more costly.

Of particular concern to employers would be the matter of fringe benefits and other fixed labor costs. As noted in previous chapters, many benefits such as health and life insurance would cost more for employees working less than full time (see Table 7.1).[6] To further complicate matters, worktime reductions would often cause increases in worker-related taxes paid by employers.[7] Any adjustment of such increased labor costs by pro-rating or other devices would likely be more complex and expensive than current standardized systems. Established and simple guidelines for determining seniority status and retirement benefits would become cumbersome. Undoubtedly, greater worklife flexibility would increase organizational costs by requiring more supervisorial effort, intricate record-keeping procedures, and new ways of assessing the performance and accountability of employees.

Personnel problems could result from conflicts borne from less standardized procedures concerning seniority rights, and worker morale could damaged due to a loss of personal influence within organizations due to unusual work patterns. There is also the danger that flexible worklives might facilitate the loss of trained employees, and possibly firm secrets, to competitors. Finally, there are fears that departures from standardized work hours would vastly complicate collective bargaining agreements and invite union hostilities. All in all, those concerned with the practical problems of administering work organizations are apt to view work-scheduling flexibility as having the overall effect of increasing the costs of operations and lowering productivity.

Of course, more flexible work patterns may also have positive impacts on work organizations. Of utmost importance to employers, increased worklife flexibility could boost productivity in some cases. Several studies have indicated that worktime reforms have improved employee morale, reduced absenteeism and counterproductive activities, and frequently increased worker output.[8] It has also been noted that increased free time adjusted to individual needs provides employees with opportunities for retraining to prevent skill obsolescence and personal renewal as a palliative for exhaustion and job boredom. In some cases, opportunities for leaves of absence and other increases of free time might allow nonproductive or "dead-ended" workers to find new and more suitable jobs to the benefit of themselves and their old organizations. It is also possible that firm tax burdens for unemployment and welfare services might be lowered in some instances.[9]

Contrary to most expectations, thoughtfully developed work scheduling innovations can enhance organizational performance. The diversity of skills among a given firm's personnel could be increased by firms hiring a greater and more heterogeneous number of workers at shorter work hours.* In some cases, work-scheduling flexibility could increase overall organizational adaptability to emergencies and fluctuations of business, as well as

---

*The use of part-time and reduced worktime to increase firm personnel diversity would be particularly attractive to small firms that can hire only a limited number of employees but still require a number of different skills.

reduce the need for prime overtime pay rates. Finally, worktime reforms are likely to be increasingly prized by employees as fringe benefits that can in some cases become acceptable substitutes for pay raises and provide an effective asset in recruiting quality personnel.[10]

In evaluating the adaptability of work organizations to more flexible work lives, it is critical to recognize that their constraints and options vary tremendously. The product type, size, structure, and stability of organizations are important considerations. For example, the work-scheduling flexibility of organizations concerned with continuous, year-round mass production is different from those concerned with seasonal or batch production. Small firms will face different constraints and options than large corporations. Likewise, the level of capital investment and nature of technologies will influence organizational flexibility.[11] The ways in which employees are organized and supervised is particularly important,[12] as is the overall stability and rate of organizational change.

Beyond the problems that must be overcome by management are those of organized labor. Unions have expressed many reservations about worklife flexibility, and many of them are well founded. Over a period of more than 100 years, organized labor has struggled to build a legal and political system that supports the institution of collective bargaining and the rights of individual workers. Widespread flexible worklives might undermine standardized worker rights such as overtime pay and job security provisions, as well as potentially complicate and fragment the worker solidarity needed for effective collective bargaining.[13] Additionally, many union leaders believe that gains in free time should not come at the expense of reductions in worker income,[14] particularly if gains in free time are fostered as work sharing. Any major movement toward flexible worklives is likely to be gained only after thorough assessment of the desires of rank-and-file union members and a careful adjustment of public statutes so that options for more flexible work scheduling do not undermine basic union concerns.

THE WORKTIMES, THEY ARE A CHANGIN'

While there is, at this time, no systematic overview of the adaptability of work organizations and unions to flexible life patterns,[15] there are a number of indications that widespread work-scheduling flexibility may be possible. Indeed, there appears to be a deluge of varied worktime experiments taking place nationally and internationally. These innovations are tampering with every dimension of worktime from the workday to the worklife. The diversity of these efforts bears testimony to the likelihood that the social forces of our times are not moving us toward some monolithic worktime reduction such as a "standard 35 hour workweek" but to a vast array of worktime reforms that will add up to overall worklife flexibility.

One of the major thrusts of current worktime innovations has been growing interest in part-time work. Not only has the portion of the work force employed in "voluntary" part-time work increased from 10.6 to 18.7 percent between 1954 and 1977,[16] but there has been a growing movement to remove part-time employment from the stigmatism of "second rate" jobs. Up to very recent times, most part-time jobs were low paying, tended to entail menial tasks, offered virtually nothing in the way of security or fringe benefits, and presented little opportunity for career advancement. Today, a growing coalition of women, youth, and older workers are advocating the creation of "permanent part-time jobs" offering fringe benefits such as health insurance and the potential for career advancement.[17] Most gains in these areas have occurred within the public sector. The federal government, many states, as well as some localities have embarked upon formal programs to increase and upgrade part-time jobs.[18] As a result, the number of permanent part-time employees in the federal civil service is reported to have increased a remarkable 20 percent in the one-year period from the end of 1976 to the end of 1977.[19] Other initiatives have sought to increase part-time work among public service jobs funded by the federal government. Within the private sector, there has been less concern with the quality of part-time jobs, but there are some indications that interest is growing.[20]

Another growing worktime reform that is somewhat akin to part-time employment has been "job splitting." This innovation entails the performance of one full-time job by two or more persons. The idea first made its appearance in California during the mid-1960s.[21] There are no figures providing a concrete indication of the incidence of job splitting, but numerous accounts suggest that the practice has grown and spread across the country.[22] This worktime reform seems applicable to many occupations. For example, there have been reports of two or more persons successfully sharing positions such as high school principal, city planner, college professor, secretarial receptionist, and many other types of work.[23] Perhaps the most remarkable case has been the sharing of the foreign minister's position in Liechtenstein.[24] There is no question that "job splitting" requires special effort and unusual cooperation by participants, but when the match of employees is appropriate, employers have found that this practice offers many unexpected benefits. Additionally, job splitting has often served the purpose of allowing persons in professional fields to maintain career attachment when they are unable to work full time or inadequate career opportunities limit chances for full-time employment in chosen fields of work.[25]

One of the most heralded types of worktime reform has been flexitime. This practice has been primarily applied to daily work hours and allows employees to arrive for work and depart at any time during the day as long as they are in attendance during specified "core hours," such as 10 A.M. to 3 P.M., and work a full workday. While there are no overall figures on the incidence of flexitime, it has been estimated that 13 percent of all firms and 6 percent of all employees within the United States were participating in flexitime programs in 1977.[26] Flexitime began during the mid-1960s in Europe and made its first American debut in the early 1970s.[27] Since that time, the practice has evolved from a rare novelty to a common idea that appears to be spreading rapidly within both the public and private sector.[28] In the "big picture" of lifetime scheduling, daily flexitime does not offer the promise of altering overall life patterns. However, the emergence and rapid assimilation of this idea has accomplished a great deal in the way of provoking thought about other forms of work-scheduling flexibility, as well as demonstrating to employers that departures from the standard "8-hour-a-day workweek" need not engender organizational anarchy. Indeed, the notion of flexitime has proven itself so manageable that some firms are beginning to experiment with the notion of "flexiweeks" and "flexi-months."[29]

Beyond the scope of the workday, there have been a number of innovations in the workweek and workmonth. Within the United States, popular attention was first drawn to workweek innovations by the wave of experiments with the "compressed workweek" that surfaced around 1970.[30] The major thrust here was the "4-day, 40-hour workweek" in which employees continued to work 40 hours a week, but put in 10 hours a day in order to gain three-day weekends. While this innovation was originally hailed as a "revolution in worktime," its growth seems to have leveled in the late 1970s.[31] However, as in the case of flexitime, attention given to the compressed workweek seems to have paved the way for a number of work-scheduling experiments within the context of weeks and months. For example, there have been reports of 3- or 3.5–day workweeks with 11- to 13-hour workdays.[32] One recent reform instigated with union cooperation at DuPont created a system of rotation between regular and night shifts in which employees work four 12-hour days between two-day weekends and receive seven days' extended leave a month. This plan has been in operation since 1974 and is considered an "all-around success" because it provides workers with free time they can use and allows plants to maintain continuous 24-hour operation.[33]

While it is often noted that the American workweek has not declined notably since the mid-1940s, it is important to realize that national averages disguise growing diversity in worktime arrangements. Indeed, analysis of worktime data shows that the small reductions in the workweek that have occurred over the last few decades have largely been the result of increased part-time work and reductions of excessively long hours.[34] More importantly, a good deal of the gains in free time during the "work years of life" have come in the form of longer vacations and paid days off. Indeed, extended vacations have become an increasingly frequent goal of collective bargaining efforts, and vacations of over six weeks' length are becoming increasingly common.[35] Of particular importance has been the recent initiative of the United Auto Workers to bargain for successive stages of paid days off with the ultimate goal of obtaining a 4-day, 32-hour workweek.[36] Such movement toward days off indicates a renewed interest on the part of organized labor toward using bargaining influence on behalf of free time. Further, such practical adjustment to days off, longer weekends, and most particularly extended vacations underscores the adaptability of work organizations to a variety of discontinuities in employee work attendance.

Some of the most interesting worktime reforms have entailed flexible mechanisms to allow individual employees the choice of foregoing income for more free time within the context of the workmonth and workyear. A much-heralded program set up by Santa Clara County in California allows employees the choice of voluntarily foregoing 5 percent of their annual income for 10.5 days' added paid vacation, 10 percent for 21 days' vacation, or as much as 20 percent for 42 days' added vacation (the level of pay is reduced proportionally for all work and vacation days). During the first year of operation, some 17 percent of all county employees requested one of these options.[37] Participation in subsequent years has declined due to increased work loads and resistance of mid-level supervisors, but these voluntary tradeoff options have become a permanent program supported by the public employee unions and top county management. Other local governments are developing similar programs.[38] One of the most notable of these is a voluntary three-month leave of absence program in which lawyers employed by a number of counties are allowed to exchange 25 percent of their annual earnings for a three-month leave each year. This program has been judged a success because it has allowed attorneys to recover from stressful work during the rest of the year, as well as provide funds for the hiring of additional lawyers.[39] Voluntary tradeoff programs of a less dramatic nature have also been developed within the private sector and federal government.*

Perhaps the most impressive move toward flexible worklives has been the development of "flexiyear contracts" by a number of private firms in Europe. The general idea of this innovation is that employer and employee negotiate on an annual basis an overall worktime agreement for a year's period. Such negotiations have opened the possibility of novel arrangements such as six months on and six months off, part-time work for part of the year (such as summer when children are home), and all manner of other options. It is claimed that such yearly negotiations improve worker morale and productivity and allow employers the predictability to plan a number of worktime arrangements that creatively meet the needs of both firm and workers.[40]

The idea of sabbaticals has also been extended beyond the academic

---

*For example, the New York Telephone and Telegraph Company allows telephone operators to take one day off each week without pay if the arrangement is made in advance. Personnel officials for the company report that most operators tend to request the day-off option.

environment in recent years. Despite some criticisms, the well-known U.S. Steel Worker sabbatical negotiated in 1967 was renewed in 1974 and is still firmly intact. This program allows up to 13 weeks' paid vacation every four years for senior workers.[41] A similar sabbatical program was negotiated for cannery workers in 1966.[42] Sabbatical leaves of up to one year have been implemented among a small number of firms. For example, the Rolm Corporation in California provides a one-year leave with pay to employees who have worked six continuous years with the firm.[43] Additionally, a number of major corporations have instigated programs allowing their executives one- to two-year "sabbaticals" for approved public service projects.[44]

These and other innovations provide evidence that the adaptability of work organizations and unions to flexible worklives is still largely untapped. Certainly, there are problems to overcome and tradeoffs to be made. However, new technologies and models of operation are being developed that allow adaptability to worktime innovations that might have been thought impossible only a few years ago. For example, the rise of flexitime has already stimulated the production of a wide array of time-keeping devices that allow supervisors an efficient and uncostly means of overseeing employee worktime.[45] Similarly, a number of large corporations are beginning to recognize that the vast computer facilities now used for computing payrolls and overtime can be applied to the task of adapting organizational operations to varied work schedules and adjusting fringe benefits to variations of individual worktime arrangements. As an illustration, computer technologies might allow more individualized worktime arrangements (even for highly interdependent assembly-line workers) through staggering each worker's schedule in the same way that the use of classrooms is planned in universities. Yet another innovation supportive of worktime reforms has been "cafeteria benefit plans" in which individual employees can choose between options such as a pay raise, $10 worth of life insurance, or added vacation.[46] Unions have been reserved about such cafeteria plans but are now finding that such approaches can facilitate member solidarity by allowing the development of a dollar-value bargaining agenda rather than internal conflicts over the priority given to life insurance as opposed to more time off.

These innovations are but a few of the mechanisms that are being developed to allow the practical implementation of increased worklife flexibility. While the task of adjusting to widespread worktime flexibility is certainly not to be underestimated, it is also important that it not be viewed as impossible. There is no law written by the hand of God that the standard workweek must be 40 hours and that employees will have two to four weeks' vacation each year. Different types of organizations and occupations will certainly confront varied obstacles to increased flexibility, but there is good reason to believe that a great deal can be done to increase the options available to all types of workers.

SOCIAL POLICY AND LIFE-CYCLE PLANNING

While the interaction among workers, unions, and employers is likely to foster important steps toward more flexible life scheduling, it is important to recognize that the government, as the custodian of common well-being, is also likely to become involved with the issue. As nonwork years become more prolonged at the extremes of the life cycle, there will be increasing social and economic costs in the form of tax burdens to those who are working and impoverishment for those who are not working. Simultaneously, the problems of extended schooling, the demand for jobs, and the desire for more free time in mid-life will cause mounting pressures for government policies to allow more flexible scheduling of education, work, and leisure over a total lifetime.

There are a number of policies and programs that governments will likely consider as mechanisms to foster more flexible life scheduling. Most of these ideas are still in their embryonic stages of development. Nonetheless, a capsule summary of some of the leading proposals will provide an outline of the social policies we might expect in coming years.

Incentives to Stimulate Voluntary Time-Income Tradeoffs

State and federal governments may consider providing subsidies and tax incentives to encourage firms to implement a number of voluntary options allowing employees to forego current or potential earnings for various forms of free time.[47] These tax incentives would be designed to cover extra costs incurred by firms providing such options. In this way firms would be compensated for added outlays for fringe benefits, more complex record keeping, and other costs. Extra incentives might be given as the range and type of tradeoff options increase. For example, a firm might be eligible to receive larger subsidies for offering opportunities for reduced workweeks, shorter workdays, and longer vacations, as opposed to only one of these options. Similarly, extra incentives might be provided to encourage firms to hire new employees to replace worktime foregone by existing employees. Many complications would have to be resolved, but such a program would have potential as a highly adaptable tool for stimulating all manner of worktime reforms.[48]

Amendment of Worktime Limitation Laws

There are now a number of proposals to reduce worktime by redefining the "standard workweek" as under 40 hours and legislating heavier overtime pay rates via amendment of the U.S. Fair Labor Standards Act and similar statutes.[49] While such legislation would likely reduce the average workweek, it would also encourage a monolithic worktime standard offering little flexibility for individual preferences. If such worktime limitations are seriously considered, an alternative approach might be to expand the time frame of worktime limitations to the year rather than the week. While such an expansion of the time frame could open possibilities for abuses of worker rights, thoughtfully designed clauses could be included to protect workers while an expansion of the time frame would encourage employer-employee negotiations of workyear contracts.[50]

Tax Laws Encouraging Collective Bargaining for More Free Time

Laws reducing or eliminating taxation of employee fringe benefits coupled with periodic wage and price controls have provided a major impetus for labor unions to shift collective bargaining priorities increasingly in favor of fringe benefits rather than leisure or pay increases. Thoughtfully designed tax law amendments might likewise encourage a shift of union negotiations for various worktime reforms.

Leave of Absence Rights

Rough legislation has been proposed to establish a national law providing workers with the right to take extended leaves of absence without pay with reemployment rights if they have worked a given number of years for their current employer.[51] Many work organizations already have leave of absence rights, particularly in the form of pregnancy and educational leaves. Reasonable government legislation to provide something along the line of an accumulative leave of absence right could provide the job security that many workers would require before seriously considering the possibility of taking an extended leave.

Sabbatical Leaves

There have been a number of recent proposals for state and federal worker sabbatical programs.[52] These proposals vary greatly in detail. Some would be mandatory programs providing full income during a year's absence, while others would be voluntary programs providing only partial income maintenance. Like the leave of absence just mentioned, these programs would also ensure reemployment rights. Existing proposals vary in terms of whether participants taking a sabbatical would be allowed to take another job.* For the most part, these proposals suggest that the

---

*Those advocating sabbaticals as a means of sharing available work suggest that participants not be allowed to take a job during leave from regular employment. Those proposing sabbaticals primarily for human enrichment suggest that a new job experience may be beneficial to both the participant and society.

incomes of participants be subsidized or maintained during the nonwork period through a system of transfer payments supported by either general tax revenues or some type of compulsory contribution procedure similar to Social Security.

Income Maintenance for Educational and Self-Renewal Leaves

There have been a variety of proposals to provide some form of income maintenance for workers leaving their jobs for an authorized purpose. Most of these proposals have entailed the provision of loans and cash subsidies for mid-life educational activities.[53] In some cases, it has been proposed that Social Security funds be drawable before retirement age by persons wishing to take mid-career leaves.[54] Finally, some advocates of "guaranteed income" have proposed that all persons should be guaranteed a subsistence income, even if they choose not to work in order to enjoy leisure.[55] Realistically, the trend toward "fiscal austerity" fostered by inflation, resistance to higher taxes, and serious questions about undermining the motivation to work[56] make most of the proposals in this group unlikely prospects.

Government Experimentation and Technical Assistance

In addition to general social policies, governments can also accomplish a great deal by applying worktime reforms to their own organization in order to test and demonstrate feasibility. Knowledge gained from these and other efforts could also be made available to interested parties through a variety of technical assistance programs.

Removal of Barriers to Life-Scheduling Flexibility

Government concern might also be directed toward removal or alteration of laws and institutions that hinder individual discretions in scheduling their lives. As an illustration, The U.S. Fair Labor Standards Act and similar statutes, which are important legal bulwarks protecting employees from worktime abuses, also present a number of rigidities that hamstring worthwhile worktime reforms.* As already noted, many payroll taxes for unemployment insurance, Social Security, and other programs frequently present disincentives to worktime innovations. A countless number of laws and institutions that present similar problems must be cautiously reviewed and revised with the intention of preserving the original purpose for which they were created while allowing flexibility for more life-scheduling discre-

---

*For example, workers desiring to work a 4-day, 40-hour workweek of 10-hour workdays often confront problems with the Fair Labor Standards Act on the basis that any worktime over 8 hours a day is subject to overtime pay.

tion. In some cases, these adjustments might be easily accomplished, and in others revisions may require tradeoffs and new balances of old and new priorities. Quite obviously, these adjustments cannot be expected to occur overnight.

Clearly, there are many social policies that might be enacted to encourage more flexible life patterns. Some represent bold strokes of "social engineering" and others less dramatic efforts. Each have their own unique problems and limitations, and all of them are relatively new and untried. Naturally, there is a likelihood that proponents of different ideas will argue the primacy of their own proposals. In assessing the value of these alternatives, it is important to recognize that there is no one approach to increasing life-pattern flexibility, and that an omnibus of approaches will be necessary to provide options to meet the needs of all groups and individuals. Current and yet-to-be presented proposals are still very much in need of further refinement and rigorous assessment, and the process of developing social policies to encourage more flexible life schedules is very much in the initial stages.

RECYCLING PEOPLE

In large measure this book has focused on facts and figures documenting social trends that may foster flexible life scheduling. Such an approach tends to downplay the less measurable humanistic issues of personal growth and fulfillment. Yet these concerns are also important, if not preeminent, and it is fitting that this volume conclude with thoughts about the importance of life scheduling to the inner meanings of human existence.

There is a story concerning a certain Mr. Creech, who allegedly wrote in the margins of his painstaking translation of Lucretius, "Memo—when I have finished my book, I must kill myself."[57] Reportedly, he carried out his resolution, a testimony to the beliefs of past ages in which life without work was held to be meaningless. Values and life styles have changed greatly since that dour Mr. Creech wrote his dismal memo. Nonetheless, most industrial nations must still be viewed as "work societies." Further, this is not likely to change. Despite the advances of technology and evolution of human values, work will certainly remain the essential and focal activity of human life. Yet it is a dismal thought that we have come to view our lives primarily in terms of preparing for work, performance of work, and finally deliverance from work. Perhaps more pertinent, it is more saddening from the standpoint of human fulfillment and growth that the virtues of learning, working, and leisure should be unduly cramped into segregated compartments of life.

It is near idiocy to believe that youth is principally for school and learning, middle age for applying what we learned in youth, and old age for reaping the rewards of a life of work. Life simply is not that way. The learning process continues to our last days. The world changes constantly around us and different stages of life impose new lessons every bit as vital as the "basics" we learn in childhood. Work is a process of self-expression and sacrifice that cannot be restricted to one portion of life without dire results. There are many faces of work, and many seem uniquely fitted to different ages. Physical toil is an experience all of us should taste, and there is no more suitable time than youth. Similarly, work requiring discipline, fully developed skills, and wisdom tends to have its natural place in the life cycle. Increasingly, it appears that those who do not confront work in youth are ill prepared—despite the best of educations—for the demands and opportunities of mid-life; and those who flee their jobs in their early sixties are all too often stranded upon an island of empty time from which there are no bridges to return. Finally, leisure seems to have become at once our most precious and wasted commodity. If anything, our time free of constraints represents the potential to renew and rebuild our spirits; and to pull the fabric of our lives together in a way that balances the meaning that comes from learning, the purposes that drive us to work, and the personal pleasures that somehow make these efforts worthwhile. All too often, it seems that "leisure" is forced upon us in ways we cannot appreciate, or made unduly harried by the pressures of mid-life.

More flexible life patterns would loosen the time binds that often prevent the natural flow of human activities, as well as nurture and renew our spirits through change and opportunities to actualize personal dreams. Of course, many life changes and dreams can be attained within the realm of work. However, others require time away from the job. Every individual has some desire to explore new experiences and possibly try fundamentally different ways of life. We all have a deeply felt yearning for what we might have been and may yet become: a desire to more freely explore things like playing the guitar, writing a book, building a house, or raising a child. Such dreams take time, and one promise of more flexible life patterns is that each individual might arrange life's activities in ways that broaden the exploration of the countless possibilities of human existence.

With due recognition for the diversity of the human species, it seems that the fullest and most productive lives are those in which individuals fluctuate through periods of action and accomplishment—which expand our awareness and solidify our sense of self—and rest and reflection—which integrate our sense of self and the world. In this way, action becomes more than reaction to an endless treadmill of unchosen challenges, and reflection more than stultifying repetition of old thoughts and experiences. The actualization of this cyclic relationship between action and renewal is essential to human growth and fulfillment, and it requires that there be a better balance of learning, work, and leisure through all stages of our lives.

In the course of history, a time appears to be upon us in which there is an opportunity to realign our values and institutions so that every person has a better opportunity to adjust the rhythm of life's experience to their own needs and temperaments. This is an opportunity that should not be cast aside lightly.

NOTES

1. Israel Shenker, "College President's Experiment: Out of the Ivory Tower," San Francisco *Chronicle*, June 12, 1973, p. 1.

2. "The Great Escape: More Affluent Adults Quit Corporate World to Lead Simpler Lives," *Wall Street Journal*, February 19, 1971, p. 1.

3. Rowland Evans and Robert Novak, "The Pension Machine," Washington *Post*, April 19, 1978, p. A13.

4. "Half-Year Stint Gives His Job More Zest," Washington *Post*, December 25, 1977, p. A15.

5. "Almost an Incentive Not to Work," Washington *Star*, April 24, 1978, Editorial page; "The Great Male Cop-Out from the Work Ethic," *Business Week*, November 14, 1977, pp. 156–66; and Bernard Lefkowitz, *Breaktime: Living Without Work in a Nine to Five World* (New York: Hawthorn Books, 1979), pp. 173–74.

6. Stanley Nollen, Brenda Eddy, and Virginia Martin, *Permanent Part-Time Employment: The Manager's Perspective* (New York: Praeger Publishers, 1978), pp. 61–83 and 114–28; Fred Best, "Individual and Firm Work Time Decisions: Comment," *Work Time and Unemployment*, Special Report No. 28, National Commission for Employment Policy, Washington, D.C., 1979.

7. For example, on the basis of 1976 unemployment insurance and Social Security tax rates, an employer would have had to pay $339 more a year for two half-time employees earning $10,000 a year each as opposed to one full-time worker earning $20,000 a year. See Robert L. Clark, *Adjusting Hours to Increase Jobs*, Special Report No. 15, National Commission for Employment Policy, Washington, D.C., September 1977, pp. 30–33.

8. Harriet Goldberg Weinstein, *A Comparison of Three Alternative Work Schedules: Flexible Work Hours, Compact Work Week, and Staggered Work Hours*, Industrial Research Unit, The Wharton School, University of Pennsylvania, 1975; *Alternatives in the World of Work*, National Center for Productivity and Quality of Working Life, Washington, D.C., Winter 1976; *Resource Packet: National Conference on Alternative Work Schedules*, National Council for Alternative Work Patterns, Washington, D.C., March 1977, pp. 29–66; "Special Flexitime Reports," *Monthly Labor Review*, February 1977, pp. 62–74.

9. Of direct concern to firms, there appear to be growing cases in which unemployment insurance or disability benefits have been used by workers to finance "extended vacations." See "The Great Male Cop-Out," op. cit. Because firm taxes for these programs vary according to the participation rates of past or existing employees, the possibility that legitimate options for more flexible worklives might reduce such misuse of public income maintenance programs opens an opportunity for reduction of firm taxes. In an indirect sense, the possibility that widespread flexible worklives might reduce unemployment also opens the possibility that general taxes for social programs might be reduced.

10. It is noteworthy that a number of county governments have recently tended to provide time-off options rather than pay increases under conditions of budget limitations. See *Leisure Sharing*, Hearings of the Select Committee on Investment Priorities and Objectives, California State Senate, Sacramento, November 1, 1977, pp. 41–66. Additionally, some private firms are experimenting with flexible benefit options. See John Perham, "New Life for Flexible Compensation," *Dun's Review*, September 1978, pp. 68–70.

11. For a general discussion of organizational constraints and options, see Jay Galbraith, *Designing Complex Organizations* (Reading, Mass.: Addison-Wesley, 1973); James Thompson,

Organizations in Action (New York: McGraw-Hill, 1967); and Curt Tausky, *Work Organizations* (Itasca, Ill.: Peacock Publishers, 1970), pp. 76–117.

12. A strict hierarchic structure with high worker specialization will face different, but not necessarily more difficult, problems in adjusting to flexible worklives than organizations typified by participative decision making and overlapping tasks. See Tausky, op. cit., pp. 24–75; George Straus et al, eds. *Organizational Behavior* (Madison, Wisc.: Industrial Relations Research Association, 1974); and Renesis Likert, *Human Organizations* (New York: McGraw-Hill, 1967).

13. John L. Zalusky, "Alternative Work Schedules: A Labor Perspective," *CUPA Journal* 28, no. 3 (Summer 1977): 54–56; "AFL-CIO Opposes Flexible Work Schedules for Federal Workers," *Daily Labor Review*, August 22, 1978, pp. A6–A8; Jeffery M. Miller, *Innovations in Working Patterns*, U.S. Trade Union Seminar on Alternative Working Patterns in Europe, Communication Workers of America, Washington, D.C., May 1978; and John D. Owen, "Flexitime: Some Problems and Solutions," *Industrial and Labor Relations Review* 30, no. 2 (January 1977): 156.

14. A recent example is a current multiunion push for reduced workweeks through legislative decree that would not reduce weekly income. See Jerry Flint, "Unions Meet Resistance in Trying to Cut Workweek," *New York Times*, April 16, 1978, p. 15.

15. For some discussion of organizational constraints concerning worktime reforms, see Weinstein, op. cit.; National Council for Alternative Work Patterns, *Resource Packet*, op. cit., pp. 29–66; and Nollen, Eddy, and Martin, op. cit., pp. 35–45; Allan R. Cohen and Herman Gordon, *Alternative Work Schedules: Integrating Individual and Organizational Needs* (Menlo Park, Calif.: Addison-Wesley, 1978); and Robert A. Lee and William McEwan Young, "A Contingency Approach to Work Week Structuring," *Personnel Review* 6, no. 2 (Spring 1977): 45–55.

16. William V. Deutermann and Scott Campbell Brown, "Voluntary Part-Time Workers: A Growing Part of the Labor Force," *Monthly Labor Review*, June 1978, p. 5.

17. Stanley Nollen, Brenda Eddy, Virginia Martin, and Douglas Monroe, *Permanent Part Time Employment: An Interpretive Review*, School of Business Administration, Georgetown University, February 1976, p. 2.

18. *Part-Time Employment and Flexible Work Hours*, Hearings before the Subcommittee on Employee Ethics and Utilization, Committee on Post Office and Civil Service, U.S. House of Representatives, 95th Cong., Serial No. 95-28, May 24, 26, June 29, July 8, and October 4, 1977; William G. Whittaker, "Alternative Work Schedules and Part-Time Career Opportunities in the Federal Government: A Legislative Review," Congressional Research Service, The Library of Congress, Economics Division, January 25, 1978; *Project JOIN: Phase I Report*, Employee Relations Division, Department of Administration, State of Wisconsin, Madison, March 1, 1977.

19. David Garfinkel, "Part-Time Work Force Doubles in 10 Years," Advertising Supplement, Washington *Post*, April 30, 1978, p. 4.

20. Nollen, Eddy, and Martin, op. cit.; and Jean B. Leed, *Part-Time Careers in Seattle* (Seattle: Focus on Part-Time Careers, 1977).

21. Judith Anderson, "A New Way of Sharing—One Job for Two," San Francisco *Chronicle*, June 5, 1973, p. 22; Gretl Meier, "Shared Job Project in California Stimulates Labor and Management Interest," *World of Work Report*, September 1976, p. 7; "Job Sharing: General Information Packet" (Palo Alto, Calif.: New Ways to Work, 1974); Fred Best, "Flexible Work Scheduling: Beyond the Forty-Hour Impasse," in *The Future of Work*, ed. Fred Best (Englewood Cliffs, N.J.: Prentice-Hall, 1973), p. 97.

22. "Job Sharing: Two for the Price of One," *Collegian*, University of Massachusetts, Amherst, March 12, 1976, p. 7; Barney Olmsted, "Job Sharing—A New Way to Work," *Personnel Journal*, February 1977, pp. 78–81; Robert Gilman, "Job Sharing is Good," *The Co-Evolution Quarterly*, Spring 1978, pp. 86–90; "Jobs: Two for the Price of One," *Time*, May 3, 1976; and Kathy Sawyer, "Job Sharing: Growing Trend," Washington *Post*, December 26, 1977, p. A1.

23. "At Filmore, Principal is Actually Two Women," Washington *Post*, December 26, 1977, p. A11; "Jobs: Two for the Price of One," op. cit.; William Arkin and Lynne R. Dobrofsky, "Job Sharing in Academia," paper delivered to the 1977 Meetings of the American Sociological Association, Chicago, September 9, 1977, and "Marriage of the Minds," *Time*, March 6, 1978, p. 68; "Jobs: Two for the Price of One," op. cit.; and "Job-Sharing Plan: A Three Year Success for City Manager," *World of Work Report*, May 1977, p. 57; *Job Sharing in the Schools: A Study of Nine Bay Area Districts* (Palo Alto, Calif.: New Ways to Work, February 1976); Gretl Meier, *Job Sharing: A New Pattern for Quality of Work and Life?* (Kalamazoo, Mich.: Upjohn Institute for Employment Research, February 1979); and Judith Michaelson, "Two Women Have Many Differences—But Same Job," Los Angeles *Times*, July 2, 1979, p. 35.

24. In this case, it must be recognized that the "job sharing" was as much a result of political expediency as anything else. See "Two for One," *Time*, May 8, 1978, p. 38.

25. Olmsted, op. cit.; and Meier, op. cit.

26. Estimates cited from a preliminary report prepared by Stanley Nollen and Virginia Martin for the American Manufacturing Association, Washington, D.C., May 1978.

27. Dennis Weintraub, "Starting the Work Day When You Want," San Francisco *Chronicle*, June 23, 1972, p. 23; Heinz Murmann, "An Elastic Work Day Catches on in Germany," Washington *Post*, August 12, 1977, p. A25; Barbara Fiss, *Flexitime: A Guide*, Bureau of Policies and Standards, U.S. Civil Service Commission, Washington, D.C., May 15, 1974, p. 2; Michael Wade, *Flexible Working Hours in Practice* (New York: John Wiley, 1973).

28. "Personnel: Rubber Hours," *Newsweek*, September 10, 1973, pp. 66–67; David T. Cook, "Punching the Clock: When You Choose," *Christian Science Monitor*, April 30, 1974, p. 1; "Special Flexitime Reports," *Monthly Labor Review*, February 1977, pp. 62–74; "Flexitimers Do It Their Way While Firms Benefit," *Commerce America*, May 23, 1977, pp. 8–11; and Frank T. Morgan, "Your (Flex) Time May Come," *Personnel Journal*, February 1977, pp. 82–96.

29. British organizational theorist William McEwan Young reports that a number of European firms are expanding the idea of flexitime to the week and month. The general notion is that the employee can work when he or she wants to within the "core hour" limitations as long as they work the required hours for the week or month. Young reports that workers tend to "hoard free time" by working longer hours at the beginning of a time period, so they can take off more time later. See William McEwan Young, "Application of Flexible Working Hours to Continuous Shift Production," unpublished paper, Loughborough (England) University of Technology, 1977.

30. Riva Poor, ed., *4 Days, 40 Hours: Reporting a Revolution in Work and Leisure* (Cambridge, Mass.: Bursk and Poor, 1970); Douglas L. Fleuter, *The Workweek Revolution* (Reading, Mass.: Addison-Wesley, 1975), pp. 3–73.

31. Since 1974, the percent of U.S. workers on 4-day workweeks appears to have stabilized between 1.3 and 1.4 percent. See Janice Neipert Hedges, "A Look at the 4-Day Workweek," *Monthly Labor Review*, October 1971, pp. 33–37; and Janice Hedges, "Six-Day Workweeks Increase; Four-Day Weeks Stable," Office of Information, U.S. Department of Labor, News Release 77–1092, December 30, 1977.

32. Poor, op. cit., pp. 133–71; Fleuter, op. cit., pp. 11–43; Max Kaplan, "A Life of Leisure," *Industrial Design*, May 1971, pp. 18–19; "Three-Day Week Gets a Trial," San Francisco *Chronicle*, April 28, 1973, p. 5.

33. "Working 12 Hour Shifts," *Wall Street Journal*, March 14, 1978, p. 1.

34. John D. Owen, "Workweeks and Leisure: An Analysis of Trends, 1948–75," *Monthly Labor Review*, August 1976, pp. 3–8.

35. U.S. Bureau of Labor Statistics, *Characteristics of Agreements Covering 1000 Workers or More*, Bulletin 1822, 1974, p. 47.

36. "Paid Personal Holidays," *Solidarity*, October 21, 1977, pp. 6–10.

37. "Testimony of Dan McCorquodale," in *Leisure Sharing*, op. cit., pp. 41–49.

38. Ibid., pp. 41–49; "Testimony of Michael Baratz" and "Testimony of Linda Gregory," in ibid., pp. 49–66.

39. "Testimony of James Hooley," in ibid., pp. 128–35.

40. Bernhard Teriet, "Flexiyear Schedules—Only a Matter of Time?" *Monthly Labor Review*, December 1977, pp. 63–64; Willi Haller, "Flexyear: The Ultimate Work Hour Concept" (New York: Interflex, Inc., 1977); and "Half-Year Stint Gives His Job More Zest," Washington *Post*, December 25, 1977, p. A15.

41. *Savings and Vacation Plan*, United Steel Workers of America and United States Steel Corporation, Revised January 1, 1964; *1974 Steel Settlement*, United Steel Workers of America, pp. 26–35.

42. Ted K. Bradshaw, "Canner Workers Sabbatical Leaves: A Report on the Study of Thirteen Week Vacations," Center for Labor Research and Education, Institute for Industrial Relations, University of California, Berkeley, 1976.

43. "Employee Leave Plan Started at Rolm Corp," uncited news article provided courtesy of New Ways to Work, Palo Alto, Calif.

44. "Xerox Sabbaticals," *Time*, September 20, 1971; "Xeroxing of Social Service," *Business World*, September 11, 1971; "Doing Good Works on Company Time: IBM Leave-for-Public Service Program," *Business World*, May 13, 1972, pp. 166–68.

45. *Plantime* (Middlesex, N.J.: Systematics, Inc., 1977); *Flextime Gazette* (Tinton Falls, N.J.: Flextime Division, Hecon Corporation, 1977); "Interflex 072" (New York: Interflex, 1977).

46. Stanley M. Nealey, "Determining Worker Preferences Among Employee Benefit Programs," *Journal of Applied Psychology* 48, no. 1 (1964): 7–12.

47. James R. Mills, "Leisure Sharing: Its Time Has Come," *State Government*, Spring 1979, pp. 75–79; Frank Schiff, "Employment Taxes and Subsidies: Comment," *Work Time and Unemployment*, Special Report No. 28, National Commission for Employment Policy, Washington, D.C., 1979; Fred Best, "Recycling People: Work Sharing Through Flexible Worklives," *The Futurist*, February 1978, p. 15; and *Leisure Sharing*, op. cit.

48. For more detailed discussion of this policy, see Fred Best, "Work Sharing: Issues, Policy Options and Assessments," Directorate of Social Affairs, Manpower and Education, Organisation for Economic Co-operation and Development, Paris, July 1979, pp. 78–91.

49. "Unions Campaign to Shrink Work Time," *Business Week*, April 24, 1978, p. 30; John Conyers, "First National all Unions Conference to Shorten the Work Week, April 11, 1978," *Congressional Record*, April 13, 1978, pp. H2896–2900.

50. Teriet, op. cit., pp. 63–64.

51. "Education and Childcare Reemployment Rights Act of 1978," proposed by Donald Riegle, U.S. Senate, 95th Cong., 2d sess., No. S.2485, January 30, 1978.

52. Donald Fraser, "Social Security Sabbaticals: A New Dimension for the Social Security System," *Congressional Record*, August 22, 1974, pp. H8939–40; Jule M. Sugarman, "The Decennial-Sabbatical Program," *Journal of the College and University Personnel Association* 28, no. 3 (Summer 1977): 47–52; Robert Rosenberg, "A Pilot Project for Extended Leaves," Working Paper No. 10, Senate Office of Research, California State Senate, Sacramento, December 1976; Barry Stern, "Feasibility of a Work Sabbatical Program," policy memorandum, Office of the Assistant Secretary for Education, U.S. Department of Health, Education and Welfare, March 18, 1975; and Dolores Melching and Merle Broberg, "A National Sabbatical System: Implications for the Aged," *Gerontologist*, April 1974, pp. 175–81.

53. Herbert A. Levine, *Paid Educational Leave*, Paper No. 6, National Institute of Education, U.S. Department of Health, Education and Welfare, March 1977; and Phillip W. Semas, "Workers' Sabbaticals Eyed as Key to Lifelong Education," *Chronicle of Higher Education*, March 18, 1974, p. 1.

54. Gosta Rehn, "For Free Choice in Working Life," *ILO Information* (U.S. Edition) 6, no. 1 (1978): 3.

55. Robert Theobald ed. *The Guaranteed Income* (Garden City, N.Y.: Doubleday, 1967).

56. There are notable arguments to the effect that subsidized nonwork at marginal income levels would not undermine motivation to work. See Best, *The Future of Work*, op. cit., pp. 126–27. At the same time, guaranteed income experiments and other income maintenance studies suggest that disincentives to work could be a major problem.

57. This is a story often told by Juanita Kreps in her speeches and writings. See *The Lifetime Allocation of Work and Income* (Durham, N.C.: Duke University Press, 1971), p. 17.

APPENDIX: SUPPLEMENTARY
REFERENCE TABLES

TABLE A.1

Comparison of Alameda County and National Survey Samples with National Data

Variable	1976 Alameda Sample	1978 National Sample	Recent BLS Data
Sex			
Male	46.9	64.3	58.7
Female	53.1	35.7	41.3
Age			
Under 20	.7	8.0	8.4
20–29	34.0	24.0	27.0
30–39	25.5	24.2	22.2
40–49	17.0	19.0	18.4
50–59	18.3	15.7	15.0
60 and over	4.4	9.2	9.2
Region			
East	0	28.5	26.6
Midwest	0	28.1	27.1
South	0	27.9	28.6
West	100.0	15.6	17.8
Race			
White	66.8	86.1	88.9
Black	17.8	8.1	11.2
Other	15.5	5.0	
Education			
Less than HS	4.9	21.3	27.2
High school	27.1	33.5	39.5
Some college	32.9	24.1	16.3
College	11.9	10.1	16.9
Graduate	23.1	10.8	
Marital status			
Married	60.8	69.4	65.3
Never married	39.2	19.2	22.5
Divorced	13.8	6.5	
Widowed	2.5	3.2	12.2
Separated	2.8	1.7	
Number of children			
None	50.2	41.3	NA*
One	21.4	19.9	NA
Two	17.3	20.1	NA

Variable	1976 Alameda Sample	1978 National Sample	Recent BLS Data
Three	7.4	11.0	NA
Four or more	3.7	7.8	NA
Occupation			
Prof-Tech	23.2	19.1	15.1
Managerial	9.9	12.6	10.8
Clerical	38.5	6.6	17.9
Sales & other	.1	6.8	6.2
Crafts	10.6	25.5	13.3
Non-farm labor	3.3	17.6	5.1
Operatives	2.6		14.9
Services	11.8	10.4	13.6
Farm	0	1.4	3.0
Family income			
Under $4,999	3.6	6.9	NA
$5,000–9,999	20.7	15.8	NA
$10,000–14,999	21.2	21.2	NA
$15,000–19,999	18.6	20.8	NA
$20,000–24,999	17.7	14.5	NA
$25,000 plus	18.2	20.8	NA

*Data not available.

Note: Data sets were not always comparable. In come cases the percentages of subcategories were interpolated to approximate comparability.

Sources: Recent Bureau of Labor Statistics data cited from *1978 Employment and Training Report of the President*, pp. 202, 233–34, 247; "Employment Situation: August 1978," News Release; and *Statistical Abstracts of the United States*, 1976, p. 11.

TABLE A.2

Generalized Time-Income Tradeoff Preferences by Selected Social Characteristics, 1978 (percentage breakdown)

Social Characteristics	More Work, More Pay	Same Work, Same Pay	Less Work, Less Pay	Correlation (Pearson r)	Number of Respondents
Total	28.0	60.7	11.3	NA*	949
Occupation				NA	
Prof-tech	25.7	61.5	12.8		179
Managerial	30.5	56.8	12.7		118
Clerical-sales	33.1	55.6	11.3		124
Skilled labor	23.0	64.9	12.1		239
Operatives-laborers	28.3	62.7	9.0		166
Service	35.7	54.1	10.2		98
Farm	23.1	69.2	7.7		13
Education				.0501 (s = .12)	
Some H.S. or less	32.5	61.6	5.9		203
High school degree	26.6	59.5	13.9		316
Some college	30.1	56.8	12.3		227
College degree	20.8	63.5	15.6		96
Some graduate school	23.0	69.0	8.0		100
Total family income				.1096 (s = .00)	
Under $4,999	41.3	49.2	9.5		63
$5,000–$9,999	30.3	57.9	11.7		145
$10,000–$14,999	29.5	62.2	8.3		193
$15,000–$19,999	30.4	58.1	11.5		191
$20,000–$24,999	21.5	66.9	11.5		130
$25,000–$34,999	16.8	68.2	15.0		107
Over $34,999	23.5	62.4	14.1		85

Social Characteristics	More Work, More Pay	Same Work, Same Pay	Less Work, Less Pay	Correlation (Pearson r)	Number of Respondents
Union affiliation				NA	
Member	25.7	64.9	9.4		202
Non-member	28.6	59.6	11.8		735
Form of payment for work				NA	
Wage	29.0	60.3	10.7		448
Salary	27.2	62.9	9.9		342
Other	26.6	57.8	15.6		154
Hours worked weekly				.0325 (s = .16)	
Under 34	30.5	57.4	12.2		197
35 – 39	32.0	58.0	10.0		100
40 – 44	27.7	63.2	9.2		437
Over 44	24.7	60.0	15.3		215
Major activity of spouse					
Men					
Not married	30.9	51.5	17.6		136
Working full time	28.0	63.1	8.9		157
Working part time	30.9	54.4	14.7		68
Unemployed & off job	26.5	58.8	14.7		34
Keeping house	23.3	69.9	6.8		206
Women					
Not married	39.1	55.7	5.2		115
Working full time	24.4	62.8	12.8		180
Working part time	36.4	36.4	27.3		11
Unemployed & off job	6.6	60.0	33.3		15
Keeping house	23.1	61.5	15.4		13
Sex				-.0892 (s = .81)	
Men	27.5	61.3	11.1		610
Women	28.9	59.6	11.5		339

Marital status		NA			
Single	35.7		12.1	52.2	182
Married	24.1		11.6	64.3	655
Div-sep-widowed	39.3		7.5	53.3	107
Number of dependents		−.0253 (s = .44)			
None	27.4		14.6	57.9	390
One	26.6		10.1	63.3	188
Two	33.2		5.3	61.6	190
Three	25.0		8.7	66.3	104
Four or more	25.6		14.9	59.5	74
Age of youngest child		−.0235 (s = .50)			
No children	29.5		15.0	55.5	366
Under 5 years	30.6		9.7	59.7	196
5 – 9 years	26.6		8.1	65.3	124
10 – 14 years	28.0		12.7	59.3	118
Over 14 years	25.2		4.5	70.3	111
Age		.1016 (s = .00)			
Under 25	40.3		9.4	50.3	171
25 – 34	27.6		14.0	58.4	257
35 – 49	28.4		10.9	60.7	285
50 – 64	11.6		10.4	71.0	221
Over 64	23.1		7.7	69.2	13
Race		NA			
White	26.1		12.2	61.7	812
Nonwhite	39.4		6.1	54.5	132

Question: "Some people would like to work more hours a week if they could be paid for it. Others would prefer to work fewer hours per week even if they earned less. How do you feel about this? Assuming that there would be no special rates for longer hours, place a mark in the box next to the answer which best reflects your feelings: (Options noted in above table)."

*Data not applicable.

Source: 1978 national survey.

TABLE A.3

Multiple Regression of Selected Predictor Variables on General Tradeoff Preferences within Selected Subsamples

Independent Variables (Predictors)	All Workers Standardized Regression Coefficients (Beta wts.)	Zero-Order Correlations (Pearson r)	Workers By Sex		Workers By Family Cycle Stage		
			Men (Beta wts.)	Women (Beta wts.)	No Children (Beta wts.)	Children under 14 (Beta wts.)	Children over 14 (Beta wts.)
Race (dummy)	-.1134*	-.1116	-.1070*	-.1188**	-.1389*	-.0943**	.1312
Socioeconomic group (SES)	.0960*	.0802	.0317*	.1676*	.1085*	.0972*	.0278*
Age (V94)	.0847*	.1589	.2085*	-.0717*	.1182*	.0247*	.2431*
Hours worked weekly (V18)	.0590*	.1036	.1127*	.0211*	-.1378*	.0448*	-.1354*
Family cycle stage (FACYCLE)	-.0404*	-.0348	-.1408*	.0501*	—	—	—
Sex (dummy)	.0383*	NA	—	—	-.0228*	.1436*	-.2975*
Union affiliation (dummy)	.0248*	.0070	.0257*	.0407*	.1112*	-.0431*	.0160**
			480				
			615				
			426				
			1				

All Workers
Multiple R = .1896
Multiple R² = .0360
Adjusted R² = .0280
Significance = .01

Men Workers
Multiple R = .2537
Multiple R² = .0644
Adjusted R² = .0540
Significance = .01

Women Workers
Multiple R = .2480
Multiple R² = .0615
Adjusted R² = .0426
Significance = .01

Workers with No Children
Multiple R = .2866
Multiple R² = .0822
Adjusted R² = .0651
Significance = .01

Workers with Children Under 14
Multiple R = .2069
Multiple R² = .0428
Adjusted R² = .0288
Significance = .01

Workers with Children Over 14
Multiple R = .4044
Multiple R² = .1635
Adjusted R² = .1118
Significance = .01

*Unstandardized coefficient greater than twice its standard error
**Unstandardized coefficient greater than 1.5 times its standard error
Source: 1978 national survey

TABLE A.4 (PART 1)

Worker Preferences among Equally Costly Options for Increased Income or Free Time (Percentage breakdown. Cost of all options equal to 2 percent pay increase)

2 Percent Time-Income Tradeoff Options	First Choice	Second Choice	Third Choice	Fourth Choice	Fifth Choice
2 Percent pay increase	35.5	18.0	16.4	16.2	14.8
10 min. reduction of ea. wkday	3.2	8.7	14.2	31.0	42.8
50 min. reduction of 1 wkday/week	17.1	22.0	27.8	23.9	9.0
5 additional days paid vacation	25.7	31.3	24.0	11.4	7.0
Earlier retirement	18.6	20.0	17.7	17.5	26.4
Total	100.0	100.0	100.0	100.0	100.0
Number respondents	950	941	929	920	922

Question: Suppose that your employer gave you a choice of the following options: A. Pay increase of 2 percent (1/50 more than your current income); B. Each workday reduced 10 minutes; C. Shortening of Friday (or any other workday) by 50 minutes; D. 5 additional days (1 workweek) of paid vacation each year; E. Earlier retirement by accumulating 7 days each year until retirement. Mark the answer spaces with the letter of the option which best reflects your own preferences: Which option would be your first choice? ( ) Which option would be your second choice? ( ) Which option would be your third choice? ( ) Which option would be your fourth choice? ( )

189

TABLE A.4 (PART 2)

Worker Preferences among Equally Costly 2 Percent Tradeoff Options by Selected Social Characteristics (first choice percentage breakdown)

Social Characteristics	2 Percent, Pay Raise	10 Minutes Off Each Workday	50 Min. Off 1 Workday Each Week	5 Days Added Vacation	Earlier Retirement	Correlation (Cramer's v)	Number of Respondents
Total	35.5	3.2	17.1	25.7	18.6	NA	950
Occupation						.0874	
Prof-tech	35.4	3.4	11.8	28.7	20.8		178
Managerial	26.1	2.5	20.2	34.5	16.8		119
Clerical-sales	33.1	4.0	21.0	26.6	15.3		124
Skilled labor	34.6	3.3	17.5	24.6	20.0		240
Operatives-laborers	40.0	3.6	18.2	21.8	16.4		165
Service	42.9	2.0	15.3	20.4	19.4		98
Farm	53.8	0	15.4	7.7	23.1		13
Education						.1221	
Some H.S. or less	43.8	3.5	14.9	13.4	24.4		201
High school degree	31.2	2.8	19.6	28.7	17.7		317
Some college	34.7	3.9	18.9	27.6	15.4		228
College degree	37.5	3.1	15.6	25.0	18.8		96
Some graduate school	31.7	3.0	11.9	36.6	16.8		101
Total family income						.1093	
Under $4,999	50.0	4.8	11.3	22.6	11.3		62
$5,000–$9,999	41.4	4.8	20.7	24.1	9.0		145
$10,000–$14,999	38.7	2.6	14.4	21.6	22.7		194
$15,000–$19,999	33.0	1.6	17.3	25.1	23.0		191
$20,000–$24,999	28.2	3.1	15.3	35.1	18.3		131
$25,000–$34,999	29.9	2.8	20.6	27.1	19.6		107
Over $34,999	31.0	2.4	14.3	29.8	22.6		84

							N
Union affiliation						.1021	
Member	33.3	3.0	16.4	20.9	26.4		201
Nonmember	35.8	3.1	17.5	27.0	16.6		737
Form of payment of work						.0696	
Wage	35.8	3.1	17.0	24.6	19.5		447
Salary	33.5	2.3	16.9	27.1	20.1		343
Other	38.7	5.2	16.8	25.8	13.5		155
Hours worked weekly						.0941	
Under 34	40.6	4.5	19.3	23.9	11.7		197
35 – 39	42.2	1.0	18.6	24.5	13.7		102
40 – 44	35.8	3.2	14.2	24.1	22.7		436
Over 44	27.0	2.3	20.0	31.2	19.1		215
Major activity of spouse						NA	
Men							
Not married	27.7	3.5	22.6	28.5	17.5		137
Working full time	34.6	2.5	9.6	25.6	27.6		156
Working part time	39.1	4.3	13.0	26.1	17.4		69
Unemployed & off job	32.4	5.9	17.6	20.6	23.5		34
Keeping house	33.0	2.9	11.7	26.7	25.7		206
Women							
Not married	47.8	2.5	13.9	25.2	10.4		115
Working full time	35.0	3.3	25.0	26.7	10.0		180
Working part time	18.2	0	36.4	36.4	9.1		11
Unemployed & off job	60.0	0	13.3	13.3	13.3		15
Keeping house	38.5	0	23.1	15.4	23.1		13
Sex						.1708	
Men	32.7	3.4	14.7	26.0	23.1		611
Women	40.4	2.7	21.2	25.1	10.6		339
Marital status							
Single	39.9	2.2	18.0	30.1	9.8		183
Married	34.2	3.2	16.2	25.6	20.8		655
Div-sep-widowed	36.4	4.7	20.6	19.6	18.7		107

Social Characteristics	2 Percent Pay Raise	10 Minutes Off Each Workday	50 Min. Off 1 Workday Each Week	5 Days Added Vacation	Earlier Retirement	Correlation (Cramer's v)	Number of Respondents
Number of dependents						.0910	
None	36.2	1.8	17.9	25.9	18.2		390
One	37.2	2.7	17.6	27.1	15.2		188
Two	35.3	4.2	12.1	25.8	22.6		190
Three	36.2	4.8	12.4	29.5	17.1		105
Four or more	27.0	6.8	29.7	16.2	20.3		74
Age of youngest child						.0846	
No children	38.3	1.9	16.4	26.0	17.5		366
Under 5 years	38.3	3.1	15.8	28.6	14.3		196
5–9 years	31.0	2.4	16.7	27.8	22.2		126
10–14 years	31.4	7.6	22.0	25.4	13.6		118
Over 14 years	33.6	4.5	14.5	20.0	27.3		110
Age						.1407	
Under 25	41.5	2.7	17.5	31.0	7.0		171
25–34	33.8	2.3	18.9	29.6	15.4		260
35–49	28.3	4.9	18.4	26.5	21.9		283
50–64	39.8	2.3	14.0	16.3	27.6		221
Over 64	69.2	0	0	23.1	7.7		13
Race						.0856	
White	33.6	3.3	17.0	27.8	18.3		813
Nonwhite	46.2	2.3	16.7	13.6	21.2		132

Question: Suppose that your employer gave you a choice of the following options: A. Pay increase of 2 percent (1/50 more than your current income); B. Each workday reduced 10 minutes; C. Shortening of Friday (or any other workday) by 50 minutes; D. 5 additional days (1 workweek) of paid vacation each year; E. Earlier retirement by accumulating 7 days each year until retirement. Mark the answer spaces with the letter of the option which best reflects your own preferences: Which option would be your first choice? ( ) Which option would be your second choice? ( ) Which option would be your third choice? ( ) Which option would be your fourth choice? ( )

TABLE A.5

Worker Preferences toward Pay Raise-Reduced Workweek Tradeoff Options by Selected Social Characteristics (percentage breakdowns)

Social Characteristics	10% Pay Raise	6% Raise & 1-2/3 Hrs. Off Wkweek	3% Raise & 2-4/5 Hrs. Off Wkweek	No Raise & 4 Hours Off Wkweek	Correlation (Pearson r)	Number of Respondents
Total	56.5	15.4	5.3	22.8	NA*	952
Socioeconomic group (SES)					.0374 (s = .13)	
Lower class	64.2	15.6	2.8	17.4		109
Lower middle class	53.0	21.5	5.0	20.5		298
Middle class	54.3	13.3	5.9	26.5		392
Upper middle class plus	64.3	7.7	5.6	22.4		143
Major activity of spouse					NA	
Men						
Not married	48.9	14.6	7.3	29.2		137
Working	61.7	11.9	5.3	21.1		227
Unemployed & off job	52.9	11.8	11.8	23.5		34
Keeping house & other	63.9	12.2	3.9	20.0		205
Women					NA	
Not married	55.2	20.7	1.7	22.4		116
Working	50.3	21.5	5.8	22.5		191
Unemployed & off job	40.0	20.0	6.7	33.3		15
Keeping house & other	61.5	15.4	7.7	15.4		13
Sex					NA	
Men	59.0	12.4	5.7	22.9		612
Women	52.1	20.9	4.4	22.6		340

193

Social Characteristics	10% Pay Raise	6% Raise & 1-2/3 Hrs. Off Wkweek	3% Raise & 2-4/5 Hrs. Off Wkweek	No Raise & 4 Hours Off Wkweek	Correlation (Pearson r)	Number of Respondents
Marital status					NA	
Single	53.6	20.2	7.1	19.1		183
Married	58.5	14.5	4.9	22.1		656
Div-sep-widowed	48.1	13.9	4.6	33.3		108
Family cycle stage (FACYCLE)					-.0484	
Single	53.7	18.1	7.4	20.7	$(s = .08)$	188
Couple without children	49.0	12.6	6.6	31.8		151
Young children	58.9	16.5	3.8	20.8		423
Children over age 14	61.9	9.5	7.6	21.0		105
Age					.0449	
Under 25	53.8	22.8	9.9	13.5	$(s = .17)$	171
25-34	58.5	15.0	3.8	22.7		260
35-49	54.9	13.7	4.9	26.4		284
50-64	57.2	13.5	4.1	25.2		222
Over 64	69.2	0	0	30.8		13
Racial-ethnic group					NA	
White	56.6	14.1	5.0	24.3		815
Nonwhite	56.8	23.5	6.1	13.6		132

Question: Which one of the following choices between a pay raise and a shorter workweek would you select?
(A) 10 percent raise and no reduction of each workweek, (B) 6 percent pay raise and a 1.6-hour reduction of each workweek, (C) 3 percent pay raise and a 2.8-hour reduction of each workweek, (D) No pay raise and a 4-hour reduction of each workweek.
*Data not applicable
Source: 1978 national survey

TABLE A.6

Worker Preferences toward Pay Raise–Added Vacation Tradeoff Options by Selected Social Characteristics (percentage breakdowns)

Social Characteristics	10% Pay Raise	6% Raise & 10 Days Added Vac.	3% Raise & 17½ Days Added Vac.	No Raise & 25 Days Added Vac.	Correlation (Pearson r)	Number of Respondents
Total	34.4	31.8	4.5	29.6		954
Socioeconomic group (SES)					.0033 (s = .46)	
Lower class	46.4	23.6	3.6	26.4		110
Lower middle class	29.3	34.4	6.4	29.4		299
Middle class	33.4	30.4	3.6	32.7		392
Upper middle class plus	37.1	35.0	4.2	23.8		143
Major activity of spouse						
Men					NA*	
Not married	29.2	27.0	5.8	38.0		137
Working	37.9	25.1	6.6	30.4		227
Unemployed & off job	29.4	17.6	8.8	4.4		34
Keeping house & other	34.5	33.5	2.4	29.6		206
Women					NA	
Not married	31.9	37.9	2.6	27.6		116
Working	35.4	41.1	3.6	19.8		192
Unemployed & off job	33.3	40.0	6.7	33.3		15
Keeping house & other	38.5	7.7	7.7	46.2		13
Sex					NA	
Men	34.3	28.2	5.1	32.5		613
Women	34.6	38.1	3.5	23.8		341

Social Characteristics	10% Pay Raise	6% Raise & 10 Days Added Vac.	3% Raise & 17½ Days Added Vac.	No Raise & 25 Days Added Vac.	Correlation (Pearson r)	Number of Respondents
Marital status					NA	
Single	28.4	36.1	5.5	30.1		183
Married	35.6	31.6	4.7	28.1		658
Div-sep-widowed	36.1	25.9	1.9	36.1		108
Family cycle stage (FACYCLE)					-.0045	
Single	33.0	32.4	4.8	29.8	(s = .45)	188
Couple without children	39.5	21.7	3.3	35.5		152
Young children	35.9	34.8	4.5	24.8		423
Children over age 14	29.5	28.6	6.7	35.2		105
Age					-.0087	
Under 25	24.0	41.5	5.8	28.7	(s = .79)	171
25–34	33.1	36.2	4.6	26.2		260
35–49	35.1	32.3	4.2	28.4		285
50–64	40.8	20.6	4.0	34.5		223
Over 64	69.2	0	0	30.8		13
Racial-ethnic group					NA	
White	33.5	31.6	4.3	30.6		817
Nonwhite	39.4	33.3	6.1	21.2		132

Question: Which one of the following choices between a pay raise and a longer paid vacation would you select? (A) 10 percent pay and no added vacation time; (B) 6 percent pay raise and 10 workdays of added vacation; (C) 3 percent pay raise and 17.5 workdays added vacation; (D) No pay raise and 25 workdays added vacation.
*Data not applicable
Source: 1978 National Survey

TABLE A.7

Worker Preferences toward Pay Raise-Sabbatical Tradeoff Options by Selected Social Characteristics (percentage breakdowns)

Social Characteristics	10% Pay Raise	6% Raise & 70 Days Leave	3% Raise & 105 Days Leave	No Raise & 150 Days Leave	Correlation (Pearson r)	Number of Respondents
Total	34.7	34.2	8.1	23.0	NA*	949
Socioeconomic group (SES)					.0407 (s = .11)	
Lower class	45.9	24.8	12.8	16.5		109
Lower middle class	32.6	36.6	8.1	22.8		298
Middle class	33.2	34.8	6.9	25.1		391
Upper middle class plus	34.8	34.0	7.8	23.4		141
Major activity of spouse					NA	
Men						
Not married	27.7	28.5	10.2	33.6		137
Working	35.7	33.9	7.5	22.9		227
Unemployed & off job	23.5	26.5	11.8	38.2		34
Keeping house & other	29.7	29.4	7.4	23.5		204
Women					NA	
Not married	34.8	13.9	9.6	35.2		115
Working	35.1	46.1	7.3	11.5		191
Unemployed & off job	33.3	46.7	6.7	13.3		15
Keeping house & other	46.2	23.1	0	30.8		13
Sex					NA	
Men	34.4	30.5	8.4	26.7		610
Women	35.1	-1.0	7.7	16.2		337

Social Characteristics	10% Pay Raise	5% Raise & 60 Days Leave	3% Raise & 105 Days Leave	No Raise & 150 Days Leave	Correlation (Pearson r)	Number of Respondents
Marital status					NA	
Single	30.8	33.5	11.0	24.7		182
Married	35.7	35.4	7.5	21.4		655
Div-sep-widowed	35.6	28.0	6.5	30.8		107
Family cycle stage (FACYCLE)					-.0279 (s = .20)	
Single	33.7	32.1	8.6	25.7		187
Couple without children	41.3	24.7	6.7	27.3		150
Young children	36.3	37.7	7.3	18.7		422
Children over age 14	33.7	30.8	8.7	26.9		104
Age					-.0073 (s = .82)	
Under 25	26.9	42.7	13.5	17.0		171
25 – 34	33.6	37.8	6.9	22.0		259
35 – 49	32.7	33.8	8.1	25.4		284
50 – 64	43.9	25.3	5.0	25.8		221
Over 64	41.7	16.7	16.7	25.0		12
Racial-ethnic group					NA	
White	34.2	34.6	7.6	23.6		813
Nonwhite	37.4	33.6	11.5	17.6		131

Question: What is your choice between a pay raise and an extended leave with pay from work after six years of work? (A) 10 percent pay raise and no leave time; (B) 6 percent pay raise and 12 workweeks' (60 workdays') paid leave; (C) 3 percent pay raise and 21 workweeks' (105 workdays') paid leave; (D) No pay raise and 30 workweeks' (150 workdays') paid leave.

*Data not applicable

Source: 1978 national survey

TABLE A.8

Worker Preferences toward Pay Raise–Earlier Retirement Tradeoff Options by Selected Social Characteristics (percentage breakdowns)

Social Characteristics	10% Pay Raise	6% Raise & 10 Days Ea. Retirmt.	3% Raise & 17½ Days Ea. Retirmt.	No Raise & 25 Days Ea. Retirmt.	Correlation (Pearson r)	Number of Respondents
Total	48.6	19.3	8.3	23.7	-.0590 (s = .04)	952
Socioeconomic group (SES)						
Lower class	47.3	23.6	6.4	22.7		110
Lower middle class	44.3	19.9	9.8	26.0		296
Middle class	50.4	16.5	7.6	25.4		393
Upper middle class plus	55.2	21.7	7.7	15.4		143
Major activity of spouse						
Men						
Not married	51.5	14.7	11.0	22.8	NA*	136
Working	53.1	13.3	6.2	27.4		226
Unemployed & off job	35.3	8.8	20.6	35.3		34
Keeping house & other	46.4	19.8	7.2	26.6		207
Women						
Not married	48.7	22.6	6.1	22.6	NA	115
Working	48.4	26.0	9.9	15.6		192
Unemployed & off job	33.3	33.3	6.7	26.7		15
Keeping house & other	38.5	23.1	7.7	30.8		13
Sex						
Men	49.0	16.3	8.3	26.3	NA	612
Women	47.9	24.7	8.2	19.1		340

Social Characteristics	10% Pay Raise	6% Raise & 10 Days Ea. Retirmt.	3% Raise & 17½ Days Ea. Retirmt.	No Raise & 25 Days Ea. Retirmt.	Correlation (Pearson r)	Number of Respondents
Marital status						
Single	56.9	18.2	9.9	14.9	NA	181
Married	47.1	20.1	8.2	24.6		658
Div-sep-widowed	43.5	17.6	6.5	32.4		108
Family cycle stage (FACYCLE)						
Single	54.3	22.0	6.5	17.2	.0597 (s = .04)	186
Couple without children	49.7	13.1	7.2	30.1		153
Young children	46.9	22.3	8.3	22.5		422
Children over age 14	48.6	16.7	6.7	28.6		105
Age						
Under 25	51.2	24.7	14.7	9.4	.1127 (s = .00)	170
25–34	50.6	22.0	8.1	19.3		259
35–49	44.4	18.0	7.7	29.9		284
50–64	46.9	15.2	4.9	33.3		224
Over 64	92.3	0	0	7.7		13
Racial-ethnic group						
White	48.5	18.8	7.8	24.9	NA	816
Nonwhite	49.6	22.1	11.5	16.8		131

Question: What is your choice between a pay raise and earlier retirement? (A) 10 percent pay raise and no change in retirement plan; (B) 6 percent pay raise, and 10 workdays' earlier retirement for each future year of work; (C) 3 percent pay raise and 17.5 workdays' earlier retirement for each future year of work; (D) No pay raise and 25 workdays' earlier retirement for each future year of work.

*Data not applicable

Source: 1978 national survey

TABLE A.9

Maximum Portion of 10-Percent Pay Raise That Workers State Willingness to Forego for Any of Five Alternative Forms of Free Time by Selected Social Characteristics (percentage breakdowns)

Social Characteristics	Nothing for Free Time	40% of Pay Raise for Free Time	70% of Pay Raise for Free Time	100% of Pay Raise for Free Time	Correlation (Pearson r)	Number of Respondents
Total	15.6	25.4	11.6	47.3	NA	955
Occupation					NA	
Prof-tech	15.6	25.0	10.6	48.9		180
Managerial	20.2	26.9	9.2	43.7		119
Clerical-sales	11.1	30.2	13.5	45.2		126
Skilled labor	15.8	21.7	11.3	51.3		240
Operatives-laborers	15.1	25.9	10.2	48.8		166
Service	17.3	25.5	18.4	38.8		98
Farm	7.7	30.8	7.7	53.8		13
Education					-.0399	
Some H.S. or less	19.7	18.7	13.3	48.3	(s = .11)	203
High school degree	14.2	25.2	10.1	50.6		318
Some college	14.4	25.8	13.5	46.3		229
College degree	12.5	37.5	8.3	41.7		96
Some graduate school	18.6	27.5	9.8	44.1		102
Total family income					.0571	
Under $4,999	19.0	25.4	11.1	44.4	(s = .04)	63
$5,000–$9,999	19.3	24.1	13.8	42.8		145
$10,000–$14,999	14.4	30.3	11.3	44.1		195
$15,000–$19,999	13.1	27.7	12.0	47.1		191
$20,000–$24,999	11.3	20.3	9.8	58.6		133
$25,000–$34,999	17.8	20.6	14.0	47.7		107
Over $34,999	15.3	24.7	8.2	51.8		85

Social Characteristics	Nothing for Free Time	40% of Pay Raise for Free Time	70% of Pay Raise for Free Time	100% of Pay Raise for Free Time	Correlation (Pearson r)	Number of Respondents
Union affiliation					NA	
Member	14.4	23.8	9.4	52.5		202
Nonmember	15.7	25.9	12.3	46.2		741
Form of payment for work					NA	
Wage	12.9	26.3	12.2	48.6		449
Salary	17.7	27.8	10.1	44.3		345
Other	17.9	17.3	13.5	51.3		156
Hours worked weekly					.0076	
Under 34	13.1	25.3	12.6	49.0	$(s = .41)$	198
35–39	16.7	35.2	14.7	33.3		102
40–44	16.2	25.1	12.3	46.3		438
Over 44	16.1	21.7	7.8	54.4		217
Major activity of spouse					NA	
Men						
Not married	13.9	17.5	14.6	54.0		137
Working full-time	17.1	24.1	7.6	51.3		158
Working part-time	23.2	21.7	11.6	43.5		69
Unemployed & off job	17.6	5.9	14.7	61.8		34
Keeping house & other	15.9	27.5	7.2	49.3		207
Women					NA	
Not married	16.4	25.0	14.7	44.0		116
Working full-time	13.3	33.7	16.0	37.0		181
Working part-time	9.1	45.5	9.1	36.4		11
Unemployed & off job	13.3	20.0	20.0	46.7		15
Keeping house & other	7.7	23.1	7.7	61.5		13
Sex					NA	
Men	16.4	22.8	9.8	51.0		614
Women	14.1	30.2	15.0	40.8		341

						N
Marital status					NA	
Single	14.2	23.0	18.0	44.8		183
Married	15.5	27.2	10.3	47.0		659
Div-sep-widowed	18.5	8.5	9.3	53.7		108
Number of dependents					-.0316 (s = .17)	
None	16.5	21.4	12.7	49.4		393
One	15.9	26.5	9.5	48.1		189
Two	16.2	25.7	12.6	45.5		191
Three	13.3	33.3	11.4	41.9		105
Four or more	12.2	32.4	9.5	45.9		74
Age of youngest child					.0220 (s = .25)	
No children	16.5	22.5	10.8	50.1		369
Under 5 years	16.3	33.2	11.2	39.3		196
5–9 years	15.7	29.9	10.2	44.1		127
10–14 years	12.7	22.0	12.7	52.5		118
Over 14 years	14.4	22.5	14.4	43.6		111
Age					.0098 (s = .38)	
Under 25	10.5	28.1	22.2	34.2		171
25–34	14.2	31.9	8.5	45.4		260
35–49	15.1	22.1	11.6	51.2		285
50–64	20.5	21.0	8.0	50.4		224
Over 64	38.5	7.7	0	53.8		13
Race					NA	
White	14.5	25.8	10.6	49.0		818
Nonwhite	22.0	21.2	18.2	35.6		132

Note: Maximum potential income-time tradeoff choice determined by computation of a composite variable (MAXTRD1) which reports the highest proportion of a potential 10-percent pay raise that each respondent states a willingness to exchange for any of five forms of potential gains of free time. For example, a respondent who states a desire to exchange 70 percent of a 10-percent pay raise for a shorter workday, 40 percent of the raise for a reduced workweek, 40 percent for added vacation, 40 percent for an extended paid leave of absence (sabbatical), and no portion of the pay raise for earlier retirement would have a maximum potential tradeoff (MAXTRD1) score of 70 percent of pay raise because the shorter workday choice elicited the highest exchange of all the available choices.

*Data not applicable

Source: 1978 national survey

TABLE A.10

Worker Preferences among Graduated Tradeoffs between Current Income and Shorter Workdays by Social Characteristics (percentage breakdowns)

Social Characteristics	Nothing	2% of Pay for 10 Min. Off Wkday	5% of Pay for 25 Min. Off Wkday	12% of Pay for 1 Hour Off Wkday	30% of Pay for 2½ Hrs. Off Wkday	50% of Pay for 4 Hrs. Off Wkday	Correlation (Pearson r)	Number of Respondents
Total	77.0	8.7	5.8	5.5	1.6	1.5	NA* NA	954
Occupation								
Prof-tech	77.8	6.1	6.1	6.7	2.8	.6		180
Managerial	80.7	5.9	5.0	4.2	1.7	2.5		191
Clerical-sales	78.6	7.1	4.0	10.3	0	0		126
Skilled labor	75.8	11.3	5.0	4.6	1.7	1.7		240
Operatives-laborers	73.9	9.1	8.5	4.8	1.8	1.8		165
Service	72.4	13.3	7.1	3.1	1.0	3.1		98
Farm	100.0	0	0	0	0	0		13
Education								
Some H.S. or less	72.8	12.9	5.9	5.0	1.0	2.5	-.0544 (s = .09)	202
High school degree	75.8	10.4	5.7	4.4	1.9	1.9		318
Some college	78.6	5.2	6.1	7.4	1.8	.9		229
College degree	80.2	7.3	4.2	7.3	1.0	0		96
Some graduate school	84.3	4.9	3.9	3.9	2.0	1.0		102
Total family income								
Under $4,999	77.4	9.6	3.2	4.8	0	4.8	.0600 (s = .07)	62
$5,000–$9,999	76.6	11.0	5.5	4.8	.7	1.4		145
$10,000–$14,999	79.5	6.2	6.7	5.1	1.5	1.0		195
$15,000–$19,999	79.6	11.0	5.2	3.1	1.0	0		191
$20,000–$24,999	78.2	8.3	4.5	5.3	2.3	1.5		133
$25,000–$34,999	74.8	6.5	6.5	7.5	2.8	1.9		107
Over $34,999	70.6	4.7	8.2	9.4	3.5	3.5		85

							NA	N
Union affiliation							NA	
Member	77.2	9.9	4.5	6.4	.5	1.5		202
Nonmember	77.0	8.5	6.1	5.1	1.9	1.4		740
Form of payment for work							NA	
Wage	72.8	10.3	6.9	6.5	1.6	2.0		448
Salary	83.2	6.7	4.6	3.5	1.4	.6		345
Other	75.0	9.0	5.0	7.0	2.0	2.0		156
Hours worked weekly							NA	
Under 34	70.7	8.1	8.1	6.1	4.5	2.5		198
35–39	76.5	11.3	3.9	4.9	0	2.9		102
40–44	78.5	9.2	5.9	5.0	.9	.5		437
Over 44	80.2	6.9	4.1	6.0	.9	1.8		217
Major activity of spouse							NA	
Men								
Not married	74.5	8.0	8.8	5.8	.7	2.2		137
Working full-time	82.3	5.1	1.9	7.0	1.3	2.5		158
Working part-time	76.8	11.6	5.8	2.5	1.4	1.4		69
Unemployed & off job	73.5	17.6	8.8	0	0	0		34
Keeping house	81.2	5.8	5.8	5.3	1.0	1.0		207
Women								
Not married	76.5	9.6	6.1	4.3	1.7	1.7		115
Working full-time	71.3	10.5	7.7	6.1	3.3	1.1		181
Working part-time	72.7	18.2	0	0	9.1	0		11
Unemployed & off job	86.7	6.7	0	6.7	0	0		15
Keeping house	69.2	15.4	7.7	7.7	0	0		13
Sex							NA	
Men	78.8	7.8	5.4	5.4	1.0	1.6		614
Women	73.8	10.3	6.5	5.6	2.6	1.2		340
Marital status							NA	
Single	73.8	8.2	9.8	6.0	1.1	1.1		183
Married	77.7	9.0	5.0	5.2	1.8	1.4		659
Div-sep-widowed	79.4	8.4	3.7	4.7	.9	2.8		107

Social Characteristics	Nothing	2% of Pay for 10 Min. Off Wkday	5% of Pay for 25 Min. Off Wkday	12% of Pay for 1 Hour Off Wkday	30% of Pay for 2½ Hrs. Off Wkday	50% of Pay for 4 Hrs. Off Wkday	Correlation (Pearson r)	Number of Respondents
Number of dependents								
None	74.0	7.9	6.9	6.6	2.3	2.3	−.0709 (s = .03)	392
One	78.3	9.0	4.2	6.3	1.1	1.1		189
Two	81.2	7.9	6.3	3.1	.5	1.0		191
Three	81.9	10.5	1.9	4.8	0	1.0		105
Four or more	73.0	10.8	8.1	4.1	4.1	0		74
Age of youngest child								
No children	74.7	7.6	6.3	7.1	1.9	2.4	−.0567 (s = .09)	368
Under 5 years	83.2	5.1	5.6	3.6	2.0	.5		196
5 – 9 years	73.2	12.6	10.2	3.1	.8	0		127
10 – 14 years	74.6	11.0	2.5	7.6	1.7	2.5		118
Over 14 years	81.1	10.8	2.7	4.5	0	.9		111
Age								
Under 25	71.9	7.6	10.5	7.0	1.8	1.2	−.0322 (s = .32)	171
25 – 34	78.5	9.2	6.2	3.8	1.2	1.2		260
35 – 49	76.1	10.2	4.9	6.3	1.4	1.1		284
50 – 64	81.3	7.1	2.7	4.9	2.2	1.8		224
Over 64	61.5	7.7	7.7	7.7	0	15.4		13
Race								
White	86.1	8.6	5.8	5.5	1.7	1.2	NA	817
Nonwhite	77.3	9.8	5.3	3.8	.8	3.0		132

Question: What is the largest portion of your current yearly income that you would be willing to give up for shorter workdays? Just call off the number that applies: (A) Nothing; (B) 2 percent (1/50) of your income for 10 minutes off each workday; (C) 5 percent (1/20) of your income for 25 minutes off each workday; (D) 12 percent (1/8) of your income for 1 hour off each workday; (E) 30 percent (3/10) of your income for 2.5 hours off each workday; (F) 50 percent (1/2) of your income for 4 hours off each workday.

*Data not applicable

Source: 1978 national survey

TABLE A.11

Multiple Regression of Selected Predictor Variables on Worker Tradeoff Preferences between Current Income and Shorter Workdays

Independent Variables (Predictors)	Standardized Regression Coefficients	Zero-Order Correlations (Pearson r)
Family cycle stage (FACYCLE)	-.0876*	-.1007
Hours worked weekly (V18)	-.0872*	-.0968
Age (V94)	-.0292*	-.0497
Race (dummy)	.0257*	.0216
Socioeconomic group (SES)	.0248*	.0044
Sex (dummy)	.0102*	.0492
Union affiliation (dummy)	-.0063**	-.0230

Multiple R = .1415.
Multiple R² = .0200.
Adjusted R² = .0119.
Significance = .025.
*Unstandardized coefficient greater than twice its standard error.
**Unstandardized coefficient greater than 1.5 times its standard error.
Source: 1978 national survey.

207

TABLE A.12

Worker Preferences toward Current Income-Reduced Workweek Tradeoff Options by Selected Social Characteristics (percentage breakdowns)

Social Characteristics	Nothing for Reduced Week	2% of Pay for 50 Min. Off Wkweek	10% of Pay for 4 Hrs. Off Wkweek	20% of Pay for 1 Day Off Wkweek	40% of Pay for 2 Days Off Wkweek	50% of Pay for 2½ Days Off Wkweek	Correlation (Pearson r)	Number of Respondents
Total	73.8	11.6	7.6	4.5	.9	1.6	NA*	953
Occupation							NA	
Prof-tech	67.6	11.2	10.6	10.1	.6	0		179
Managerial	80.7	8.4	5.9	1.7	0	3.4		119
Clerical-sales	75.4	12.7	4.8	5.6	.8	.8		126
Skilled labor	73.3	13.8	6.3	3.8	1.3	1.7		240
Operatives-laborers	70.9	11.5	10.9	3.0	1.2	2.4		165
Service	74.5	12.2	7.1	2.0	2.0	2.0		98
Farm	92.3	7.7	0	0	0	0		13
Education							−.0101 (s = .38)	
Some H.S. or less	74.8	9.4	8.4	3.5	1.0	3.0		202
High school degree	75.5	12.6	6.0	2.5	1.3	2.2		318
Some college	71.5	12.7	7.9	6.1	.9	.9		228
College degree	71.9	14.6	6.3	6.3	1.0	0		96
Some graduate school	74.5	8.8	9.8	6.9	0	0		102
Total family income							.1105 (s = .16)	
Under $4,999	74.2	6.5	6.5	6.5	3.2	3.2		62
$5,000 – $9,999	73.8	12.5	7.6	4.1	1.4	1.4		145
$10,000 – $14,999	77.8	11.3	5.7	2.6	.5	2.1		194
$15,000 – $19,999	77.0	13.1	5.2	3.7	0	1.0		191
$20,000 – $24,999	70.7	14.3	6.8	4.5	2.3	1.5		133
$25,000 – $34,999	70.1	10.3	11.2	6.5	0	1.9		107
Over $34,999	64.7	10.6	14.1	8.2	1.2	1.2		85

							N	
Union affiliation								NA
Member	75.7	9.9	7.4	4.0	1.0	2.0	202	
Nonmember	73.2	12.2	7.7	4.6	1.0	13.5	739	
Hours worked weekly								$-.0978$ (s = .00)
Under 34	67.6	10.6	8.6	8.1	1.5	3.5	198	
35–39	70.6	16.7	2.0	5.9	2.0	2.9	102	
40–44	76.9	11.7	7.6	2.7	.5	.7	437	
Over 44	74.5	10.2	9.3	4.2	.9	.9	216	
Major activity of spouse								
Men								NA
Not married	67.2	14.6	6.6	7.3	1.5	2.9	137	
Working full time	79.1	8.2	8.2	1.3	.6	2.5	158	
Working part time	71.0	14.5	8.7	5.8	0	0	69	
Unemployed & off job	76.5	11.8	8.8	2.9	0	0	34	
Keeping house & other	81.1	7.8	6.8	2.4	.5	1.5	206	
Women								NA
Not married	75.7	12.2	3.5	7.0	.9	.9	115	
Working full time	63.5	17.7	9.4	6.6	1.1	1.7	181	
Working part time	81.8	9.1	0	0	9.1	0	11	
Unemployed & off job	80.0	6.7	13.3	0	0	0	15	
Keeping house & other	84.6	0	15.4	0	0	0	13	
Sex								NA
Men	75.7	10.3	7.7	3.8	.8	1.8	613	
Women	70.3	14.1	7.4	5.9	1.2	1.2	340	
Marital status								NA
Single	65.0	16.4	8.2	8.2	1.1	1.1	183	
Married	75.2	10.8	8.1	3.5	.9	1.5	658	
Div-sep-widowed	80.4	9.3	2.8	3.7	.9	2.8	107	
Number of dependents								$-.0887$ (s = .01)
None	69.8	11.5	8.4	6.1	1.5	2.6	391	
One	76.2	11.1	9.0	2.1	.5	1.1	189	

Social Characteristics	Nothing for Reduced Week	2% of Pay for 50 Min. Off Wkweek	10% of Pay for 4 Hrs. Off Wkweek	20% of Pay for 1 Day Off Wkweek	40% of Pay for 2 Days Off Wkweek	50% of Pay for 2½ Days Off Wkweek	Correlation (Pearson r)	Number of Respondents
Two	78.0	11.5	7.3	2.1	.5	.5		191
Three	75.2	12.4	5.7	4.8	0	1.9		105
Four or more	77.0	12.2	2.7	8.1	0	0		74
Age of youngest child							$-.0853$	
No children	70.0	11.7	8.7	5.7	1.6	2.2	$(s = .01)$	367
Under 5 years	77.0	11.2	7.1	2.6	1.0	1.0		196
5–9 years	74.0	13.4	6.3	5.5	0	.8		127
10–14 years	73.7	11.0	9.3	3.4	0	2.5		118
Over 14 years	80.2	10.8	6.3	2.7	0	0		111
Age							$-.0776$	
Under 25	63.2	17.0	9.4	7.0	2.3	1.2	$(s = .01)$	171
25–34	72.3	13.5	9.2	3.1	.8	1.2		260
35–49	75.7	10.6	6.7	5.6	.4	10.6		284
50–64	81.2	7.6	5.4	3.1	.9	1.8		223
Over 64	69.2	0	7.7	0	0	23.1		13
Race							NA	
White	73.8	11.6	7.7	4.7	1.0	1.2		816
Nonwhite	75.0	11.4	5.3	3.8	.8	3.8		132

Question: What is the largest portion of your current yearly income that you would be willing to give up for shorter workweeks? (A) Nothing; (B) 2 percent ($\frac{1}{50}$) of your income for 50 minutes off 1 workday a week; (C) 10 percent ($\frac{1}{10}$) of your income for 4 hours off 1 workday a week; (D) 20 percent ($\frac{1}{5}$) of your income for 1 full workday off each week; (E) 40 percent ($\frac{4}{10}$) of your income for 2 full workdays off each week; (F) 50 percent ($\frac{1}{2}$) of your income for 2 full workdays off each week.

*Data not applicable

Source: 1978 national survey

TABLE A.13

Worker Preferences among Graduated Tradeoffs between Current Income and Added Vacation by Social Characteristics (percentage breakdown)

Social Characteristics	Nothing	2% of Pay for 5 Days Vacation	5% of Pay for 12½ Days Vac.	10% of Pay for 25 Days Vacation	20% of Pay for 50 Days Vacation	33% of Pay for 87½ Days Vac.	Correlation (Pearson r)	Number of Respondents
Total	57.9	23.2	8.5	6.2	2.2	2.0	NA*	952
Occupation							NA	
Prof-tech	55.3	24.6	7.8	8.4	1.1	2.8		179
Managerial	63.7	17.6	10.9	.8	3.4	3.4		119
Clerical-sales	56.3	28.6	4.0	6.7	2.4	0		126
Skilled labor	61.1	23.8	7.5	6.3	.8	.4		239
Operatives-laborers	53.9	20.0	13.9	6.7	2.4	3.0		165
Service	49.0	27.6	8.2	5.1	6.1	4.1		98
Farm	92.3	7.7	0	0	0	0		13
Education							.0076 (s = .82)	
Some H.S. or less	63.2	18.4	6.5	7.0	2.0	2.0		201
High school degree	58.2	22.6	8.8	5.3	2.2	2.8		318
Some college	51.3	25.4	11.8	7.0	3.1	1.3		228
College degree	58.3	26.0	6.3	5.2	2.1	2.1		96
Some graduate school	58.8	27.5	4.9	6.9	1.0	1.0		102
Total family income							.0513 (s = .12)	
Under $4,999	59.7	22.6	4.8	3.2	4.8	4.8		62
$5,000–$9,999	57.6	19.4	14.6	3.5	4.2	.7		144
$10,000–$14,999	59.8	25.3	7.2	4.6	1.0	2.1		194
$15,000–$19,999	59.7	26.2	6.3	5.2	1.0	1.6		191
$20,000–$24,999	53.4	27.1	6.0	9.0	2.3	2.3		133
$25,000–$34,999	58.9	17.8	10.3	8.4	2.8	1.9		107
Over $34,999	52.9	22.4	10.6	10.6	1.2	2.4		85

Social Characteristics	Nothing	2% of Pay for 5 Days Vacation	5% of Pay for 12½ Days Vac.	10% of Pay for 25 Days Vacation	20% of Pay for 50 Days Vacation	33% of Pay for 87½ Days Vac.	Correlation (Pearson r)	Number of Respondents
Union affiliation							NA	
Member	62.7	17.4	10.4	5.5	1.0	3.0		201
Nonmember	56.4	24.9	8.1	6.4	2.6	1.6		739
Form of payment for work							NA	
Wage	55.9	23.9	9.8	6.3	2.0	2.0		447
Salary	59.4	24.9	7.0	4.3	2.6	1.7		345
Other	60.0	16.8	8.4	10.3	1.9	2.6		155
Hours worked weekly							-.0757	
Under 34	47.5	26.8	9.6	10.1	2.5	3.5	(s = .02)	198
35–39	61.8	24.5	6.9	6.9	0	0		102
40–44	60.6	21.8	7.8	5.0	2.5	2.3		436
Over 44	60.2	22.2	9.7	4.6	2.3	.9		216
Major activity of spouse							NA	
Men								
Not married	50.4	24.8	10.9	6.6	2.2	5.1		137
Working full-time	62.7	17.7	10.1	5.1	2.5	1.9		158
Working part-time	55.1	30.4	4.3	5.8	2.9	1.4		69
Unemployed & off job	50.0	26.5	11.8	11.8	0	0		34
Keeping house	71.2	15.1	7.3	3.4	2.0	1.0		205
Women								
Not married	54.8	26.1	6.1	7.0	3.5	2.6		115
Working full-time	45.3	33.7	9.9	7.7	1.7	1.7		181
Working part-time	63.6	27.3	0	9.1	0	0		11
Unemployed & off job	80.0	6.7	13.3	0	0	0		15
Keeping house	84.6	7.7	0	7.7	0	0		13
Sex							NA	
Men	61.1	20.3	8.5	5.9	2.1	2.1		612
Women	52.1	28.5	8.5	6.8	2.4	1.8		340

	A	B	C	D	E	F		N
Marital status							NA	
Single	45.4	27.9	13.7	8.7	2.2	2.2		183
Married	60.0	22.8	7.9	5.8	2.1	1.4		657
Div-sep-widowed	66.3	18.7	2.8	3.7	2.8	5.6		107
Number of dependents							−.1116 (s = .00)	
None	54.9	22.6	9.7	7.4	2.1	3.3		390
One	52.4	25.9	10.6	5.8	3.2	2.1		189
Two	62.8	26.2	4.2	4.2	2.1	.5		191
Three	67.6	18.1	8.6	3.8	1.9	0		105
Four or more	63.5	18.9	8.1	8.1	1.4	0		74
Age of youngest child							−.0718 (s = .03)	
No children	54.9	22.7	9.8	7.4	2.2	3.0		366
Under 5 years	58.2	25.0	8.2	5.1	2.6	1.0		196
5–9 years	55.9	27.6	11.0	3.1	2.4	0		127
10–14 years	61.0	22.0	4.2	9.3	2.5	.8		118
Over 14 years	64.9	19.8	7.2	5.4	.9	1.8		111
Age							−.1217 (s = .00)	
Under 25	39.2	35.7	14.0	8.8	1.2	1.2		171
25–34	53.1	25.8	10.8	5.4	2.7	2.3		260
35–49	63.4	20.1	7.0	6.0	2.5	1.1		284
50–64	70.7	15.8	3.6	5.4	2.3	2.3		222
Over 64	61.5	0	7.7	7.7	0	23.1		13
Race							NA	
White	56.9	24.7	8.5	6.3	2.1	1.6		815
Nonwhite	65.2	15.2	6.8	5.3	3.0	4.6		132

Question: What is the largest portion of your current yearly income that you would be willing to give up in exchange for more paid vacation time? Just call off the letter that applies: (A) Nothing; (B) 2 percent (1/50) of your income for 5 workdays' added paid vacation each year; (C) 5 percent (1/20) of your income for 12.5 workdays' added paid vacation each year; (D) 10 percent (1/10) of your income for 25 workdays' added paid vacation each year; (E) 20 percent (1/5) of your income for 50 workdays' (10 workweeks) added paid vacation each year; (F) 33 percent (1/3) of your income for 87.5 workdays (17.5 workweeks) added paid vacation each year.

*Data not applicable

Source: 1978 national survey

TABLE A.14

Worker Preferences among Graduated Tradeoffs between Current Income and Extended Leaves with Pay Every Seventh Year by Social Characteristics (percentage breakdown)

Social Characteristics	Nothing	2% of Pay for 7 Weeks Leave	5% of Pay for 17½ Weeks Leave	10% of Pay for 35 Wks Leave	15% of Pay for 52 Wks Leave	Correlation (Pearson r)	Number of Respondents
Total	57.9	24.4	8.0	4.8	4.8	NA*	951
Occupation						NA	
Prof-tech	53.6	25.1	10.6	6.1	4.5		179
Managerial	61.3	24.4	5.0	3.4	5.9		119
Clerical-sales	57.1	24.6	7.1	7.1	4.0		126
Skilled labor	63.9	21.8	8.0	4.2	2.1		238
Operatives-laborers	55.8	24.2	9.1	4.8	6.1		165
Service	49.0	30.6	7.1	4.1	9.2		98
Farm	76.9	23.1	0	0	0		13
Education						.0455 (s = .16)	
Some H.S. or less	60.2	24.4	8.5	2.5	4.5		201
High school degree	59.7	25.8	4.7	4.4	5.3		318
Some college	53.3	24.2	12.3	5.7	4.4		227
College degree	58.3	22.9	7.3	6.3	5.2		96
Some graduate school	58.8	21.6	6.9	7.8	4.9		102
Total family income						.0513 (s = .12)	
Under $4,999	57.4	23.0	6.6	4.9	8.2		61
$5,000–$9,999	59.0	21.5	10.4	3.5	5.6		144
$10,000–$14,999	62.4	24.7	7.2	3.1	2.6		194
$15,000–$19,999	58.6	26.2	6.8	3.7	4.7		191
$20,000–$24,999	53.4	26.3	5.3	9.0	6.0		133
$25,000–$34,999	59.8	23.4	11.2	3.7	1.9		107
Over $34,999	47.1	23.5	9.4	9.4	10.6		85

Union affiliation							
Member	61.7	21.4	8.5	2.5	6.0	NA	201
Nonmember	57.2	24.9	8.0	5.4	4.5		738
Form of payment for work							
Wage	55.4	26.0	9.4	5.6	3.6	NA	446
Salary	61.2	22.9	6.7	3.2	6.1		345
Other	58.7	23.2	7.1	5.8	5.2		155
Hours worked weekly							
Under 34	49.5	27.3	12.6	4.5	6.1	$-.0626$	198
35 – 39	53.9	27.5	8.8	6.9	2.9	$(s = .05)$	102
40 – 44	61.6	22.1	6.7	4.1	5.5		435
Over 44	58.3	22.6	7.8	7.0	4.3		115
Major activity of spouse							
Men							
Not married	52.2	23.5	13.2	4.4	6.6	NA	136
Working full time	62.7	21.5	5.7	7.6	2.5		158
Working part time	58.0	26.1	2.9	5.8	7.2		69
Unemployed & off job	54.3	30.4	6.5	4.3	4.3		46
Keeping house	71.5	17.1	6.7	2.6	2.1		193
Women							
Not married	50.4	25.2	9.6	7.0	7.8	NA	115
Working full time	47.5	32.0	10.5	3.3	6.6		181
Working part time	54.5	36.4	0	9.1	0		11
Unemployed & off job	69.2	23.1	3.8	3.8	0		26
Keeping house	100.0	0	0	0	0		2
Sex							
Men	61.7	21.9	7.4	4.9	4.1	NA	611
Women	51.2	28.8	5.1	4.7	6.2		340
Marital status							
Single	48.9	23.1	15.4	7.1	5.5	NA	182
Married	60.6	24.5	6.5	4.1	4.3		657
Div-sep-widowed	57.9	26.2	4.7	3.7	7.5		107

Social Characteristics	Nothing	2% of Pay for 7 Weeks Leave	5% of Pay for 17½ Weeks Leave	10% of Pay for 35 Wks Leave	15% of Pay for 52 Wks Leave	Correlation (Pearson r)	Number of Respondents
Number of dependents							
None	57.3	22.1	9.5	4.9	6.2	-.0775 (s = -.02)	389
One	51.9	29.6	7.4	5.3	5.8		189
Two	60.2	24.6	7.3	4.2	3.7		191
Three	64.8	21.9	4.8	6.7	1.9		105
Four or more	62.2	24.3	8.1	2.7	2.7		74
Age of youngest child							
No children	57.0	23.0	9.6	4.9	5.5	-.0401 (s = -.23)	365
Under 5 years	59.2	23.5	9.7	3.1	4.6		196
5 - 9 years	49.6	35.4	5.5	4.7	4.7		127
10 - 14 years	60.2	21.2	3.4	11.0	4.2		118
Over 14 years	64.0	22.5	8.1	2.7	2.7		111
Age							
Under 25	39.4	35.3	14.7	4.7	5.9	-.1621 (s = .00)	170
25 - 34	54.6	24.6	10.0	5.4	5.4		260
35 - 49	60.9	23.6	5.6	6.0	3.9		284
50 - 64	72.1	17.6	3.2	3.2	4.1		222
Over 64	69.2	0	15.4	0	15.4		13
Race							
White	57.5	25.8	7.2	5.0	4.4	NA	814
Nonwhite	62.1	15.9	11.4	3.8	6.8		132

Question: What is the largest portion of your current yearly income that you would be willing to give up in exchange for an extended leave with pay every seventh year? (A) Nothing; (B) 2 percent ($\frac{1}{50}$) of your yearly income for 7 workweeks' paid leave after six years of work; (C) 5 percent ($\frac{1}{20}$) of your yearly income for 17.5 workweeks' of paid leave after six years of work; (D) 10 percent ($\frac{1}{10}$) of your yearly income for 35 workweeks' paid leave after six years of work; (E) 15 percent ($\frac{3}{20}$) of your yearly income for 52 workweeks' of paid leave after six years of work.

*Data not applicable

Source: 1978 national survey

TABLE A.15

Worker Preferences toward Current Income-Earlier Retirement Tradeoff Options by Selected Social Characteristics (percentage breakdowns)

Social Characteristics	Nothing for Earlier Retirement	2% of Pay for 5 Days Ea. Retirmnt.	5% of Pay for 12½ Days Ea. Retirmnt.	10% of Pay for 25 Days Ea. Retirmnt.	20% of Pay for 50 Days Ea. Retirmnt.	Correlation (Pearson r)	Number of Respondents
Total	64.0	17.6	8.1	5.9	4.4	NA*	951
						NA	
Occupation							
Prof-tech	69.8	11.2	10.1	5.0	3.9		179
Managerial	65.5	16.0	8.4	5.0	5.0		119
Clerical-sales	69.8	16.7	7.9	3.2	2.4		126
Skilled labor	62.5	20.4	7.5	6.7	2.9		240
Operatives-laborers	57.7	17.8	9.8	7.4	7.4		163
Service	53.1	27.6	4.1	9.2	6.1		98
Farm	84.6	15.4	0	0	0		13
Education						-.0656 (s = .04)	
Some H.S. or less	61.7	18.9	7.0	6.5	6.0		201
High school degree	60.4	20.1	7.5	6.9	5.0		318
Some college	64.3	18.5	9.3	4.8	3.1		227
College degree	69.8	8.3	11.5	6.3	4.2		96
Some graduate school	74.5	13.7	5.9	2.9	2.9		102
Total family income						.0147 (s = .66)	
Under $4,999	64.5	14.5	6.5	6.5	8.1		62
$5,000-$9,999	63.2	22.2	6.9	4.9	2.8		144
$10,000-$14,999	62.7	19.2	8.3	7.3	2.6		193
$15,000-$19,999	62.3	17.3	8.4	8.9	3.1		191
$20,000-$24,999	69.2	12.0	9.0	1.5	8.3		133
$25,000-$34,999	66.4	17.8	8.4	3.7	3.7		107
Over $34,999	58.8	15.3	9.4	8.2	8.2		85

Social Characteristics	Nothing for Earlier Retirement	2% of Pay for 5 Days Ea. Retirmnt.	5% of Pay for 12½ Days Ea. Retirmnt.	10% of Pay for 25 Days Ea. Retirmnt.	20% of Pay for 50 Days Ea. Retirmnt.	Correlation (Pearson r)	Number of Respondents
Union affiliation						NA	
Member	61.2	22.9	6.0	5.5	4.5		201
Nonmember	64.8	16.1	8.8	6.0	4.8		738
Hours worked weekly						-.0901 (s = .01)	
Under 34	57.1	14.6	11.6	8.6	8.1		198
35–39	61.8	26.5	3.9	4.9	2.9		102
40–44	64.8	18.4	8.3	4.4	4.1		435
Over 44	69.9	14.4	6.5	6.9	2.3		216
Major activity of spouse							
Men						NA	
Not married	64.7	17.6	9.6	3.7	4.4		136
Working full time	67.7	14.6	7.0	6.3	4.4		158
Working part time	63.8	21.7	7.2	5.8	1.4		69
Unemployed & off job	44.1	32.4	2.9	14.7	5.9		34
Keeping house & other	70.0	15.5	5.6	7.0	1.9		213
Women						NA	
Not married	64.3	16.5	7.8	5.2	6.1		115
Working full time	56.1	20.0	11.7	5.0	7.2		180
Working part time	81.8	9.1	0	9.1	0		11
Unemployed & off job	66.7	6.7	6.7	6.7	13.3		15
Keeping house & other	61.5	23.1	15.4	0	0		13
Sex						NA	
Men	65.8	17.3	7.2	6.4	3.3		612
Women	60.8	18.0	9.7	5.0	6.5		339
Marital status						NA	
Single	62.1	17.6	12.6	4.9	2.7		182
Married	63.8	18.0	7.3	6.4	4.6		657
Div-sep-widowed	69.2	15.9	4.7	3.7	6.5		107

	A	B	C	D	E		N
Number of dependents							
None	64.1	16.4	8.5	6.7	4.4	-.0235 (s = -.47)	390
One	63.5	18.0	7.9	5.8	4.8		189
Two	66.5	16.8	7.9	3.1	5.8		191
Three	63.5	19.2	6.7	9.6	1.0		104
Four or more	62.2	23.0	5.4	4.1	5.4		74
Age of youngest child							
No children	64.8	17.5	7.9	5.5	4.4	.0295 (s = .37)	366
Under 5 years	66.3	15.8	9.2	4.6	4.1		196
5–9 years	63.0	21.3	7.9	6.3	1.6		127
10–14 years	61.5	17.1	6.8	8.5	6.0		117
Over 14 years	62.2	19.8	7.2	3.6	7.2		111
Age							
Under 25	57.1	19.4	14.1	5.3	4.1	-.0651 (s = .05)	170
25–34	63.8	15.4	11.5	6.5	2.7		260
35–49	61.1	21.9	5.3	4.9	6.7		283
50–64	71.7	14.3	3.1	7.2	3.6		223
Over 64	84.6	0	7.7	0	7.7		13
Race							
White	65.0	16.6	8.1	6.1	4.2	NA	815
Nonwhite	58.0	24.4	6.9	4.6	6.1		131

Question: What is the largest portion of your current year's income that you would be willing to give up in exchange for earlier retirement? (A) Nothing; (B) 2 percent ($\frac{1}{50}$) of your income for earlier retirement at a rate of 5 workdays' for every year worked until retirement; (C) 5 percent ($\frac{1}{20}$) of your income for earlier retirement at a rate of 12.5 workdays for every year worked until retirement (D) 10 percent ($\frac{1}{10}$) of your income for earlier retirement at a rate of 25 workdays for every year worked until retirement; (E) 20 percent ($\frac{1}{5}$) of your income for earlier retirement at a rate of 50 workdays for every year worked until retirement.

*Data not applicable

Source: 1978 national survey

219

TABLE A.16

Maximum Portion of Current Income That Workers Prefer to Exchange for Any of Five Forms of Free Time (percentage breakdown)

Social Characteristics	Nothing for Time	2% for Time	5% for Time	10% for Time	12% for Time	15% for Time	20% for Time	30% or 33% for Time	40% or 50% for Time	Correlation (Pearson r)	Number of Respondents
Total	40.7	23.6	9.7	10.0	8.1	4.0	2.1	.9	.9	NA*	955
Occupation											
Prof-tech	38.3	25.6	7.2	12.8	7.8	3.9	2.2	2.2	0	NA	180
Managerial	41.2	23.5	10.9	10.9	5.9	4.2	0	0	3.4		119
Clerical-sales	42.1	27.8	6.3	6.3	10.3	5.6	1.6	0	0		126
Skilled labor	43.8	22.1	11.3	11.3	5.0	2.9	2.1	1.3	.4		240
Operatives-laborers	38.2	17.6	13.3	9.1	12.1	4.8	3.0	.6	1.2		165
Service	34.7	26.5	9.2	9.2	10.2	3.1	4.1	1.0	2.0		98
Farm	69.2	30.8	0	0	0	0	0	0	0		13
Education										.0056 (s = .43)	
Some H.S. or less	44.6	19.3	10.9	9.4	7.4	3.0	3.5	.5	1.5		202
High school degree	39.9	26.4	8.5	9.1	7.5	3.8	2.2	.9	1.6		318
Some college	37.1	23.6	12.7	9.2	9.2	4.8	2.2	.9	.4		229
College degree	41.7	20.8	8.3	14.6	6.3	6.3	1.0	1.0	0		96
Some graduate school	42.2	26.5	6.9	9.8	9.8	2.9	0	2.0	0		102
Total family income										.0480 (s = .0731)	
Under $4,999	43.5	17.7	6.5	6.5	17.7	1.6	3.2	0	3.2		62
$5,000 – $9,999	42.1	22.1	13.1	6.9	7.6	5.5	1.4	.7	.7		145
$10,000 – $14,999	44.6	25.1	7.7	10.8	5.1	3.1	2.1	.5	1.0		195
$15,000 – $19,999	40.3	26.7	11.0	9.9	7.3	1.0	3.1	.5	0		191
$20,000 – $24,999	35.3	23.3	11.3	11.3	9.0	5.3	1.5	2.3	.8		133
$25,000 – $34,999	48.8	20.6	8.4	8.4	9.3	3.7	.9	.9	1.9		107
Over $34,999	29.4	23.5	8.2	14.1	8.2	9.4	3.5	2.4	1.2		85

Union affiliation											
Member	42.1	25.7	10.9	5.9	5.9	3.5	4.5	.5	1.0		202
Nonmember	40.3	22.8	9.5	11.2	8.8	4.1	1.5	1.1	.8		740
Form of payment for work										NA	
Wage	39.1	22.8	12.1	8.5	9.8	3.8	2.0	.9	1.1		448
Salary	41.7	26.4	9.0	9.6	6.1	2.9	2.6	1.2	.6		345
Other	30.2	23.8	6.3	18.3	8.7	8.7	1.6	.8	1.6		156
Hours worked weekly										.1237 (s = .00)	
Under 34	32.3	23.2	8.1	12.6	10.1	7.1	2.0	2.0	2.5		198
35 – 39	39.2	26.5	10.8	8.8	4.9	5.9	2.0	2.0	0		102
40 – 44	40.5	24.9	11.4	8.7	8.7	2.3	2.5	.5	.5		437
Over 44	49.3	19.8	7.4	10.6	6.5	3.7	1.4	.5	.9		217
Major activity of spouse										NA	
Men											
Not married	37.2	22.6	9.5	12.4	5.8	5.8	4.4	0	2.2		137
Working fulltime	46.2	18.4	8.9	10.8	8.2	3.8	1.3	1.9	.6		158
Working parttime	40.6	27.5	8.7	10.1	7.2	2.9	0	2.9	0		69
Unemployed & off job	39.1	23.9	8.7	17.4	6.5	2.2	2.2	0	0		46
Keeping house	52.8	20.0	9.7	7.2	4.6	2.6	2.1	.5	.5		196
Women											
Not married	35.7	25.2	10.4	4.3	17.4	4.3	.9	.9	.9		115
Working fulltime	28.2	28.2	13.3	11.6	8.8	4.4	3.3	.6	1.7		181
Working parttime	45.5	36.4	0	9.1	0	0	0	9.1	0		11
Unemployed & off job	42.3	30.8	3.8	7.7	11.5	3.8	0	0	0		26
Keeping house	100.0	0	0	0	0	0	0	0	0		2
Sex										NA	
Men	45.0	21.3	9.1	10.6	6.2	3.9	2.1	1.0	.8		614
Women	32.9	27.6	10.9	8.8	11.5	4.1	2.1	.9	1.2		340
Marital status										NA	
Single	32.2	22.4	11.5	15.3	9.3	6.6	1.6	.5	.5		183
Married	42.0	23.7	10.0	9.6	7.1	3.6	2.0	1.2	.8		659
Div-sep-widowed	46.7	25.2	5.6	3.7	11.2	.9	3.7	0	2.8		107

Social Characteristics	Nothing for Time	2% for Time	5% for Time	10% for Time	12% for Time	15% for Time	20% for Time	30% or 33% for Time	40% or 50% for Time	Correlation (Pearson r)	Number of Respondents
Number of dependents											
None	38.5	22.4	9.2	10.5	8.9	4.8	2.6	1.3	1.8	.1088 (s = .00)	392
One	38.6	21.2	11.1	12.2	10.1	4.2	1.1	1.1	.5		189
Two	43.5	24.6	9.4	9.9	7.3	3.1	1.6	.5	0		191
Three	48.6	23.8	10.5	7.6	5.7	1.0	1.9	0	1.0		105
Four or more	40.5	33.8	8.1	5.4	4.1	2.7	4.1	1.4	0		74
Age of youngest child											
No children	38.6	23.4	8.2	10.6	9.5	5.2	1.9	.8	1.9	-.0465 (s = .08)	368
Under 5 years	44.4	23.5	13.3	7.1	4.6	3.6	1.5	1.5	.5		196
5 – 9 years	37.0	28.3	11.8	12.6	5.5	2.4	2.4	0	0		127
10 – 14 years	39.8	21.2	7.6	11.9	11.9	2.5	3.4	.8	.8		118
Over 14 years	45.0	23.4	9.0	8.1	9.0	2.7	2.7	0	0		111
Age											
Under 25	26.3	26.3	16.4	12.3	7.6	7.6	1.8	1.2	.6	.1070 (s = .00)	171
25 – 34	38.8	21.9	11.9	13.1	8.1	3.5	1.2	.8	.8		260
35 – 49	40.8	25.7	7.4	8.8	9.5	3.9	2.8	.7	.4		284
50 – 64	52.7	21.4	5.4	6.7	7.1	2.2	1.8	1.3	1.3		224
Over 64	61.5	0	7.7	0	0	0	15.4	0	15.4		13
Race											
White	40.0	24.1	9.4	10.9	8.0	4.0	1.8	1.0	.7	NA	817
Nonwhite	46.2	20.5	11.4	3.8	8.3	3.0	3.8	.8	2.3		132

Note: Maximum current income-time tradeoff choice determined by computation of a composite (MAXTRD2) variable which reports the highest proportion of current earnings that each respondent states a willingness to exchange for any of five forms of potential gains of free time. For example, a respondent who states a desire to exchange 5 percent of current earnings for a shorter workday, 10 percent for a reduced workweek, 10 percent for added vacation, 15 percent for a sabbatical leave, and 2 percent for earlier retirement in paired choices between income and each of these five forms of free time would have a maximum current tradeoff (MAXTRD2) score of 15 percent because the sabbatical leave choice elicited the highest exchange of all the available choices.

*Data not applicable

Source: 1978 national survey

TABLE A.17

Maximum Portion of Current Income That Worker Would Exchange for Any of Five Forms of Free Time by Sex, Major Activity of Spouse, and Age of Youngest Child (percentage breakdown)

Tradeoff Preferences by Sex	Not Married				Working Spouse			
	No Child	Youngest Child under 6	Youngest Child 6–14	Youngest Child over 14	No Child	Youngest Child under 6	Youngest Child 6–14	Youngest Child over 14
Men								
Nothing	52.0	55.6	60.0	60.0	39.4	50.0	41.6	51.9
2% of pay for time	18.2	1.5	1.5	.8	22.7	19.6	20.8	22.2
5% of pay for time	10.7	11.1	6.7	0	6.1	10.9	10.4	7.4
10% of pay for time	14.6		6.7	20.0	12.1	4.3	13.0	11.1
12% or 15% of pay for time	12.6		6.7	0	16.7	10.9	11.7	3.7
20% of pay for time	3.9	11.1	6.7	0	0	0	1.3	3.7
30% or 40% of pay for time	2.9		0	0	3.0	4.3	1.3	0
Total percent	100.0	100.0	100.0	100.0	100.0	100.0	100.0	100.0
Number of respondents	(103)	(9)	(15)	(5)	(66)	(46)	(77)	(27)
Women								
Nothing	33.3	50.0	31.6	50.0	40.0	18.9	27.7	32.1
2% of pay for time	23.6	20.0	42.1	10.0	25.0	28.3	35.4	21.4
5% of pay for time	9.7	10.0	10.5	10.0	2.5	26.3	7.7	14.3
10% of pay for time	5.6		5.3	0	10.0	13.2	12.3	7.1
12% or 15% of pay for time	25.0	20.0	5.3	30.0	15.0	9.4	10.8	17.9
20% of pay for time	0		5.3	0	0	0	6.2	7.1
30% or 40% of pay for time	2.8		0	0	7.5	3.8	0	0
Total percent	100.0	100.0	100.0	100.0	100.0	100.0	100.0	100.0
Number of respondents	(72)	(10)	(19)	(10)	(40)	(53)	(65)	(28)

| | Spouse Keeps House or Other | | | |
Tradeoff Preferences by Sex	No Child	Youngest Child under 6	Youngest Child 6–14	Youngest Child over 14
Men				
Nothing	53.0	54.2	44.3	47.2
2% of pay for time	16.7	25.0	16.4	30.6
5% of pay for time	10.6	6.9	11.5	8.3
10% of pay for time	9.1	6.9	13.1	5.6
12% or 15% of pay for time	6.1	4.2	13.1	8.3
20% of pay for time	4.5	2.8	0	0
30% or 40% of pay for time	0	0	1.6	0
Total percent	100.0	100.0	100.0	100.0
Number of respondents	(66)	(72)	(61)	(36)
Women				
Nothing	38.5	83.3	33.3	33.3
2% of pay for time	46.2	0	16.7	33.3
5% of pay for time	0	0	16.7	0
10% of pay for time	7.7	0	16.7	0
12% or 15% of pay for time	7.7	16.7	16.7	33.3
20% of pay for time	0	0	0	0
30% or 40% of pay for time	0	0	0	0
Total percent	100.0	100.0	100.0	100.0
Number of respondents	(13)	(6)	(6)	(3)

Note: Maximum current income-time tradeoff choice determined by computation of a composite (MAXTRD2) variable that reports the highest portion of current earnings that each respondent states a willingness to exchange for any of five forms of potential added free time. For example, a respondent who states a desire to exchange 5 percent of earnings for a shorter workday, 10 percent for a reduced workweek, 10 percent for added vacation, 15 percent for a sabbatical leave, and 2 percent for earlier retirement in paired choices between current income and each of these five forms of free time would have a maximum current tradeoff (MAXTRD2) score of 15 percent because the sabbatical leave choice elicited the highest exchange of all available options.

Source: 1978 national survey

TABLE A.18

Worker Preferences toward Flexitime by Selected Social Characteristics (percentage breakdown)

Social Characteristics	Strongly Disfavor (1)	Disfavor (2-4)	Indifferent (5)	Favor (6-8)	Strongly Favor (9)	Correlation (Pearson r)	Number Respondents
Total	10.9	6.4	9.8	24.3	48.6	NA*	745
Age (v31)						−.2954	
Under 25	2.4	4.7	8.2	12.9	71.8	(s = .00)	85
25–29	2.5	1.9	7.6	15.9	72.0		157
30–39	6.0	4.4	8.2	18.6	62.8		183
40–49	18.3	4.2	15.0	14.2	48.3		120
50–59	21.5	6.9	12.7	12.7	47.0		134
Over 59	27.5	3.4	13.8	10.3	44.8		29
Number of children (v40)						−.0971	
None	5.7	4.5	8.0	15.5	66.3	(s = .03)	264
One	8.9	2.4	9.8	18.7	60.2		123
Two	15.9	4.6	11.3	13.9	54.3		151
Three	12.4	3.1	15.5	10.3	58.8		92
Four	23.5	7.3	14.5	10.9	43.6		55
Over four	25.0	7.1	3.6	21.4	42.9		28
Family cycle stage						−.1257	
Single	3.3	5.3	7.5	8.3	75.2	(s = .00)	133
Married couple	3.7	3.7	9.3	23.4	59.8		107
New nest	8.2	1.8	10.0	19.1	60.9		110
Old nest	19.5	4.9	14.6	11.6	49.4		164
Empty nest	22.2	3.7	18.5	13.0	42.6		54
Single parent	10.2	2.3	6.8	14.8	65.9		88
Survivor	18.4	7.9	5.3	23.7	44.7		38

225

Social Characteristics	Strongly Disfavor (1)	Disfavor (2-4)	Indifferent (5)	Favor (6-8)	Strongly Favor (9)	Correlation (Pearson r)	Number Respondents
Occupation (v42)						NA	
Prof-tech	6.0	5.4	9.0	16.8	62.9		167
Managerial	20.5	8.2	12.3	16.4	42.5		73
Clerical	4.6	2.8	5.7	13.9	73.0		281
Crafts	28.2	1.3	15.4	11.5	43.6		78
Nonfarm labor	20.0	15.0	20.0	5.0	35.0		20
Operatives	35.3	23.5	5.9	11.8	23.5		17
Service	15.0	1.3	18.8	16.3	48.8		80
Total family income (v46)						.0924	
Under $4,999	8.0	0	8.0	4.0	80.0	(s = .02)	25
$5,000-$9,999	8.6	5.7	7.1	9.3	69.3		140
$10,000-$14,999	8.6	4.6	10.6	15.9	60.3		151
$15,000-$19,999	13.4	6.3	8.7	16.5	55.1		127
$20,000-$24,999	16.7	4.0	11.1	13.5	54.8		126
$25,000-$34,999	9.2	2.0	14.3	21.4	53.1		98
Over $34,999	6.1	6.1	15.2	21.2	51.5		33
Education (v56)						-.1003	
Some H.S. or less	33.3	0	10.0	10.0	46.7	(s = .01)	30
High school degree	13.5	7.9	11.9	9.5	57.1		126
Technical school	20.3	2.7	16.2	9.5	51.4		74
Some college	9.6	3.8	9.6	17.5	59.6		240
College degree	5.6	3.4	9.0	10.1	71.9		89
Some graduate school	11.0	4.1	4.1	19.2	61.6		73
Advanced degree	3.2	5.3	11.6	22.1	57.9		95
Sex (v32)						-.1929	
Male	15.2	4.5	13.4	17.6	49.4	(s = .00)	336
Female	7.4	4.6	7.7	12.3	67.9		390

Question: "Some employees are allowed to start the workday anytime within a three-hour period between 7 A.M. and 10 A.M. as long as they work a full eight hours a day. This means that they may leave as early as 3 P.M. or as late as 6 P.M. Please circle the number on the following scale which best represents how strongly you favor or disfavor this basic idea."
Source: 1976 Alameda County survey.
*Data not applicable

TABLE A.19

Worker Preferences toward Alternative Workweek Schedules by Selected Social Characteristics (first choice percentage breakdowns)

Social Characteristics	6-Hour Days, 6-Day Weeks	8-Hour Days, 5-Day Weeks	10-Hour Days, 4-Day Weeks	13.5-Hour Days, 3-Day Weeks	Correlation (Pearson r)	Number of Respondents
Order of choice (totals)						
First	1.5	32.2	55.3	11.0		754
Second	6.0	39.8	35.9	18.4		739
Third	16.6	28.7	5.4	49.3		691
Fourth	79.9	0	0	20.1		652
Age (v31)					−.2052	
Under 25	1.2	30.6	60.0	8.2	(s = .00)	85
25–29	.6	21.1	68.1	10.2		166
30–39	1.1	24.6	56.1	18.2		187
40–49	.8	38.5	54.9	5.7		122
50–59	0	48.9	45.2	5.9		135
Over 59	3.5	51.7	44.8	0		29
Number of children (v40)					−.0826	
None	.7	25.7	61.3	12.3	(s = .04)	269
One	2.3	40.3	48.1	9.3		129
Two	0	36.4	53.2	10.4		154
Three	1.0	31.0	65.0	3.0		100
Four	3.6	48.2	39.3	8.9		56
Over four	3.6	28.6	57.1	10.7		28
Family cycle stage (FACYCLE)					−.1592	
Single	1.5	23.4	66.4	8.8	(s = .00)	137
Married couple	0	25.9	57.4	16.7		108
New nest	1.9	30.7	57.0	11.4		114

Social Characteristics	6-Hour Days, 6-Day Weeks	8-Hour Days, 5-Day Weeks	10-Hour Days, 4-Day Weeks	13.5-Hour Days, 3-Day Weeks	Correlation (Pearson r)	Number of Respondents
Old nest	1.8	32.7	58.9	6.5		168
Empty nest	0	53.7	40.7	5.6		54
Single parent	3.3	40.0	46.7	10.0		90
Survivor	0	48.8	46.3	4.9		41
Total family income (v46)					−.0718	
Under $4,999	4.2	37.5	54.2	4.2	(s = .08)	24
$5,000 – $9,999	1.4	32.2	56.2	10.3		146
$10,000 – $14,999	.7	37.5	55.9	5.9		152
$15,000 – $19,999	0	34.4	57.3	8.4		131
$20,000 – $24,999	2.4	27.6	57.5	12.6		127
$25,000 – $34,999	1.0	25.3	52.9	14.7		99
Over $35,000	2.9	29.4	52.9	14.7		34
Occupation (v42)					NA*	
Prof-tech	.6	25.1	62.6	11.7		171
Managerial	1.4	35.6	49.4	13.6		73
Clerical	1.4	32.5	57.4	8.7		289
Crafts	3.8	50.0	40.0	6.3		80
Nonfarm labor	5.6	33.3	55.6	5.6		18
Operatives	5.9	64.7	29.4	0		17
Service	0	28.6	58.3	13.1		84
Education (v56)					−.1757	
Some H.S. or less	0	79.3	13.8	6.9	(s = .00)	29
High school degree	1.6	41.1	53.5	3.9		129
Technical school	0	44.2	42.9	13.0		77
Some college	1.6	26.3	63.0	9.1		243
College degree	2.2	28.6	61.5	7.7		91
Some graduate school	0	26.3	60.5	13.2		76

Social Characteristics	6-Hour Days, 6-Day Weeks	8-Hour Days, 5-Day Weeks	10-Hour Days, 4-Day Weeks	13.5-Hour Days, 3-Day Weeks	Correlation (Pearson r)	Number of Respondents
Advanced degree	1.0	23.5	56.1	19.4		98
Sex (v32)					$-.0319$	
Male	1.2	29.9	59.3	9.6	$(s = .43)$	344
Female	1.0	24.5	53.9	10.6		397

Question: Assume that you must work a total of 40 hours each week, but that you are given a choice between the following schedules: (A) Working 6.5 hours a day for 6 days a week with 1 day off each week; (B) Working 8 hours a day for 5 days a week with 2 days off each week; (C) Working 10 hours a day for 4 days a week with 3 days off each week; and (D) Working 13.5 hours a day for 3 days a week with 4 days off each week. Which option would you choose first? ( ) Second? ( ) Third? ( )

*Data not applicable

Source: 1976 Alameda County survey

TABLE A.20

Worker Preferences toward Workyear Schedules by Selected Social Characterisitcs (first choice percentage breakdowns)

Social Characteristics	50 Weeks Work & 2 Weeks Vac.	45 Weeks Work & 8 Weeks Vac.	40 Weeks Work & 12 Wks. Vac.	Zero Order Correlations (Pearson r)	Number of Respondents
Order of choice (totals)					
First	18.6	48.4	32.0		751
Second	23.2	46.5	30.3		727
Third	58.2	4.1	37.7		NA
Age (v31)				−.1894	
Under 25	11.8	60.0	28.2	(s = .00)	85
25–29	14.5	46.7	38.8		165
30–39	14.7	50.0	51.6		184
40–49	18.0	54.9	27.0		122
50–59	30.9	45.6	23.5		136
Over 59	26.7	50.0	23.3		30
Number of children (v40)				−.0987	
None	12.1	52.1	35.8	(s = .02)	265
One	21.1	54.0	24.8		161
Two	23.8	46.0	30.2		126
Three	27.8	42.6	29.6		54
Over three	17.9	39.3	42.9		28
Family cycle stage (FACYCLE)				−.1077	
Single	14.9	53.2	31.9	(s = .01)	47
Married couple	12.0	45.4	42.6		108
New nest	26.5	39.8	33.6		113
Old nest	23.8	48.2	28.0		168
Empty nest	28.6	48.2	23.2		56
Single parent	13.8	59.8	26.4		87

				Correlation	N
Life change history (LFHIST)				.1946 (s = .00)	
Very linear	23.4	52.7	23.8		239
Moderately linear	19.9	48.6	31.4		296
Moderately flexible	9.8	50.0	4C.2		122
Very flexible	5.9	49.0	45.1		51
Socioeconomic class (SES)				.1425 (s = .00)	
Lower	50.0	43.8	6.3		16
Lower-middle	20.2	50.6	29.2		168
Middle	19.4	50.5	30.1		392
Upper-middle	11.1	48.4	40.5		153
Occupation (v42)				NA*	
Prof-tech	11.2	43.8	45.0		169
Managerial	16.9	56.3	25.8		71
Clerical	16.5	59.1	24.4		279
Crafts	40.5	37.8	21.6		74
Nonfarm labor	44.4	33.3	22.2		18
Operatives	17.6	35.3	47.1		17
Service	14.3	45.2	40.5		84
Total family income (v46)				-.0780 (s = .07)	
Under $4,999	12.0	68.0	20.0		25
$5,000 – $9,999	19.1	48.9	31.9		141
$10,000 – $14,999	22.0	53.3	24.7		150
$15,000 – $19,999	14.8	53.1	32.0		128
$20,000 – $24,999	24.0	40.0	36.0		125
$25,000 – $34,999	12.6	51.6	35.8		95
Over $34,999	11.8	44.1	44.1		34
Education (v56)				-.1957 (s = .00)	
Some H.S. or less	43.8	40.6	15.6		32
High school degree	27.3	51.6	21.1		128
Technical school	25.0	48.7	26.3		76
Some college	17.4	50.4	32.2		242
College degree	15.6	52.2	32.2		90

Social Characteristics	50 Weeks Work & 2 Weeks Vac.	45 Weeks Work & 8 Weeks Vac.	40 Weeks Work & 12 Wks. Vac.	Zero Order Correlations (Pearson r)	Number of Respondents
Some graduate school	12.0	57.3	30.7		75
Advanced degree	8.2	42.9	49.0		98
Sex (v32)				.0542	
Male	20.6	42.7	36.7	(s = .21)	335
Female	15.8	57.4	26.9		385
Race (v34/dummy)				NA	
White	15.8	50.2	34.0		482
Black	14.5	62.1	23.4		124
Oriental	24.1	46.3	29.6		54
Mexican-American	39.3	35.7	25.0		28
Other	32.0	40.0	28.0		25

Question: Assume that you must work an average of 40 hours a week but that it is possible to schedule your work over an entire year in one of the following ways: (A) Fifty 40-hour workweeks with 2 weeks' paid vacation each year; (B) Forty-four 45-hour workweeks with 8 weeks' paid vacation each year; (C) Forty 50-hour workweeks with 12 weeks' paid vacation every year. Which option would you choose first? ( ) Which would you choose second? ( )

*Data not applicable

Source: 1976 Alameda County survey

TABLE A.21

Worker Preferences toward School Scheduling Flexibility by Selected Social Characteristics (percentage breakdowns)

Social Characteristics	Flexible School Schedule	Traditional Linear School Schedule	Correlation (Cramer's v)	Number of Respondents
Total	51.3	48.3	NA*	951
Occupation			.0674	
Prof-tech	53.1	46.9		179
Managerial	49.6	50.4		119
Clerical-sales	46.8	53.2		126
Skilled labor	52.1	47.9		240
Operatives-laborers	57.3	42.7		164
Service	51.0	49.0		'98
Farm	41.7	58.3		12
Education			.0838	
Some H.S. or less	52.2	47.8		203
High school degree	48.7	51.3		316
Some college	53.7	46.3		229
College degree	51.6	48.4		95
Some graduate school	54.9	45.1		102
Total family income			.0905	
Under $4,999	55.6	44.4		63
$5,000–$9,999	52.1	47.9		144
$10,000–$14,999	55.4	44.6		195
$15,000–$19,999	51.6	48.4		190
$20,000–$24,999	50.0	50.0		132
$25,000–$34,999	40.2	59.8		107
Over $34,999	51.8	48.2		85

Social Characteristics	Flexible School Schedule	Traditional Linear School Schedule	Correlation (Cramer's v)	Number of Respondents
Union affiliation				
Member	51.5	48.5	.0387	202
Nonmember	51.7	48.3	(Phi)	737
Form of payment for work				
Wage	51.3	48.7	.0792	448
Salary	53.5	46.5		344
Other	47.4	52.6		154
Hours worked weekly				
Under 34	53.5	46.5	.1034	198
35 – 39	48.0	52.0		102
40 – 44	50.1	49.9		435
Over 44	54.2	45.8		216
Major activity of spouse				
Men			NA	
Not married	58.5	41.5		135
Working fulltime	54.4	45.6		158
Working parttime	44.9	55.1		69
Unemployed & off job	55.9	44.1		34
Keeping house & other	48.1	51.9		206
Women			NA	
Not married	50.9	49.1		116
Working fulltime	47.8	52.2		180
Working parttime	45.5	54.5		11
Unemployed & off job	60.0	40.0		15
Keeping house & other	46.2	53.8		13
Sex			.0315	
Men	52.7	47.3	(Phi)	611
Women	49.4	50.6		340

				Phi
Marital status				.0494
Single	54.9	45.1	182	
Married	50.2	49.8	657	
Div-sep-widowed	55.1	44.9	107	
Number of dependents				.0763
None	51.3	48.7	390	
One	57.1	42.9	189	
Two	51.8	48.2	191	
Three	47.6	52.4	105	
Four or more	42.5	57.5	73	
Age of youngest child				.1067
No children	50.0	50.0	366	
Under 5 years	59.2	40.8	196	
5 – 9 years	51.6	48.4	126	
10 – 14 years	49.2	50.8	118	
Over 14 years	40.5	59.5	111	
Age				.1165
Under 25	52.9	47.1	170	
25 – 34	57.7	42.3	260	
35 – 49	46.3	53.7	283	
50 – 64	50.2	49.8	223	
Over 64	53.8	46.2	13	
Race				.0560 (Phi)
White	51.4	48.5	814	
Nonwhite	52.3	47.7	132	

Question: In general, which of the following approaches for the education of young persons do you think would be best? (A) Continuous attendance in school (except summers) until all formal high school or college has been completed and the young person is ready to begin work in a chosen occupation; (B) Continuous attendance in school (except summers) through junior high school, followed by more-or-less equal alterations between work experiences and schooling until the young person has finished high school or college and is ready to begin work in a chosen occupation.

*Data not applicable

Source: 1978 national survey

TABLE A.22

Worker Retirement-Age Worktime Preferences by Selected Social Characteristics (percentage breakdowns)

Social Characteristics	No Work at All	Part-week Work	Part-year Work	Full-time Work	Not Sure	Correlation (Cramer's v)	Number of Respondents
Total	23.1	44.9	10.4	9.1	12.5	NA*	955
Occupation						.1402	
Prof-tech	19.4	50.6	13.3	11.1	5.6		180
Managerial	18.5	45.4	10.9	9.2	16.0		130
Clerical-sales	22.2	48.4	13.5	3.2	12.7		126
Skilled labor	27.1	43.8	9.6	6.3	13.3		240
Operatives-laborers	34.9	34.3	6.0	10.2	14.5		166
Service	11.2	48.0	8.2	16.3	16.3		98
Farm	0	61.5	15.4	15.4	7.7		13
Education						.1363	
Some H.S. or less	26.1	39.4	6.9	8.9	18.7		203
High school degree	26.4	44.3	8.5	8.2	12.6		318
Some college	20.1	43.7	13.5	10.5	12.2		229
College degree	19.8	51.0	14.6	7.3	7.3		96
Some graduate school	16.7	54.9	12.7	10.8	4.9		102
Total family income						.0944	
Under $4,999	19.0	52.4	7.9	9.5	11.1		63
$5,000–$9,999	13.1	48.3	11.0	11.7	15.9		145
$10,000–$14,999	24.6	44.6	10.8	6.2	13.8		195
$15,000–$19,999	27.7	46.1	8.9	6.8	10.5		191
$20,000–$24,999	26.3	42.1	12.0	10.5	9.0		133
$25,000–$34,999	28.0	47.7	12.1	2.8	9.3		107
Over $34,999	22.4	40.0	11.8	15.3	10.6		85

							N
Union affiliation							
Member	33.7	40.1	9.4	4.5	12.4		202
Nonmember	20.5	46.2	10.4	10.3	12.3		741
Major activity of spouse							
Men						NA	
Not married	17.5	48.2	10.2	10.2	12.9		137
Working full-time	30.4	37.3	7.6	8.9	15.8		158
Working part-time	27.5	39.1	18.8	8.7	5.8		69
Unemployed & off job	23.5	44.2	11.8	8.8	14.7		34
Keeping house & other	24.2	47.3	10.6	9.2	8.7		207
Women						NA	
Not married	8.6	51.7	12.9	13.8	12.9		116
Working full-time	28.2	42.5	8.8	4.4	16.0		181
Working part-time	36.4	36.4	9.1	9.1	9.1		11
Unemployed & off job	20.0	40.0	6.7	20.0	13.3		15
Keeping house & other	23.1	61.5	0	15.4	0		13
Sex						.0559	
Men	24.4	44.0	10.7	9.3	11.6		614
Women	20.8	46.6	9.7	8.8	14.1		341
Marital status						.0863	
Single	13.7	49.2	10.9	13.1	13.1		183
Married	26.9	43.1	10.0	8.0	12.0		659
Div-sep-widowed	16.7	49.1	12.0	8.3	13.9		108
Number of dependents						.0741	
None	19.3	49.9	9.7	9.2	12.0		393
One	22.8	42.9	9.0	10.6	14.8		189
Two	29.8	35.6	13.6	8.9	12.0		191
Three	24.8	46.7	10.5	9.5	8.6		105
Four or more	25.7	45.9	9.5	4.1	14.9		74
Age of youngest child						.0774	
No children	19.0	50.4	9.8	9.5	11.4		369
Under 5 years	21.4	43.4	13.3	7.1	14.8		196
5 - 9 years	24.4	38.6	12.6	11.8	12.6		127

Social Characteristics	No Work at All	Part-week Work	Part-year Work	Full-time Work	Not Sure	Correlation (Cramer's v)	Number of Respondents
10–14 years	29.7	43.2	5.9	7.6	13.6		118
Over 14 years	31.5	39.6	9.0	9.9	9.9		111
Age						.1276	
Under 25	14.6	42.7	9.4	14.6	18.7		171
25–34	19.2	46.9	14.6	7.3	11.9		260
35–49	29.1	40.7	12.3	6.0	11.9		285
50–64	27.7	48.2	4.5	10.3	9.4		224
Over 64	7.7	76.9	0	15.4	0		13
Race						.0809	
White	21.8	45.5	11.2	9.2	12.3		818
Nonwhite	31.1	41.7	4.5	9.1	13.6		132

Question: Considering your expected financial situation and ability to stay in or change your current line of work when you reach retirement age, which of the following worktime options would you personally prefer at age 65? (A) No work at all; (B) Work part time or short workweeks year around (with vacations); (C) Work full time for only a portion of the year; (D) Work full time year around (with vacations); (E) Not sure.

*Data not applicable

Source: 1978 national survey

TABLE A.23

Older Population Retirement-Age Worktime Preferences by Selected Social Characteristics (percentage breakdowns)

Social Characteristics	No Work at All	Work Part Week All Year	Work Full Time Part Year	Work Full Time All Year	Not Sure	Correlation (Cramer's v)	Number of Respondents
Total	33.6	42.5	3.4	8.9	11.5	NA*	494
Major activity						.1437	
Working full time	26.0	48.0	5.2	11.6	9.2		173
Working part time	21.8	58.2	1.8	10.9	7.3		55
Unemployed or off job	34.0	46.8	4.3	6.4	8.5		47
Retired	50.0	29.5	2.5	4.9	13.1		122
School	0	0	0	0	0		0
Keeping house	33.7	36.8	2.1	9.5	17.9		95
Hours worked weekly						.1362	
Not working	40.4	35.9	2.4	7.3	13.9		245
Under 35	22.0	55.9	3.4	10.2	8.5		59
35–39	29.2	37.5	4.2	16.7	12.5		24
40–44	31.3	48.7	3.5	7.8	8.7		115
Over 44	20.0	48.0	8.0	14.0	10.0		50
Age						.1114	
50–64	31.2	44.9	3.1	9.1	11.7		385
Over 64	42.2	33.9	4.6	8.3	11.0		109
Race						.1215	
White	35.1	40.0	3.8	9.0	12.1		422
Nonwhite	24.6	56.5	1.4	8.7	8.7		69

Social Characteristics	No Work at All	Work Part Week All Year	Work Full Time Part Year	Work Full Time All Year	Not Sure	Correlation (Cramer's v)	Number of Respondents
Sex						.1255	
Men	34.5	45.1	4.3	7.8	8.2		255
Women	32.6	39.7	2.5	10.0	15.1		239
Occupation						.1872	
Prof-tech	37.7	37.7	5.2	11.7	7.8		77
Manager	23.6	49.1	1.8	9.1	16.4		55
Clerical-sales	33.8	45.5	7.8	3.9	9.1		77
Skilled labor	39.4	38.5	2.8	5.5	13.8		109
Operatives-laborers	41.0	38.5	1.3	5.1	14.1		78
Service	22.2	48.1	0	20.4	9.3		54
Farm	14.3	28.6	14.3	35.7	7.1		14
Education						.1369	
Elementary or less	30.1	41.7	1.9	11.7	14.6		103
Some high school	31.5	44.6	1.1	10.9	12.0		92
High school degree	33.6	43.8	4.1	5.5	13.0		146
Some college	41.3	38.8	6.3	8.8	5.0		80
College degree	40.0	42.9	2.9	8.6	5.7		35
Graduate school	28.6	40.0	5.7	11.4	14.3		35
Family cycle stage						.1130	
Single	26.2	54.2	2.8	7.5	9.3		107
Couple without children	38.1	37.2	4.1	6.4	14.2		218
Children under age 14	29.8	44.7	2.1	14.9	8.5		47
Children over age 14	37.9	42.4	4.5	9.1	6.1		66
Total family income						.1143	
Under $4,999	28.8	46.3	2.5	11.3	11.3		80
$5,000–$9,999	30.1	46.7	1.9	8.4	12.1		107
$10,000–$14,999	35.6	45.6	2.2	6.7	10.0		90

Social Characteristics	No Work at All	Work Part Week All Year	Work Full Time Part Year	Work Full Time All Year	Not Sure	Correlation (Cramer's v)	Number of Respondents
$15,000–$19,999	35.1	41.6	3.9	5.2	14.3		77
$20,000–$24,999	42.9	26.5	6.1	14.3	10.2		49
$25,000–$34,999	31.4	54.3	5.7	2.9	5.7		35
Over $34,999	37.5	40.6	9.4	9.4	3.1		32
Maximum current tradeoff choice						.1236	
No part of pay for time	34.3	43.9	2.6	10.9	8.3		230
2%–5% of pay for time	32.8	40.9	4.4	8.8	13.1		137
10%–12% of pay for time	29.4	45.6	5.9	7.4	11.8		68
15%–50% of pay for time	37.3	37.3	1.7	3.4	20.3		59

Question: Considering your expected financial situation and ability to stay in or change your current line of work when you reach retirement age, which of the following worktime options would you personally prefer at age 65? (A) No work at all; (B) Work part time or short workweeks year around (with vacations). (C) Work full time for only a portion of the year; (D) Work full time year around (with vacations); (E) Not sure.

*Data not applicable

Source: 1978 national survey

241

TABLE A.24

Worker Preferences among Life-Scheduling Options by Selected Social Characteristics (first choice percentage breakdowns)

Social Characteristics	Linear Lifeplan	Moderate Cyclic Lifeplan	Full Cyclic Lifeplan	Correlation (Pearson r)	Number Respondents
Total	20.7	33.0	46.3	NA*	709
Age (v31)				-.1429	
Under 25	12.3	38.3	49.5	(s = .00)	81
25 – 29	11.0	37.2	51.8		164
30 – 39	17.3	31.8	50.9		179
40 – 49	19.8	40.5	39.6		111
50 – 59	37.3	25.4	37.3		134
Over 59	33.3	26.7	40.0		30
Number of children (v40)				-.0425	
None	13.4	35.9	50.8	(s = .33)	262
One	22.4	34.6	42.9		156
Two	15.8	34.2	50.0		120
Three	22.4	34.7	42.9		49
Over three	39.1	26.1	34.8		23
Family cycle stage (FACYCLE)				-.0550	
Single	21.3	31.9	46.8	(s = .21)	47
Married couple	12.3	40.6	47.2		106
New nest	18.2	39.1	42.7		110
Old nest	27.9	33.1	39.0		154
Empty nest	40.0	29.1	30.9		55
Single parent	11.9	28.6	59.5		84
Life change history (LFHIST)				-.2755	
Very linear	31.1	36.9	32.0	(s = .00)	225
Moderately linear	18.0	33.5	48.6		278

					N
Moderately flexible	10.7	36.4	52.9		121
Very flexible	0	23.5	76.5		51
Socioeconomic class (SES)				-.0829 (s = .06)	
Lower	23.1	38.5	38.5		13
Lower-middle	26.4	29.4	44.2		163
Middle	20.3	36.8	42.9		380
Upper-middle	14.7	27.3	58.0		143
Occupation (v42)				NA	
Prof-tech	14.4	27.5	58.1		167
Managerial	19.1	42.6	38.2		68
Clerical	16.1	36.9	47.1		274
Crafts	33.3	31.9	34.7		72
Nonfarm labor	31.6	31.6	36.8		19
Operatives	7.7	38.5	53.8		13
Service	38.9	27.8	33.3		72
Total family income (v46)				.0178 (s = .68)	
Under $4,999	12.0	36.0	52.0		25
$5,000–$9,999	17.3	33.1	49.6		133
$10,000–$14,999	22.8	34.5	42.8		145
$15,000–$19,999	21.3	33.1	45.7		127
$20,000–$24,999	22.1	28.7	49.2		122
$25,000–$34,999	24.2	36.3	39.5		91
Over $34,999	13.3	46.7	40.0		30
Education (v56)				-.1331 (s = .00)	
Some H.S. or less	40.0	20.0	40.0		25
High school degree	26.4	33.6	40.0		125
Technical school	36.6	32.4	31.0		71
Some college	18.8	35.0	46.2		234
College degree	17.0	29.5	53.4		88
Some graduate school	8.1	40.5	51.4		74
Advanced degree	13.3	30.6	56.1		98

Social Characteristics	Linear Lifeplan	Moderate Cyclic Lifeplan	Full Cyclic Lifeplan	Correlation (Pearson r)	Number Respondents
Sex (v32)				-.0933	
Male	26.8	30.8	42.4	(s = .03)	321
Female	15.4	35.6	48.9		376
Race (v34)				NA	
White	21.4	33.3	45.3		472
Black	18.6	36.3	45.1		113
Oriental	22.0	30.0	48.0		50
Mexican-American	13.8	44.8	41.4		29
Other	17.4	26.1	56.5		23

Question: See Table 10.1
*Data not applicable
Source: 1976 Alameda County survey

TABLE A.25

Worker Choices among Life-Scheduling Options by Selected Life-Scheduling Preference Indicators

Life-Scheduling Preference Indicators	Distribution of Indicator	Life-Scheduling Options				Correlation (Pearson r)	Number of Respondents
		Linear Lifeplan	Moderate Cyclic Plan	Full Cyclic Lifeplan			
Total	100.0	20.7	33.0	46.3		NA*	709
Expect to return to school (v91)						.2937	
Very unlikely (1–3)	21.0	29.7	38.6	31.7		(s = .00)	145
Possibly (4–6)	48.8	23.5	33.3	43.2			336
Very likely (7–9)	30.2	8.2	30.3	61.5			208
School scheduling preferences (v93)						.3504	
Traditional, linear schedule	40.2	35.8	36.5	27.7		(s = .00)	274
Nontraditional, flexible schedule	59.8	10.6	31.4	58.0			407
Expect to change occupation (v80)						.2149	
Very unlikely (1–3)	21.5	34.0	30.6	35.4		(s = .00)	147
Possibly (4–6)	42.7	20.2	36.3	43.5			292
Very likely (7–9)	35.8	13.1	31.4	55.5			245
Desire for work &/or job change (v81)						.1843	
Change work and employer	20.2	11.7	29.9	58.4			137
Change employer but not work	17.8	13.2	34.7	52.1			121
Change work but not employer	22.4	16.4	40.8	42.8			152
Same work and same employer	39.6	30.1	30.1	39.8			269
Desirability of rotating jobs (v83)						.1314	
Oppose (1–3)	11.7	23.5	28.4	48.1		(s = .00)	81
Mixed (4–6)	37.9	26.3	33.6	40.1			262
Favor (7–9)	50.4	15.5	33.8	50.7			349

Life-Scheduling Preference Indicators	Distribution of Indicator	Life-Scheduling Options			Correlation (Pearson r)	Number of Respondents
		Linear Lifeplan	Moderate Cyclic Plan	Full Cyclic Lifeplan		
Importance of on- and off-job time (v85)					.2114	
Job activities more important	36.2	27.2	35.4	37.4	(s = .00)	246
Job & off job equally important	34.9	19.7	33.2	47.1		238
Off-job activities more important	28.9	11.7	31.5	56.9		197
Sex-role flexibility (v98)					.3180	
Oppose flexibility (1–4)	33.8	33.2	34.9	31.9	(s = .00)	229
Neutral (5)	28.3	18.8	33.3	47.9		192
Favor flexibility (6–9)	37.9	8.6	32.7	58.8		257
Workyear scheduling preferences (v22)					.1722	
40 hr. wks., 2 wks. vacation	18.3	38.2	28.2	33.6	(s = .00)	131
45 hr. wks., 8 wks. vacation	49.9	16.6	36.5	46.9		356
50 hr. wks., 12 wks. vacation	31.8	17.2	30.4	52.4		227
Pay-vacation-job quality choice (v84)					NA	
10 percent pay increase	27.8	30.6	34.7	34.7		193
Better quality work	28.4	17.8	29.9	52.3		197
Added 5 weeks paid vacation	43.7	15.8	34.7	49.5		303
Graduated tradeoff choices (v24)					.1722	
Nothing	51.6	26.1	45.8	28.0	(s = .00)	371
2 percent for 5 days vacation	21.1	14.5	59.9	25.7		152
5 percent for 12½ days vacation	12.1	9.2	60.9	29.9		87
10 percent for 25 days vacation	8.3	5.0	45.0	50.0		60
20 percent for 50 days vacation	6.8	6.1	30.6	63.3		49

246

Life-Scheduling Preference Indicators	Distribution of Indicator	Life-Scheduling Options			Correlation (Pearson r)	Number of Respondents
		Linear Lifeplan	Moderate Cyclic Plan	Full Cyclic Lifeplan		
Retirement-age activity options (v95)					.1039 (s = .01)	
Desire to work fulltime	5.0	34.3	20.0	45.7		35
Desire to work parttime	48.7	17.3	32.3	50.4		341
Not sure about working	17.7	14.5	39.5	46.0		124
Desire no work at retirement age	28.6	28.0	34.5	37.5		200

Question: See Table 10.1
*Data not applicable
Source: 1976 Alameda County survey

TABLE A.26

Correlation Matrix of Life-Scheduling Preference Indicators (zero-order Pearson's r measures of correlation)

Life-Scheduling Preference Indicators	Lifeplan Choice (v27)	v91	v93	v69	v80	v83	v85	v98	v87	v22	v24
Expect to return to school (v91)	.301										
School sched. preferences (v93)	.351	.230									
Work & job satisfaction (v69)	.182	-.206	-.092								
Expect occupational change (v80)	.215	.365	.130	-.383							
Desire for job rotation (v83)	.131	.173	.029	-.069	.174						
On/off job time importance (v85)	.211	.139	.191	-.302	.230	.072					
Sex-role flexibility (v98)	.318	.260	.309	-.147	.221	.096	.279				
Leisure satisfaction (v87)	-.045	-.025	-.041	.073	-.010	.095	.073	-.058			
Workyear sched. preferences (v22)	.172	.095	.123	-.046	.089	.048	.105	.141	.031		
Grad. Time-income choice (v24)	.206	.169	.222	-.042	.188	.074	.166	.277	.006	.237	
Retirement-age preferences (v95)	.104	-.142	-.140	.035	-.115	-.037	.023	-.167	.079	-.043	-.083

Questions:
Expect to return to school (v91): "Do you expect that you may need or desire to attend full-time school sometime during the rest of your life?" (Responses on ten-point Likert Scale ranging from 1 = "Definitely Will Not" to 10 = "Definitely Will.")

School scheduling preferences (v93): "In general, which of the following approaches for the education of young persons do you think would be best? ( ) Continuous attendance in school (except summers) until all formal high school or college education has been completed and the young person is ready to begin work in a chosen occupation. ( ) Continuous attendance in school (except summers) through Junior High School, followed by more-or-less equal alterations between work experiences and schooling until the young person has finished high school or college and is ready to begin work in a chosen occupation."

Work and job satisfaction (v69): "On the whole, would you say that you are satisfied or dissatisfied with your current job (or last job if not now working)?" (Responses on a nine point Likert Scale with 1 = "Very Dissatisfied" and 9 = "Very Satisfied.")

Expect occupational change (v80): "Do you expect to change your occupation or career sometime during the rest of your life?" (Responses on a nine-point Likert Scale with 1 = "Definitely Will Not" and 9 = "Definitely Will.")

Desire for job rotation (v83): "In a situation where workers have more skills and training than necessary for the performance of available jobs, would you favor or oppose a plan whereby all qualified persons take turns between desirable and undesirable jobs so that all persons would have the chance to apply their talents as well as share in the performance of less attractive but necessary tasks?" (Responses on a nine-point Likert Scale with 1 = "Strongly Oppose" to 9 = "Strongly Favor.")

On and off job time importance (v85): "How much importance do you place on what you do *on* the job as compared to what you do *off* the job? ( ) On-job activities much more important. ( ) On-job activities somewhat more important. ( ) On-job activities about the same importance. ( ) On-job activities somewhat less important. ( ) On-job activities much less important."

Sex-role flexibility (v98): "Do you favor or oppose the idea that women should work more in paying jobs than they do now, and that men should devote more time to child rearing and housekeeping duties?" (Responses on a nine-point Likert Scale with 1 = "Strongly Oppose" and 9 = "Strongly Favor.")

Leisure satisfaction (v87): "In general, how satisfied are you with the way you are spending your time *off* the job?" (Responses on a nine-point Likert Scale with 1 = "Very Dissatisfied" and 9 = "Very Satisfied.")

Workyear scheduling preferences (v22): "Assume that you must work an average of 40 hours a week but that it is possible to schedule your work over an entire year in one of the following ways: (A) Fifty 40-hour workweeks with 2 weeks' paid vacation each year. (B) Forty-four 45-hour workweeks with 8 weeks' paid vacation each year. (C) Forty 50-hour workweeks with 12 weeks' paid vacation every year. Which option would you choose first? ( ) Which would you choose second? ( )"

Graduated time-income tradeoff choices (v24): "What is the largest portion of your current yearly income that you would be willing to give up in exchange for more vacation time? ( ) Nothing. ( ) 2 percent ($\frac{1}{50}$) of your income for 5 days' (1 workweek) additional paid vacation time each year. ( ) 5 percent ($\frac{1}{20}$) of your income for 12.5 days (2.5 workweeks) additional paid vacation each year. ( ) 10 percent ($\frac{1}{10}$) of your income for 25 days' (5 workweeks) additional paid vacation each year. ( ) 20 percent ($\frac{1}{5}$) of your income for 50 days' (10 workweeks) additional paid vacation each year."

Retirement-age activity preferences (v95): "If possible, would you like to continue working after retirement age? ( ) No. ( ) Yes, part time. ( ) Yes, full time. ( ) Not sure."

Source: 1976 Alameda County survey

TABLE A.27

Multiple Regression of Selected Predictor Variables on Life-Scheduling Preferences within Selected Subsamples (Alameda County Sample)

Independent Variables (predictors)	All Workers Standardized Regression Coefficients (Beta wts.)	Zero-Order Correlations (Pearson r)	Workers by Sex		Workers by Family Cycle Stage		
			Men	Women	No Children	Children under 21	Children over 21
Expect return to school (V91)	.2287*	.3318	.1830*	.2570*	.2120*	.2919*	-.2473
Life-scheduling history (LFHST)	.2116*	.3120	.2333*	.2106*	.2215*	.2024*	.3773
Sex-role flexibility (V98)	.1452*	.3090	.2232*	.0512*	.1642*	.1362*	.2315*
Family cycle stage (FACYCLE)	-.0888*	-.1836	.0357*	-.3108*	—	—	
Socioeconomic status (SES)	.0627*	.0772	.0014*	.1502	.0128**	.1306**	-.0753*
Expect occupation change (V80)	.0588*	.2338	.0492*	.0710*	.0831*	.0776*	.0887*
Age (V31)	.0520*	-.1779	.0090*	.1891*	.0226*	.0795*	-.1741
Length of workweek (V52)	-.0446*	-.0805	-.0019*	-.0820*	.0298*	-.0785*	-.1882
Sex (V32)	-.0432*	-.1324	—	—	-.1099*	-.0013**	.1794*
Degree financial worry (V51)	-.0050*	-.0212	-.0936*	.0867*	.0574*	-.0514*	-.0598*
Expected no. children (V97)	.0035*	-.0269	.0615*	-.1092*	-.0274*	.0122*	.1870

All Workers	Men Workers	Women Workers	Workers with No Children	Workers with Children under 21	Workers with Children over 21
Multiple R = .4710	Multiple R = .4632	Multiple R = .5349	Multiple R = .4791	Multiple R = .4682	Multiple R = .5584
Multiple R² = .2219	Multiple R² = .2146	Multiple R² = .2861	Multiple R² = .2296	Multiple R² = .2192	Multiple R² = .3118
Adjusted R² = .2044	Adjusted R² = .1829	Adjusted R² = .2550	Adjusted R² = .1929	Adjusted R² = .1801	Adjusted R² = .0898
Significance = .01	Significance = .01	Significance = .01	Significance = .01	Significance = .01	Not Significant

*Unstandardized coefficient greater than twice its standard error.

**Unstandardized coefficient greater than 1.5 times its standard error.

Source: 1976 Alameda County survey

ANNOTATED
BIBLIOGRAPHY

This bibliography presents selected reading references grouped into the following areas:

1. Trends and Data on Work Time and Life Scheduling
2. Speculations on Life Scheduling
3. Education and Work
4. Changing Sex Roles and Family Structure
5. Old Age and Retirement
6. Unemployment and Work Sharing
7. Values Toward Work Time and Leisure
8. Innovations and Institutional Changes

Each reference is followed by a brief comment indicating its particular relevance to life scheduling.

TRENDS AND DATA ON WORK
TIME AND LIFE SCHEDULING

Best, Fred and Barry Stern, "Education, Work and Leisure—Must They Come in That Order?" *Monthly Labor Review* (July 1977) pp. 3–9 (Data oriented discussion of life scheduling trends and resulting social problems).

Bowen, William and Aldrich Finegan, *The Economics of Labor Force Participation*, (Princeton, N.J.: Princeton University Press, 1969) (Major study of the patterns of labor force participation which demonstrates that competition for employment tends to drive younger and older persons out of the labor force).

Career Thresholds, Volume 6, Research and Development Monograph No. 16, (Washington, D.C.: U.S. Department of Labor, 1977) (Report on longitudinal survey research with valuable data on the patterns of entrance and withdrawal from the labor force among the younger population as it grows older).

Deuterman, William V. and Scott C. Brown, "Voluntary Part-Time Workers: A Growing Part of the Labor Force," *Monthly Labor Review* (June 1978) pp. 3–10. (One of the most comprehensive discussions of recent national data on the growth of voluntary part-time work, with emphasis on the types of persons employed part-time).

Dual Careers, Volume 4, Research and Development Monograph No. 21 (Washington, D.C.: U.S. Department of Labor, 1976) (Longitudinal survey study of the labor force activity of women).

Estes, Richard and Harold Wilensky, "Life Cycle Squeeze and Morale Curve," *Social Problems* (February 1978) pp. 277–92 (Life satisfaction study demonstrating the financial and occupational demands of mid-life).

Fullerton, Howard and James Byrne, "Length of Working Lives for Men and Women," *Monthly Labor Review* (February 1976) pp. 31–35 (Summary of past and recent Bureau of Labor Statistics computations showing the portion of overall lifespans that men and women spend holding jobs).

Ghez, Gilbert R. and Gary S. Becker, *The Allocation of Time and Goods Over the Life Cycle* (New York: Columbia University Press, 1975) (Econometric analysis of lifetime decisions and trends concerning the earning and use of income).

Hedges, Janice Neipert and Geoffrey Moore, "Trends in Labor and Leisure," *Monthly Labor Review* (February 1971) pp. 3–11 (Slightly dated but superb overview of work time trends).

Hedges, Janice, "How Many Days Make a Workweek?" *Monthly Labor Review* (April 1975) pp. 19–36 (Analysis of national data to assess the incidence of modified workweeks of all types).

Henle, Peter, "Recent Growth of Paid Leisure for U.S. Workers" *Monthly Labor Review* (March 1962) pp. 249–257. (Early documentation of shift in emphasis from shorter workweeks to extended time away from work as the most preferred form of leisure).

Kreps, Juanita, *The Lifetime Allocation of Work and Income* (Durham, N.C.: Duke University Press, 1971) (Classic study of trends and reasons for compression of work activity into the middle of life, with particular attention given to old age and retirement).

Owen, John, *The Price of Leisure* (Montreal, Canada: McGill-Queens University Press, 1970) (Review of theories concerning work-time tradeoff decisions followed by analysis of data to test theories).

Pre-Retirement Years, Volume 4, Manpower Research Monograph No. 15, (Washington, D.C.: U.S. Department of Labor, 1975) (Report on longitudinal surveys on the decision to work or retire among late middle aged workers as they grow older).

Wilensky, Harold, "The Uneven Distribution of Leisure," *Social Problems*, (Summer 1961), pp. 32–56 (Internationally recognized article showing that leisure is distributed differently among occupational strata, and that the higher status and best educated workers tend to have less leisure than other workers).

SPECULATIONS ON LIFE SCHEDULING

Best, Fred, "The Time of Our Lives: The Parameters of Lifetime Distribution of Education, Work and Leisure," *Society and Leisure*, Vol. 1, No. 1 (May 1978) pp. 95–124 (Review of historic data concerning the distribution of work over lifespans which also updates earlier 1965 computations by Juanita Kreps and Joseph Spengler projecting potential gains of free time from economic growth; also discusses alternative life scheduling patterns that may emerge if individuals had more freedom to choose between work and leisure).

Bolles, Richard, *The Three Boxes of Life: And How to Get Out of Them* (San

Francisco: Ten Speed Press, 1978) (Anecdotal discussion of how individuals can alter their personal life styles and schedules).

Butler, Robert, "The Burnt-Out and the Bored," *The Washington Post*, (January 1969) pp. 58, 60 (Widely circulated news column which popularized the idea of more flexible life scheduling in order to engender more personal growth and learning throughout life).

Evans, Archibald, *Flexibility in Working Life*, (Paris: Organisation for Economic Co-operation and Development, 1973) (One of the earliest comprehensive discussions of flexible life scheduling which draws heavily on international data).

Kahn, Herman and Anthony Weiner, *The Year 2000* (New York: Collier-MacMillan Company, 1965) pp. 193–202, 213–17 (Thoughtful but unduly optimistic discussion of how expected economic affluence would allow major reductions of work time by the year 2000).

Kreps, Juanita and Joseph Spengler, "Future Options for More Free Time" in Fred Best (ed.), *The Future of Work* (Englewood Cliffs, N.J.: Prentice-Hall, 1973) pp. 87–92 (Reprint of classic computations based on 1965 data showing how much free time might be gained if different portions of projected economic growth were foregone for leisure up to the year 1985).

Rehn, Gosta, *Prospective View on Patterns of Working Time* (Paris: Organisation for Economic Co-operation and Development, 1972) (Wide ranging and thoughtful discussion of how changes within industrial societies are making it desirable and necessary to increase work and life scheduling options).

Thompson, William Irwin, "Walking Out of the University," *Harper's Magazine*, (September 1973) pp. 70–76 (Brilliant expressionistic essay which explores the possibility that human growth and learning occurs in cycles throughout life and that continuous revolution of learning, work, and play might be better than the existing school-work-retirement lockstep).

Wirtz, Willard and the National Manpower Institute, *The Boundless Resource* (Washington, D.C.: New Republic Book Company, 1975) (A recent and major volume on the topic of life scheduling flexibility written by a consortium of policy makers and academics working under the leadership of former Secretary of Labor Willard Wirtz).

EDUCATION AND WORK

Berg, Ivar, *Education and Work: The Great Training Robbery* (New York: Praeger Publishers, 1970) (Famous ground breaking study documenting the emergence of under-utilization of educational achievement and providing evidence indicating that associated job dissatisfaction may reduce productivity on the job).

Erickson, Eric, *Childhood and Society*, second ed. (New York: W.W. Norton 1963) pp. 247–74 (Part of this book presents the author's famous framework of life stages and the need for varying types of growth and learning throughout life).

Freeman, Richard, *The Over-Educated American* (New York: Academic Press, 1976) (Economic study documenting the growth of under-utilized educational attainment and the decline of financial returns for higher levels of schooling).

Gould, Roger, "The Phases of Adult Life: A Study of Developmental Psychology," *American Journal of Psychiatry* (November 1972) (Discussion of recent thought and research about stages of change and growth in adult life).

Hershey, Cary, "Educated Labor and Social Change," in Phillip Ritterbush (ed.),

Talent Waste (Washington, D.C.: Acropolis Books, 1972) pp. 46–64 (Early exploration of "new working class theory" in which it is postulated that discontent among workers with underutilized education would be a major force for social change).

Jencks, Christopher et. al., *Inequality* (New York: Harper & Row Books, 1972) (One of the more recent of many studies of the social stratification process which shows that social achievement in terms of earnings, occupational advancement and educational attainment is due mostly to family background and "luck" rather than "meritocratic" sorting out of the most qualified and motivated persons).

Levitan, Sar and William Johnston, "Job Redesign, Reform and Enrichment— Exploring the Limitations," *Monthly Labor Review* (July 1973) pp. 35–41 (Critical discussion of the limits of the "quality of work" reforms which have been advocated in recent years).

O'Toole, James, *Work in America* (Cambridge, Mass.: MIT Press, 1974) (Classic and widely read critique of American working conditions and argument for work reforms to meet the higher human needs for personal growth, social belongingness, and self-esteem).

Pascal, Anthony, "Mid-Life Redirection of Careers: Introduction," in *An Evaluation of Policy Related Research on Programs for Mid-Life Career Redirection*, Volume II (Santa Monica: Rand Corporation, 1975) (Policy oriented discussion of the need for "lifelong learning" and retraining throughout the life cycle).

Rodriquez, Orlando, "Occupational Shifts and Educational Upgrading of the American Labor Force Between 1950 and 1970," *Sociology of Education*, (January 1978) pp. 55–67 (Excellent analysis of data showing that educational attainment has increased dramatically within all occupational groups).

Sommers, Dixie and Alan Eck, "Occupational Mobility in the American Labor Force," *Monthly Labor Review* (January 1977) pp. 3–17 (Excellent analysis of national data to determine how much workers with different social characteristics change their jobs and occupations).

Stern, Barry, *Toward a Federal Policy on Education and Work*, U.S. Department of Health, Education and Welfare (Washington, D.C.: Government Printing Office, 1977) (Thought provoking data-based examination of current relationships between education and work with discussion of potential alternative policies).

Vermilye, Dyckman W., (ed.), *Relating Work and Education* (Washington, D.C.: Jossey-Bass Publishers, 1977) (Wide scoped anthology dealing with many issues of the emerging relationships between education and work).

Young, Anne McDougall, "Going Back to School at 35 and Over," *Monthly Labor Review* (July 1977) pp. 43–45 (Latest of several reports on special national data on the proportion of persons over age thirty-five who are enrolled in degree granting school programs).

CHANGING SEX ROLES AND FAMILY STRUCTURE

Best, Fred, "Changing Sex Roles and Worklife Scheduling," *Psychology of Women Quarterly* (Winter 1980) (Detailed analysis of exploratory survey data concerning work time preferences which shows a high association between values and behaviors in favor of non-traditional sex roles and the desire for alternative work time arrangements).

Giele, Janet Zollinger, "Changing Sex Roles and Family Structure," *Social Policy* (January–February 1979) pp. 32–43 (Insightful and provocative discussion of changing sex and family roles with particular attention given to the likely growth in demand for more flexible work time conditions).

Goode, William J., *World Revolution and Family Patterns* (New York: The Free Press, 1970) (Prize winning international study of the impact of industrialization and other social changes on sex roles and family life).

Hayghe, Howard, "Families and the Rise of Working Wives—An Overview," *Monthly Labor Review* (May 1976) pp. 12–19 (Summary of national labor force data showing the growth and family characteristics of working wives).

Hedges, Janice Neipert and Jeanne K. Barnett, "Working Women and the Division of Household Tasks," *Monthly Labor Review* (April 1972) pp. 9–14 (Review of data indicating the unequal division of household chores between spouses in dual-earner households).

Kreps, Juanita, "Do All Women Want to Work: The Economics of Their Choice," in Louise Kapp (ed.), *The Future of the Family* (New York: Simon and Schuster, 1972) pp. 224–34 (Theoretical discussion of the reasons women seek employment and the impact of their job activities on family roles and the use of time).

Mason, Karen Oppenheim, John L. Czaika, and Sava Arber, "Change in U.S. Women's Sex Role Attitudes, 1964–1974," *American Sociological Review* (August 1976) pp. 573–96 (Review and statistical comparison of five national surveys to determine the nature and extent of sex role value change).

Polit, Denise, "The Implications of Non-Traditional Work Schedules for Women," *The Urban and Social Change Review*, 2 (1978) pp. 37–42 (Discussion of the importance of work scheduling options to women who seek to balance job holding and family responsibilities).

Robinson, John P., *How Americans Use Time* (New York: Praeger Publishers, 1977) (Important analysis of two comparable national time budget studies undertaken in 1965 and 1975, the results of which indicate notable shifts in the use of time within family units).

Sawhill, Isabel V., "Economic Perspectives on the Family," *Daedalus* (Spring 1977) pp. 115–25 (Discussion of the impact of increased employment of women on the structure of the family from the standpoint of economic theory).

Smith, Ralph, *The Subtle Revolution* (Washington, D.C.: The Urban Institute, 1979) (Major study of the causes, impacts, and future of working women; particularly important for its critique of Department of Labor projections of women's labor force participation).

Women's Changing Roles at Home and on the Job, Special Report No. 26 (Washington, D.C.: National Commission for Employment Policy, 1979) (Highly informative compendium which analyzes national longitudinal survey data about working women to examine decisions to work, impact on employment on socio-economic standing, and alterations of values).

Young, Michael and Peter Willmott, *The Symmetrical Family* (New York: Pantheon Publishers, 1973) (Treatise which discusses the long-term implications of current sex and family role changes, most particularly the rise of egalitarian relationships between men and women).

OLD AGE AND RETIREMENT

Best, Fred, "Retirement and the Lifetime Distribution of Work," *Aging and Work* (Summer 1979) pp. 173–181 (Discussion of emerging problems in today's retirement system and the need for flexible retirement ages and work time options for the elderly).

Bixby, Lenore F., "Retirement Patterns in the United States: Research and Policy Interaction," *Social Security Bulletin* (August 1[76]) pp. 3–19 (Review of several social security studies concerning the age of retirement, reasons for retirement, and characteristics of retirees).

Butler, Robert, *Why Survive? Being Old in America* (New York: Harper & Row, 1973) pp. 102, 353 (Prize winning book which discusses the problems of the older population with some attention to the relevance of flexible life scheduling).

Havighurst, Robert J., "Alternative Work Schedules: Implications for Older Workers," *The Journal of the College and University Personnel Association* (Summer 1977) pp. 60–65 (Discussion of the importance of alternative work time options to older persons who wish to keep working).

Henle, Peter, "Recent Trends in Retirement Benefits Related to Earnings," *Monthly Labor Review* (June 1972) pp. 12–20 (Analysis of available data concerning the issue of whether and under what conditions pensions provide adequate funds to maintain the living standards of recipients).

Meier, Elizabeth and Elizabeth Kerr, "Capabilities of Middle Aged and Older Workers: A Survey of Literature," *Industrial Gerontology* (Summer 1976) pp. 147–56 (Discussion of recent data on the effects of aging on intellectual and physical job capabilities).

Meier, Elizabeth, *Aging in America: Implications for Employment*, Report No. 7, (Washington, D.C.: National Council for the Aging, 1977) (Often cited report based on a 1974 Harris survey on retirement sponsored by the National Council for the Aging).

Kittner, Dorothy R., "Forced Retirement: How Common Is It?," *Monthly Labor Review* (December 1977) pp. 60–61 (Review of available national data on retirement programs which finds that explicit forced retirement provisions are relatively rare, but that secondary conditions create significant pressures to retire at or before age sixty-five).

Munnell, Alicia, *The Future of Social Security* (Washington, D.C.: The Brookings Institution, 1977) (Important book which marshals existing data and projections to assess the costs and policy options of providing adequate pension programs in the future).

Neugarten, Bernice (ed.), *Middle Age and Aging* (Chicago: University of Chicago Press, 1975) (Extremely valuable and informative compendium concerning all aspects of the impact of aging on human behavior, containing numerous studies on the effect of aging on job performance, reasons for retirement, and self-concept of older persons).

Rones, Philip L., "Older Men—The Choice Between Work and Retirement," *Monthly Labor Review* (November 1978) pp. 3–10 (One of the best available articles summarizing national data on the work time and retirement decisions of older men—an excellent introductory article).

Sheppard, Harold and Sara Rix, *The Graying of Working America* (New York: The

Free Press, 1977) (Excellent, wide scoped data-based discussion of older populations now and in the future, with particular attention given to the problem of financing pension programs for the large post-World War II "baby boom" generation).

Zalusky, John, "Shorter Workyears—Earlier Retirement," *AFL-CIO American Federationist* (August 1977) (Review of collective bargaining accomplishments and trends concerning retirement age and pension benefits).

UNEMPLOYMENT AND WORK SHARING

Best, Fred, *Work Sharing: Policy Options and Assessments* (Paris: Organisation for Economic Co-operation and Development, June 1979) (Detailed summary of the pros and cons of reducing work time to spread employment and assessment of seventeen major work sharing policy options).

Ginzberg, Eli, "The Job Problem," *Scientific American* (November 1977) pp. 43–51 (Thoughtful, data-based assessment of the extent and nature of unemployment in the United States).

Henle, Peter, "Work Sharing as an Alternative to Layoffs," Congressional Research Service, U.S. Congress (Washington, D.C.: July 1976) (Review of past and existing use of work sharing through collective bargaining in the United States and government programs abroad).

Kreps, Juanita, "Some Time Dimensions of Manpower Policy," in Eli Ginzberg (ed.), *Jobs for Americans* (Englewood Cliffs, N.J.: Prentice-Hall, 1975) (Perceptive discussion of the issues which complicate the use of work sharing to combat unemployment).

Leisure Sharing, Hearings of the Select Committee on Investment Priorities and Objectives, California State Senate, Sacramento, California, November 1, 1977 (Transcript of wide scoped legislative hearings which are particularly important because of testimonies reporting working examples of numerous approaches to work sharing).

Levitan, Sar and Richard Belous, *Shorter Hours, Shorter Weeks: Spreading the Work to Reduce Unemployment* (Baltimore: Johns Hopkins University Press, 1977) (Interesting booklet which reviews work sharing programs in Europe and explores potential future acceptability of such approaches in the United States).

National Commission on Technology, Automation and Economic Progress, *Technology and the American Economy*, Vol. 1 (Feburary 1966) (Summary report of the Commission's deliberations which is important to the topic of work sharing because of its discussion of the small effect of automation on unemployment and the supply of jobs).

Reynolds, Lloyd G., *Labor Economics and Labor Relations* (Englewood Cliffs, N.J.: Prentice-Hall, 1970) pp. 46–50, 576–83 (Sample of traditional rejection of work sharing by economists on the grounds that workers do not wish to exchange earnings for leisure and that it would lessen pressures to reduce joblessness through other approaches).

Work Time and Employment, Special Report No. 28, National Commission for Employment Policy (Washington, D.C.: October 1978) (Widely scoped compendium prepared to examine various work sharing issues and policies; important because it contains the viewpoints of persons who favor and oppose work sharing).

VALUES TOWARD WORK TIME AND LEISURE

Bell, Daniel, *The Coming of Post-Industrial Society* (New York: Basic Books, 1973) pp. 456–74 (Controversial but brilliant speculations about the future of late-industrial societies, with some thought-provoking discussion about increasing scarcity of time).

Best, Fred, "Preferences on Worklife Scheduling and Work-Leisure Tradeoffs," *Monthly Labor Review* (June 1978) pp. 31–37 (Summary of findings from a 1976 exploratory survey of 791 varied county employees on the topic of work and life scheduling preferences).

Best, Fred and James Wright, "The Effect of Scheduling on Time-Income Trade-offs," *Social Forces* 57, No. 1 (September 1978) pp. 136–53 (Report on pilot survey study on work and life scheduling preferences accompanied by review of relevant economic theory and social policy implications).

Best, Fred, Phillip Bosserman, and Barry Stern, "Income-Time Tradeoff Preferences of U.S. Workers: A Review of Literature and Indicators," *Leisure Sciences* 2, No. 2 (Summer 1979) pp. 119–41 (Summary of a longer 150-page report prepared for the U.S. Department of H.E.W. to assess the desire of American workers to trade income for more free time on the basis of available behavioral and attitudinal data).

Best, Fred, *Exchanging Earnings for Leisure: Findings of an Exploratory National Survey on Work Time Preferences*, Special Monograph, Office of Research and Development, Employment and Training Administration (Washington, D.C.: U.S. Department of Labor, 1980) (Full report summarizing the findings of a 1978 nationally representative survey study on work time preferences).

Chapman, Brad L. and Robert Otteman, "Employees' Preferences for Various Compensation and Fringe Benefit Options," *The Personnel Administrator* (November 1975) pp. 30–36 (Important exploratory survey study which shows that accidental samples of workers prefer longer vacations to equally valuable pay raises or benefits).

deGrazia, Sebastian, *Of Time, Work and Leisure* (Garden City, N.Y.: Doubleday, 1968) (Philosophical treatise on the changing definitions of work and leisure from Hellenic times to modern society).

Kaplan, Max, *Leisure: Theory and Policy* (New York: John Wiley and Sons, 1975) (Theoretical discussion of leisure from virtually every imaginable vantage point).

Linder, Staffan, *The Harried Leisure Class* (New York: Columbia University Press, 1970) (Economic discussion of the value of time focusing on the premise that high levels of affluence and diversified consumer options have left individuals with inadequate amounts of time to utilize their earnings).

Martin, Virginia, *Hours of Work When Workers Can Choose* (Washington, D.C.: Business and Professional Women's Foundation, 1975) (Study which reviews managerial responses to alternative work arrangements accompanied by comprehensive bibliography).

Nealey, S.M. and J.G. Goodale, "Workers Preferences Among Time-Off Benefits and Pay," *Journal of Applied Psychology* 5, No. 4 (1967) pp. 354–61 (Pioneer survey study of time-income tradeoff preferences which suggests that the ways potential free time gains are scheduled are an important determinant of willingness to forego income for time).

INNOVATIONS AND INSTITUTIONAL CHANGES

Alternative Work Schedule Directory: First Edition (Washington, D.C.: National Council for Alternative Work Patterns, 1978) (Short case descriptions of 290 firms that have applied alternative work time arrangements such as permanent part-time employment, job-splitting, and flexitime).

Best, Fred and Barry Stern, "Lifetime Distribution of Education, Work and Leisure: Research, Speculations and Policy Implications," *Review of Sports and Leisure*, October 1977 (Discussion of social forces likely to foster more flexible life patterns, with attention given to social policy options and implications).

Best, Fred, "Short-Time Compensation and Work Sharing" (Washington, D.C.: National Commission for Employment Policy, April 1978) (Analysis of proposals to provide part-week unemployment insurance benefits to work groups experiencing reduced workweeks as an alternative to layoffs; with attention given to existing programs in Europe, history of the concept in the United States, and a preliminary cost-benefit assessment of potential impacts).

Bradshaw, Ted K., "Cannery Workers Sabbatical Leaves: A Report on the Study of Thirteen Week Vacations," Center for Labor Research and Education, Institute for Industrial Relations (Berkeley: University of California, 1976) (Study of union negotiated sabbatical leave program).

Cohen, Allan and Herman Gadon, *Alternative Work Schedules: Integrating Individual and Organizational Needs* (New York: Addison-Wesley Publishing Company, 1978) (Treatise dealing with organizational constraints and options concerning alternative work time arrangements).

Hodgco, Janice Neipert, "A Look at the 4-Day Workweek," *Monthly Labor Review* (October 1971) pp. 33–37 (First use of national labor data to assess the growth of the much heralded 4-day, 40 hour workweek).

Nollen, Stanley, Brenda Eddy, and Virginia Martin, *Permanent Part-Time Employment: The Manager's Perspective* (New York, Praeger Publishers, 1978) (A major study of the effects of part-time employment on perceived worker productivity, turnover and morale; with discussions of the managerial pros and cons of other work time innovations).

Meier, Gretle, *Job-Sharing: A New Pattern for Quality of Work and Life?* (Kalamazoo, Mich.: W. E. Upjohn Institute for Employment Research, February 1979) (Study of the organizational impacts of job-splitting, a work time reform in which two or more persons hold one job).

Miller, Jeffrey M., *Innovations in Working Patterns*, U.S. Trade Union Seminar on Alternative Working Patterns in Europe, Communications Workers of America (Washington, D.C.: May 1978) (Report of the findings of a union task force which toured Europe to investigate work time innovations abroad).

Mills, James R., "Leisure Sharing: Its Time Has Come," *State Government* (Spring 1979) pp. 75–79 (General discussion of the idea of stimulating voluntary options for the exchange of earnings for more free time which would lead to the creation of jobs for those currently unemployed).

Olmsted, Barney, "Job-Sharing—A New Way to Work," *Personnel Journal* (February 1977) (One of the original and most widely read discussions of job-splitting).

Owen, John D., "Flexitime: Some Problems and Solutions," *Industrial and Labor Relations Review* 30, No. 2 (January 1977) (Excellent discussion of the pros and cons of "flexitime).

Owen, John D., "Work Time: The Traditional Workweek and Its Alternatives," *Employment and Training Report of the President* (Washington, D.C.: U.S. Department of Labor, 1979) pp. 75–92 (Review of work time trends accompanied by descriptions of major work time reforms and their growth in recent years).

"Paid Personal Holidays," *Solidarity*, October 21, 1977, pp. 6–10 (Brief description of the staggered days-off program negotiated by the United Auto Workers in order to preserve jobs thought to be threatened by automation).

Poor, Riva (ed.), *4 Days, 40 Hours: Reporting a Revolution in Work and Leisure* (Cambridge, Mass.: Bursk and Poor Publishing, 1970) (Highly publicized case descriptions of early compressed workweek experiences).

Project JOIN: Phase 1 Report, Employees Relations Division, Department of Administration, State of Wisconsin, Madison, March 1977 (Initial report of state program to increase voluntary part-time work options among public employees and measure the performance of participating workers).

Rosenberg, Robert, "A Pilot Project for Extended Leaves," Working Paper No. 10, Senate Office of Research, California State Senate, Sacramento, California, December 1976 (Thoughtful discussion of the need for work sharing as a means of reducing unemployment, with particular attention given to sabbatical leaves).

Sugarman, Jule M., "The Decennial-Sabbatical Program," *Journal of College and University Personnel Association* 28, No. 3 (Summer 1977) pp. 47–52 (Discussion of the need to establish a national workers sabbatical program in order to free people for voluntary social service, meet human needs for personal renewal, and spread available jobs among a larger number of persons desiring to work).

Terlet, Bernhardt, "Flexiyear Schedules—Only a Matter of Time," *Monthly Labor Review* (December 1977) pp. 63–64 (Review and discussion of European innovations which allow employees to re-negotiate the length and scheduling of work time each year on a regular basis).

"Testimony of Dan McCorquodale," *Leisure Sharing*, Hearings of the Select Committee on Investment Priorities and Objectives, California State Senate, Sacramento, California, November 1, 1977, pp. 41–49 (Important review of county program allowing employees to voluntarily forego 5, 10, or 20 percent of annual income for $10\frac{1}{2}$, 21, or 42 days of added vacation time).

"Unions Campaign to Shrink Work Time," *Business Week*, April 24, 1978 (Journalistic account on national organized labor campaign to share work by amending the Fair Labor Standards Act so that the standard workweek is reduced from 40 to 35 hours and double pay required for overtime).

Weinstein, Harriet G., *A Comparison of Three Alternative Work Schedules: Flexible Work Hours, Compact Workweeks and Staggered Work Hours*, Industrial Research Unit, The Wharton School, University of Pennsylvania, Philadelphia, Pennsylvania, 1975 (Case studies of three distinct worktime innovations).

"Work Sharing Programs Under UI," *California Public Employee Relations* (June 1979) pp. 13–15 (Brief description of the California "shared work unemployment compensation" program which allows partial UI to employees experiencing reduced workweeks as an alternative to layoffs).

Zalusky, John L., "Alternative Work Schedules: A Labor Perspective," *Journal of the College and University Personnel Association* 28, No. 3 (Summer 1977) pp. 54–56 (Informative and critical review of several work time innovations from vantage point of the AFL-CIO, with some attention given to union efforts to better work time conditions for workers).

INDEX

adults in college, 37, 38–39

age: effect on desire to work and earn more, 129; effect on tradeoff preferences, 120–21, 134

Alameda County survey, 127, 153, 156, 157

alternative life patterns, consideration of, 12–19; outlining the options, 12–14; shape of time to come, 14–19; support for, 12–19, 21–22, 60

amendment of worktime limitation laws, 171–72

American Express Company, 65

Arabic writings, support of work breaks, 20

Arber, Sara, 59

Arizona, first-old age pension in U.S., 66

attitudes toward worktime, 111–16

baby boom generation: in labor force, 33, 93; in retirement, 67, 78

Boyer, Ernest, 23

Bellamy, Edward 66

Bismarck, Otto von, 66, 72

BLS projections, 94

Bosserman, Phillip, 22

Boston, early sabbatical program, 21

Bronfenbrenner, Urie, 24

Brown, Zenia, 24

Bureau of Labor Statistics, 6, 14, 60, 108

Bureau of the Census, 65

Butler, Robert, 22

Byrne, James, 37

cafeteria benefit plan, 170

Cantril, Albert, 115

capital investments, effect on job creation, 96

career-related work experience, 34–35

Chapman, 114

child labor laws, 33

children, effect on desire for leisure time, 126

Christian faith, support of work breaks, 21

Coleman, John, 163–64

college-educated workers in U.S. labor force, 4

competition for jobs, 9, 89

compressed workweek, 168

compulsory education, 33

computer facilities, application to adapting organizational operations, 170

consensus for new life patterns, emerging, 103–58

consumer expenditure trends, 116–19

Converse, Philip, 115

core hours, 148, 168

cost-cutting policies, 86

counterculture, 22

cyclic life plan, 17

Czaika, John, 59

Department of Labor, 115

dependents, declining responsibilities for, 50

desire for free time, importance and nature of, 113, 115

discontent among workers, 4

dropping out, 22

Drucker, Peter, 23

dual careers, 52

dual-earner families, effect on tradeoff choices, 132–134; rise of, 126; value of time for, 145

DuPont, 168

Eck, Alan, 37

economic growth, population trends and future of retirement, 67–70; rate of, 91, 95, 96

Edison Electric Institute, 96

education; changing nature, 32–34, 45; compulsory, 33; effect on desire for free time, 131; effect on desire to

ABOUT THE AUTHOR

FRED BEST is a policy analyst for the U.S. Department of Labor and is currently on special assignment to the Office of the Director of the California Employment Development Department. Previously he held positions with the National Commission for Employment Policy, the U.S. Department of Commerce, and the U.S. Department of Health, Education and Welfare.

Dr. Best has published widely concerning the changing nature of work. His books and monographs include *The Future of Work*, *Exchanging Earnings for Leisure*, and *Shared Work Compensation*. His articles have appeared in journals including the *Monthly Labor Review*, *Social Forces*, and *Aging and Work*.

Dr. Best holds a B.A. in economics and history and an M.B.A. from the University of California at Berkeley, and a Ph.D. in sociology from the University of Massachusetts at Amherst.